Consuming Passions

Medieval History and Culture
Volume 20

Studies in Medieval History and Culture

Edited by
Francis G. Gentry
Professor of German
Pennsylvania State University

A Routledge Series

STUDIES IN MEDIEVAL HISTORY AND CULTURE

FRANCIS G. GENTRY, *General Editor*

CONSUMING PASSIONS

The Uses of Cannibalism in Late Medieval and Early Modern Europe

Merrall Llewelyn Price

Routledge
New York & London

Published in 2003 by
Routledge
29 West 35th Street
New York, NY 10001
www.routledge-ny.com

Published in Great Britain by
Routledge
11 New Fetter Lane
London EC4P 4EE
www.routledge.co.uk

Routledge is an imprint of the Taylor & Francis Group
Printed in the United States of America on acid-free paper.

BV
823
.P75
2003

10 9 8 7 6 5 4 3 2 1

Library of Congress Cataloging-in-Publication Data
Price, Merrall Llewelyn.
    Consuming passions : the uses of cannibalism in late medieval and early
modern Europe / by Merrall Llewelyn Price.
        p. cm. — (Studies in medieval history and culture ; v. 20)
    Includes bibliographical references and index
    ISBN 0-415-96699-X (alk. paper)
    1. Lord's Supper—Catholic Church—History—Middle Ages, 600–1500.
2. Cannibalism—History—To 1500. 3. Lord's Supper—Catholic Church—
History—16th century. 4. Cannibalism—History—16th century.
I. Title. II. Series.
BV823.P75 2003
394'.9'094—dc21   2003006144

Series Editor Foreword

Far from providing just a musty whiff of yesteryear, research in Medieval Studies enters the new century as fresh and vigorous as never before. Scholars representing all disciplines and generations are consistently producing works of research of the highest caliber, utilizing new approaches and methodologies. Volumes in the Medieval History and Culture series will include studies on individual works and authors of Latin and vernacular literatures, historical personalities and events, theological and philosophical issues, and new critical approaches to medieval literature and culture.

Momentous changes have occurred in Medieval Studies in the past thirty years in teaching as well as in scholarship. Thus the goal of the Medieval History and Culture series is to enhance research in the field by providing an outlet for monographs by scholars in the early stages of their careers on all topics related to the broad scope of Medieval Studies, while at the same time pointing to and highlighting new directions that will shape and define scholarly discourse in the future.

Francis G. Gentry

Contents

List of Illustrations

Acknowledgments

THANKS ARE DUE IN PARTICULAR TO TOM HAHN, WHOSE INSIGHTS and fondness for cannibalism puns were inexhaustible. I'd also like to extend my appreciation to the interlibrary loan departments at Rochester and Huntsville, to Alan Lupack and the staff of the Robbins Library, and to the many colleagues, associates, and friends who gave their unstinted assistance during this project, including, but not limited to, Russell Peck, Sarah Higley, Eve Salisbury, Cristelle Baskins, Melissa Bernstein, and Andi Hubbard.

Portions of this project have appeared as part of the article "Bitter Milk: The *Vasa Menstrualis* and the Cannibal(ized) Virgin," *College Literature* 28.1, (Winter 2001): 144–154, and a version of chapter four has appeared as "Imperial Violence and the Monstrous Mother: Cannibalism at the Siege of Jerusalem," in *Domestic Violence in Medieval Texts,* ed. Eve Salisbury, Georgiana Donavin, and Merrall Llewelyn Price. Gainesville: Florida UP, 2002. 272–298.

Anglo-Saxon and Middle English orthography has been modernized in accordance with standard publication practices.

CONSUMING PASSIONS

Chapter One
The Man-Eating Body

FROM APPROXIMATELY THE FIRST CRUSADE TO THE PERIOD OF INITIAL exploration of the Atlantic frontier, medieval Christian Europe saw the development and reification of a protocolonialist ideology associated first with eastward and then with westward expansion, and marked by a concurrent interest in what Peter Hulme, using the type of corporeal metaphors I examine in this project, calls "the purging of heretics and pagans from within the body of Christendom."[1]

Approximately contemporary with this evolving ethos was an increased concern with the real meaning of the central ceremony of Christianity—the eucharistic meal.[2] Gary Macy has suggested that the late medieval engagement of the church with the nature of the eucharist was actually manifest as early as the beginning of the eleventh century,[3] and this fascination would continue long after the defining moments of Lateran IV and the Council of Trent. Not only did the twelfth century mark the inception of a period when the eucharistic sacrament, with its new resonance, would be given less frequently and with more drama than in the past, but it was also the century during which eucharistic miracles began to proliferate in sermons and in collections of *exempla.*[4]

This coincidence of chronology between the beginnings of colonial incorporation and the reification of an encompassing theory of theophagy manifests itself in a proliferation of late medieval and early modern texts—literary, legal, and geopolitical—that actively explore the idea of the consumption of human flesh by other human beings. These texts function to solidify cultural and Christian identity at the same time as they address the cultural anxieties implicit in the act of eating the human flesh of the divine; as Peter Hulme has noted, "boundaries of community are often created by accusing those outside the boundary of the very practice on which the integrity of that community is founded."[5] Indeed, the parallels between the Christian eucharist and the un-Christian cannibalism being described are often noted, and serve in most cases to heighten the horror of the cannibal-istic act.[6]

This is not, however, to suggest that cultural discussions of human/divine consumption were new in the late Middle Ages—on the con-trary, there is a vigorous classical and early medieval tradition of anthro-pophagy.[7] In Greek mythology the world begins in an incestuous cannibal-ism in which the consuming desire of the parent is interrogated, as Cronos, who has castrated his own father at the urging of his mother/grandmother Gaia, consumes his children by his wife and sister, Rhea, to secure his rule. Instead of consuming Zeus, he is fooled by his wife into swallowing a stone, and, on reaching adulthood, Zeus defeats his father and forces him to dis-gorge his immortal and undigested siblings. Moreover, a filial cannibalism will continue to shadow Zeus throughout his dominion; his son Zagreus is torn to pieces and consumed by the Titans, and Zeus arrives too late to save more than the heart, which he feeds to his current amour, Semele, who is thereby made pregnant with Dionysus.

Neither does Zeus himself escape the temptations of cannibalism: on two occasions, he is served a stew of human meat. Once the Arcadian tyrant Lycaon attempts to test Zeus's divinity by presenting him with the prepared flesh of a hostage, and is punished by being transformed into a sublinguistic werewolf, thereby meriting inclusion in Ovid's *Metamorphoses*: "He fled in terror, reached the silent fields, / And howled and tried to speak. No use at all!"[8] On the second occasion, the perpetrator is one of Zeus's many sons, Tantalus, whose name is permanently associated with desire for forbidden food. Tantalus stews his own son, Pelops, and serves him to the gods, but only the distracted mother Demeter eats of the dish, consuming a piece of Pelops's shoulder, which is replaced with ivory when the boy is divinely reconstituted. However, in a brutal act of compulsive familial reinscription, one of Pelops's sons, Atreus, takes his revenge on his brother Thyestes for the latter's adultery with Atreus's wife Aerope by killing Thyestes's sons, and cooking all of their bodies except for their hands and feet. This meat is pre-sented to Thyestes at a sumptuous banquet, and after Thyestes has eaten, his brother produces the dismembered hands and feet of the children, thus pre-cipitating the curse of the house of Atreus.

The only narrative of Greek mythological cannibalism which involves a female (and maternal) perpetrator is also one of familial infanticidal revenge—the story of Procne and Philomela, the first sister married to Ares's son Tereus, King of Thrace, and the latter raped and silenced by him after he has conceived an overwhelming desire for her. Despite the fact that Tereus has cut out her tongue, Philomela is able to communicate her story to her sister by weaving a narrative tapestry. In response to the monstrosity of the father, Procne then kills their son Itys, cooks him, and serves his body to her husband, who flies into a homicidal rage and pursues both sisters.[9] Before more slaughter can ensue, all three are translated into birds; Philomela's voice is returned to her, since her new form is that of a nightingale.

Moreover, anthropophages litter the pages of classical geography and romance as well as theology. The Greeks "envisioned rings of progressively more primitive social development surrounding a Mediterranean hearth; in the furthest ring, at the banks of the Ocean, social primitivism becomes absolute."[10] As the archetype of (anti)social primitivism and the antithesis of culture, the anthropophagous peoples were placed well beyond the *oikumene*, at the extreme edges of the known world—in the far north, such as Ireland, or Scythia, or well to the south or east, such as Ethiopia and India. Grouped, particularly in their Indian manifestations, with other monstrous races transgressing physical, human, or gender norms, such as Amazons, Blemmye, Sciapods, and Monoculi, the Anthropophages, sometimes human but for their diet, and sometimes hideous hybrids of man and beast, retreated as the edges of the known world extended.

Despite the relative lateness of the marvelous races interpolations into their pages, the Alexander romances were perhaps the most influential, and certainly the most widespread, of the repositories of classical/medieval geoteratography. The Alexander legend ranges some of the monstrous races in battle against the mighty Alexander, including bands of ferocious animalistic warriors, sometimes described as cynocephalic (dog-headed), sometimes as merely hairy and barking. In some versions of the *Pseudo-Callisthenes*, Alexander isolates such a prelinguistic, hairy man. Operating on stereotypes of uncivilized hypermasculine sexuality, Alexander attempts to capture his prey by tempting him with a naked woman: "And I ordered a woman to undress and go to him on the chance that he might be vanquished by lust."[11] Unfortunately for both Alexander and the woman in question, the experiment triggers the creature's gastronomic rather than sexual appetite: "But he took the woman and went far away, where, in fact, he ate her."[12] The wildmen are not the only cannibals encountered by Alexander, as his enclosure of the savage nations behind the Caspian Gates is partially predicated upon their cannibalistic behavior. The Anglo-Norman *Alexander* of Thomas of Kent features a battle between Alexander's men and the bloodthirsty people of Gog and Magog, during which some unfortunate Macedonians have their brains sucked out by the enemy.[13] Moreover, the Greek *Pseudo-Callisthenes* includes the "Kynecephaloi" among the nations shut in by Alexander behind the Caspian Gates,[14] and indeed, cites his reasons for doing so as the fact that these peoples "ate the flesh of human beings and drank the blood of animals (and beasts) like water; for their dead they buried not, but ate," and because Alexander "feared that through such a diet they might pollute the earth by their vile pollutions."[15]

Later versions than *Pseudo-Callisthenes* contain more explicit details about the noxious diet of the soon-to-be enclosed barbarians. The late seventh-century *Pseudo-Methodius* details that the "children of Japhet"

> ate in cups every kind of defiled and filthy thing, that is, dogs, rats, serpents, dead men's flesh, aborted and unformed bodies, and those which are not yet formed in the womb in their essential features . . . both those of beasts of burden and also every type of unclean and untamed beast. Moreover, they do not even bury their dead but often eat them.[16]

Furthermore, their release in the endtimes will manifest divine wrath in similar brutal and voracious form:

> Then the Gates of the North will be opened and the strength of those nations which Alexander shut up there will go forth. The whole earth will be terrified at the sight of them; men will be afraid and flee in terror to hide themselves in mountains and caves and graves. They will die of fright and very many will be wasted with fear. There will be no one to bury the bodies. The tribes which will go forth from the North will eat the flesh of men and will drink the blood of beasts like water. They will eat unclean serpents, scorpions, and every kind of filthy and abominable beast and reptile which crawls the earth. They will consume the dead bodies of beasts of burden and even women's abortions. They will slay the young and take them from their mothers and eat them.[17]

These children of Japhet are identified in an early sixth-century Alexandrian romance, also Syrian, the *Christian Legend Concerning Alexander*, as a race of Huns descended from Noah's son Japhet, whom legend has it was suckled by a bitch after the death of his mother, imbibing her traits as well as her milk. A late fourth-century sermon imputes similar bloodthirsty habits to the Huns, who allegedly "eat the flesh of infants and drink the blood of women."[18]

But, as David White points out, the actual identity of the man-eating tribes behind Alexander's Gate is hardly important, since texts could easily be revised to accommodate the predations of any invading barbarian, causing the serial association of the cannibalistic hordes with "the Scythians, Parthians, Huns, Alans, Arabians, Turks, Mongols, and a host of other real or imagined races."[19] Having said that, however, it is interesting to note that later recensions of the legend, notably those of Peter Comestor and Godfrey of Viterbo, associate the nations behind the gates with the lost tribes of Israel, a connection between Judaism and anthropophagy which has a long history, and which surfaces again in early European encounters with the people of the New World.[20]

However, in the thirteenth century, as the Mongolian threat encroached on eastern Europe, the identity of not merely Alexander's barbarians but also of the quintessential rapacious cannibalistic horde became fixed as Tartar, as the title of Gregory Guzman's essay suggests. Ivo of Narbonne maintained in 1242 that the Mongol soldiers were cynocephalic cannibals, chewing the bodies of the fallen enemy "like so much bread," and Vincent of Beauvais envisioned an army of "infernal leeches," sucking the blood from their captives.[21] Simon of Saint-Quentin's *Historia Tartarorum* of 1248 informs its readers that the Tartars "devour human flesh like lions, but prefer it roasted by fire rather than boiled," adding that they eat this meat sometimes out of necessity, sometimes out of pleasure, and sometimes in order to strike fear and terror in the people who will hear of it."[22] The most obviously propagandist piece of writing on this topic, complete with a graphic illustration, appears as the entry under 1243 in the *Chronica Majora* of Matthew Paris:

> The Tartar chiefs, with the houndish cannibals their followers, fed upon the flesh of their carcasses, as if they had been bread, and left nothing but bones for the vultures. But, wonderful to tell, the vultures, hungry and ravenous, would not condescend to eat the remnants of flesh, if any by chance were left. The old and ugly women were given to their dog-headed cannibals—anthropophagi as they are called—to be their daily food; but those who were beautiful were saved alive, to be stifled and overwhelmed by the number of their ravishers, in spite of all their cries and lamentations. Virgins were deflowered until they died of exhaustion; then their breasts were cut off to be kept as dainties for their chiefs, and their bodies furnished a jovial banquet to the savages.[23]

It is hard to imagine a rhetoric more deliberately designed to outrage, inflame and rally feeling against the conquerors. It has it all—a cannibalism that is far worse than bestial, since even the vultures refuse the bodies of their victims, the daily devouring of the elderly and those unfortunate or fortunate enough to be considered ugly, the repeated rape of beautiful virgins, and a sexual mutilation reminiscent of the religious pornography[24] of the lives of saints like Barbara and Agnes. The goal of such a discourse is transparent, even when the terms themselves are subject to slippage, as was the designation Mongol/Tartar/Turk/ Moslem, particularly during the period of concerted Ottoman expansion in the fifteenth century.[25]

Certainly one logical catalyst for the development of ethno- and geoteratological discourses of cannibalism from the eleventh century onward would be the crusade ethos, and indeed, there are occasions where the expected accusations of cannibalism against the Saracens, or against their allies, appear in crusade literature, such as *Floovant*, in which the French forces are warned of the possibility of postmartial consumption,[26] or the *Conquete de Jerusalem*, where cannibalistic Blemmyae fight on the Saracen side.[27] However, the most interesting and most unlikely contribution of the literature of this period is the appearance of a Christian cannibalism. Guibert of Nogent, whose own vexed relationship with consumption is discussed in chapter three, chronicles the existence in Syria and Palestine of a ferocious band of vagabond survivors of the disastrous first crusade, known as the Trudentes, or Tafurs.[28] Said to be originally Frankish but under the control of a Norman (or Flemish) nobleman, the Tafurs are regarded by Guibert and other contemporary chroniclers as effective warriors with a useful reputation for ferocity, but also as something of an embarrassment. The twelfth-century vernacular poems *La Conquete de Jérusalem* and *La Chanson d'Antioche*, on the other hand, view the Tafurs and their hideous reputation as definite assets to the French and Christian cause. Norman Cohn argues that the *Conquete de Jérusalem* is useful primarily as "a guide to the psychology rather than to the external history of the People's Crusade in the East; and what it tells of the Tafurs is their legend," while "[t]he *Chanson d'Antioche* gives a soberer, less flattering and no doubt factually more accurate account of the Tafurs."[29] The "factual account," which claims to be the work of an eyewitness, Richard the Pilgrim, details the siege of Antioch in 1098, where the crusaders were themselves beset by famine, surrounded as they were by a further ring of Moslem soldiers. At the suggestion of Peter the Hermit, the Tafurs resolve their famine by roasting and eating some of the fallen Moslems within sight (and smell) of the enemy, and compound their offense by desecrating graveyards and devouring the recently buried bodies.

Contemporary chroniclers of the crusade also described siege cannibalism by the Christian troops, although without the note of vengeful glee sounded in the *Chanson d'Antioche*. Fulcher of Chartres, for instance, includes the following in his report of the siege of Ma'arra in 1098: "I shudder to say that many of our men, terribly tormented by the madness of starvation, cut pieces of flesh from the buttocks of the Saracens lying there dead. These pieces they cooked and ate, savagely devouring the flesh while it was insufficiently roasted. In this way, the besiegers were harmed more than the besieged.[30] Similarly, Raymond d'Aguilers wrote that the anthropophagy of the Frankish army, whether strategic or starvation cannibalism, not only appalled the enemy, but also impacted public opinion at home, even forcing some to rethink the ethics and the wisdom of the eastern campaign.[31] Despite acknowledging evidence for some Christian cannibalism at Antioch and at Ma'arra, Jonathan Riley-Smith remains dubious about the historical existence of a fearsomely cannibalistic Frankish contingent as described in Lewis Sumberg's influential essay,[32] reiterating that such an idea "seems to me to make the evidence provided by the *Chanson d'Antioche* carry more weight than it can bear."[33]

The allegations of the *Chanson d'Antioche* include the suggestion that Godfrey of Bouillon, far from discouraging the Tafurs from their grisly repast, in fact endorsed it, going so far as to donate a bottle of his best wine for their king to wash down his meal (ll. 4096–106). This lighthearted Christian attitude to anthropophagy reappears in the late thirteenth or early fourteenth century in a Middle English poem, "King Richard Coer de Lyon," in which crusade cannibalism is attributed to the king himself.[34] In the Holy Land for the Third Crusade, Richard becomes deathly ill, and feels that he will never recover unless he partakes of pork, a flesh that is obviously unavailable in his current circumstances. The king seems doomed until one of his men, inspired by the Blessed Virgin, remembers both the ample supply of Saracen prisoners of war, and the possibilities of spice and a little culinary skill:

> The sooth to say at words few
> Slayn and sodden was the hethene schrewe;
> Beffore the kyng it was forth brougt.
> Quod hys men: "Lord, we haue pork sougt;
> Etes, and southes off the browys swote,   *brow's sweat*
> Thorwg grace off God it schal be youre boote."   *benefit*
> Beffore Kyng Rychard karf a knygte:
> He eete ffastere than he karue mygte.
> The kyng eet the fflesch, and gnew the bones,
> And drank wel afftyr, for the nones   *occasion*
> (ll. 3104–12).

Believing he has consumed the pork necessary for his recovery, the king recuperates rapidly, until he is well enough to demand the head of the pig. When he is shown the head of a Saracen, instead of expressing the horror and disgust one might expect, Richard is delighted at the fact that Saracens are so tasty, and at the fact that this discovery means the defeat of famine in the Christian camp (ll. 3194–226).

In fact, Richard finds a further way to capitalize on his innovation. Shortly thereafter, he invites representatives of the Saracens to a feast, ostensibly to broker a peace agreement, but before they arrive, he has the most noble of his prisoners-of-war killed, giving his marshall the following instructions:

And are the hedes be of smyten   *before*
Loke euery name be wryten
Vpon a scrowe of parchemyn   *scroll*
And bere the hedes to the kechyn,
And in a cawdroun thou hem caste,
And bydde the cook sethe hem ffaste;
And loke that he the her off stryppe,
Off hed, off berd, and eke off lyppe....
Lay euery hed on a platere;
Bryng it hoot forthal in thyn hand,
Vpward hys vys, the teeth grennand....   *visage*
Hys name faste aboue hys browe,
What he hygte, and off what kyn born(e)
                          (ll. 3417–24; 3428–30; 3432–3433).

Faced with the English king carving the head before him and eating heartily, in addition to the carefully labeled grinning horrors on their own plates, the Saracen ambassadors flee, and Richard warns their retreating backs that, compared to Saracen meat "ther is no fflesch so norysschaunt / Vnto an Ynglyssche Cristen-man" (ll. 3548–3549), and that the English will leave only when the Saracens "be eaten euerylkon" (l. 3562). The Saracens immediately return to their Sultan, and the story is reiterated once more in the form of their outraged narrative, which includes their description of Richard, truly lionhearted, tearing into the human head before him: "With teeth he grond the flessch ful harde, / As a wood lyoun he ffarde, / With hys eyen stepe and grym..." (ll. 3599–3611).

The tone of this piece is, like that of the *Chanson d'Antioche*, difficult to characterize. The anonymous poet opens Richard's humanity to question, inventing or perhaps reattributing a legend of his parentage that claims that his mother (here named Cassodorien rather than the historical Eleanor of Aquitaine) was a daemon physically unable to stand witnessing the elevation of the host that marked the moment of transformation into the body and blood of Christ. One day a Christian earl tries to force her to do so, but she breaks free and, gripping her daughter and younger son, John, flies through the church roof in her attempt to escape. She drops John, breaking his thigh, but she and her daughter are never seen again (ll.185–234).[35] Certainly Richard's own devilish glee and fiendish skill at psychological warfare are important parts of the poem. Indeed, the English king's barbarity causes the Saracen ambassadors to whisper to one another, "this is the deuelys brothir, / that slees oure men and thus hem eetes!" (ll. 3484–85). Yet the poet never indicts Richard for his actions, but rather uses the incidences of cannibalism to celebrate his courage, cleverness, and charisma. By no means, then, is the poem an acknowledgement of the brutality of Christian imperialism. In an odd turnabout, by doing to the human enemy what humans do only to animals, the king in his authority effectively denies their humanity rather than his own. The fact that the meat that the flesh of the Saracens is said to resemble is the proscribed pork is a further sly assault on Moslem religion and culture.

Despite the prevalent horror of cannibalism in late medieval texts, and even, so to speak, in the teeth of it, the ultimate attitude toward the act clearly depended, to some degree, on context. In the accounts of the Tafurs, although cannibalism is transparently seen as brutal, it also proves to have a certain utility. There exists, then, a category of useful cannibals, some of whom appear again, in the familiar guise of Gog and Magog, in the supposed *Letter of Prester John*:

> We have in our country still another kind of men who feed only on raw flesh of men and women and do not hesitate to die. And when one of them passes away, be it their father or mother, they gobble him up without cooking him. They hold that it is good and natural to eat human flesh and they do it for the redemption of their sins.[36] This nation is cursed by God and it is called Gog and Magog and there are more of them than of all other peoples. With the coming of the Antichrist they will spread over the whole world, for they are his friends and allies. . . . None the less we take many of them with us into war, whenever we wish to wage one, and we give them license and permission to eat our enemies, so that of a thousand not a single remains who is not devoured and consumed. But later we send them home, because, if they were to stay with us longer, they would eat us all.[37]

Such a fate would indeed seem the downside of acquiring such voracious allies. But despite the obvious utility of cannibal allies in wartime, it is the domestic ritual funerary cannibalism described at the beginning of the passage that is perhaps the most popular type encountered in medieval travel texts. "Sir John Mandeville," for instance, includes a section on Dondun, in the Andaman Islands, where, following a spiritually prescribed euthanasia, a similar funeral custom exists:

> And after that thei choppen all the body in smale peces & preyen all his frendes to comen & eten of him that is ded & thei senden for all the mynstrall of the contree & maken a solempne feste. . . . And thei seyn also that men eten here flesch for to delyueven hem out of peyne, For if the wormes of the erthe eten hem the soule scholde suffre gret payne . . .[38]

Josephine Bennett argues that Mandeville's source here is the itinerary of Friar Odoric of Pordenone, c. 1330,[39] but the closeness of both texts to Marco Polo's account of the inhabitants of Dragoian is remarkable.

Mandeville is manifestly less critical of the inhabitants for their practices than are either Odoric or Marco Polo, displaying some of the tolerance for almost all non-Christian cultures which marks his chronicle (the distinct exception is Judaism).[40] However, he immediately follows this episode with an exhaustive catalog of Plinian monstrosities, featuring Cyclopes, Blemmye, people with holes for eyes, with giant lips, Pygmies, people with giant ears, with feet like horses, ape people, Hermaphrodites, knee walkers, people with enormous feet, apple smellers, and so on, suggesting, perhaps, that a degree of incredulity may also taint his account of the funerary practice.

Mandeville goes on, however, to describe an even more interesting mortuary ritual in Tibet, where filial mourning is marked by prayerful ritual dismemberment and the removal of the flesh by birds of prey and carrion birds:

> And after that, as preestes amonges vs syngen for the *Subuenite, sancti Dei, & cetera*, right so tho prestes syngen with high voys in hire langage: Beholdeth how so worthi a man & how gode a man this was, that the Aungeles of god comen for to sechen him & for to bryngen him in to paradys. . . . And whan thei ben at mete, the sone let brynge forth the hede of his fader and there of he geveth of the flesch to his most specyall frendes in stede of entremess or a sukkarke. And of the brayn panne he leteth make a cuppe & there of drynketh he & his other frendes also, with gret deuocioun . . .[41]

His source for this is clearly Odoric, in his section "45: Concerning the realm of Tibet, where dwelleth the Pope of the Idolaters," where the friar gives an account of a funeral ritual very much like that of Mandeville, with the latter excluding only Odoric's disapproval: "And they say by acting in this way they show their great respect for their father. And many other preposterous and abominable customs have they."[42]

In contrast to Odoric's disapproval, Mandeville's lack of condemnation is both extraordinary and unprecedented, even within his own text. His readers have already encountered a clear eucharistic parallel, peculiar, as far as I know, to Mandeville, in which he indicts the people of Milke [Malacca?], near Java, for their voracious and, worse, sacrilegious cannibalism: ". . . There is a full cursed peple for thei delyten in nothing more than for to fighten & to sle men And thei drynken gladyest mannes blood the whiche thei clepen DIEU . . ."[43] At this point, the ritual practice of a cannibalism very like communion serves merely to render the experience more depraved. Not so, however, by the time Mandeville discusses the Tibetan mortuary ritual. Stephen Greenblatt notes that the acknowledgment of the parallels between pagan ritual dismemberment and cannibalism and Christian liturgical and eucharistic practice in this passage is an acknowledgement that, for Mandeville, rather than further anathemizing the former ceremonies, imbues them with a sense of the Christian sacred. He sees this moment in Mandeville's text as one that marks the development of the author from his "possessive insistence on the core orthodox Christian belief to an open acceptance of many coexisting beliefs."[44] Nevertheless, the Christian eucharist does not remain untouched by this resemblance; rather, the parallels open it to a revisiting, revealing its rather unsettling strangeness to Mandeville, and to the peoples he encounters, sometimes accompanying other signs of deficient culture, like indiscriminate sex, common ownership, lack of agricultural and technological development, and gigantic or cyno-cephalic appearance.[45] Odoric's interest in cannibalism is clearly no match for that of Mandeville, since each of the former's episodes of anthropophagy is reproduced in the latter, together with additional instances. However, Odoric's evident horror is reflected in his discussion of cannibalism as prac-ticed on the island of Lamori, where, one version explains, the inhabitants practice a racially specific form of exocannibalism, eating only white men: "black men, like themselves, they eat not."[46] This suspiciously specific caveat demonstrates a fear of personal consumption which will emerge again in the radical racial othering found in the early European chronicles of the New World.

Marco Polo's concern, on the other hand, is almost entirely, and typi-cally, with practical details. He mentions on more than one occasion that death by natural causes disqualifies a body for consumption,[47] and points to the utilitarian practices of Zipangu (Japan), where prisoners are consumed only if they cannot raise their own ransom money. In order to make up for the financial loss, the captors make a gourmet celebration out of the occa-sion; they invite "all their relations and friends, and putting their prisoner to death, dress and eat the body, in a convivial manner, asserting that human flesh surpasses every other in the excellence of its flavour."[48] Indeed, Marco may have felt that he had to consider the practical details, since he himself, forced by contrary winds to bivouac on the island of Samara (Sumatra?) might have fallen victim to the voracious savages if it were not for his pru-dent defensive strategies: "in order to guard against mischief from the savage natives, who seek for opportunities of seizing stragglers, putting them to death, and eating them, he caused a large and deep ditch to be dug around him on the land side."[49] However, since he also made arrangements to trade victuals with the same natives, it may be assumed that their diet was not exclusively cannibalistic.[50] Of course, the question of precisely who informed the explorer about the supposed dietary habits of the peoples of Samara remains open.

The practical concerns about and utilitarian application of cannibalistic tendencies also appear in the earliest English text detailing a race of man-eating monsters, the ninth- or tenth-century *Andreas*. This poem is the account of the evangelical mission of Matthew to Mermedonia, where "There was no plenty of bread / for the men in that plain nor water's drink / to enjoy, but they ate blood and skin, / the flesh-home of men, of those who came from afar."[51] Ungraciously, his hosts blind him and imprison him to await consumption. His prayers for deliverance are answered in the form of Andrew and his disciples, who brave storm-tossed waters to reach him. The prison guards fall dead and the prison gates open at Andrew's touch, and he sends Matthew (who seems, in this version, to have quietly regained his sight) and his own followers away. Without their victim, the anthropophages face starvation, and draw lots for a new victim. In an ironic eucharistic parody, the chosen fare, referred to as "*tha collenferhth*," the bold one, offers his young son instead; the text comments: "*hie tha lac hrathe / thegon to thance*"—quickly they took that sacrifice with thanks (ll. 1111–2). But such a fundamentally false and futile, because literal, communion cannot be allowed; through Andrew, God causes their weapons to melt like wax, and in revenge, they seize and torture Andrew horribly for three days. He is divinely healed on the fourth day, and he causes a great flood to spring forth, drowning many of the Mermedonians. The remainder survive only because of Andrew's pity, as he causes the mountain to swallow up both the water and the worst of the people. Then angels restore and baptize the youthful drowned, and Andrew returns to his mission.

This legend was enormously geographically widespread, with extant versions in Greek, Latin, Old French, Syriac, Coptic, Ethiopic and Arabic, as well as Old English—indeed, Robert Boenig has argued that the cult of Andrew was among the most important of the medieval apostolic cults.[52] Certainly the mission to central Asia was both early and important in the spread of Christianity. The earliest sources suggest that Thomas was sent to Parthia and Andrew to Scythia, whereas later evangelical sources suggest, as does *Andreas*, that Matthias, or Matthias and Andrew, or Andrew and Bartholomew, are sent to a conflated Scythia/Parthia. The fourteenth-century *Ethiopic Contendings of the Apostles* is perhaps the most interesting of these, since it takes the extraordinary step of appropriating cannibalism as a vehicle for evangelism.

In this legend, Bartholomew and Andrew sorrow because their evangelical mission seems to be failing. The Angel of God transports them to the City of Cannibals, and as the disciples sleep, the angel appears before a dog-headed cannibal, convinces him of the power of God, and baptizes him in fire. The angel provides him with both the linguistic ability to communicate with the apostles and the self-control to refrain from eating them.[53] Nevertheless, the apostles are naturally alarmed at his "exceedingly terrible" appearance:

> He was four cubits in height and his face was like unto that of a great dog, and his eyes were like unto lamps of fire which burned brightly, and his teeth were like unto the tusks of a wild boar, and the nails of his hands were like unto curved reaping hooks, and the nails of his toes were like unto the claws of a lion, and the hair had come down over his arms to look like the mane of a lion, and his whole appearance was awful and terrifying.[54]

God removes their fear, and Andrew finds that the creature's name, appropriately enough, is Hasum [Abominable], but in the light of his recent conversion, the apostle bestows the name "Christian" upon him. All three travel to the city of Bartos, which has previously been infiltrated by Satan, and when the gates crumble before them, the townspeople send "hungry and savage beasts" to attack not Christian, whose fearsome head is covered, but the disciples themselves. After checking with Andrew, Christian prays that his savage nature be returned, and even increased, to God's glory, and he becomes "exceedingly wroth." He "leaped upon all the wild beasts that were among the multitudes of people who were gathered together, and he slew them forthwith, and tore out their bowels and devoured their flesh."[55] The men of the city are terrified, and seven hundred men and three nobles die. God surrounds the city with fire, whereupon the people acknowledge God's power and entreat him to use it to save them from tooth and flame. The apostles lay hands on Christian, and he again becomes as "gentle as a lamb."[56]

The text is ambiguous—just who or what is Christian/Abominable devouring? Is it the wild beasts, or the multitudes of people? If it is the former, as the syntax of Budge's translation seems to suggest, how do the men and nobles die? And is the city of Bartos to be identified with the City of Cannibals which is Christian's hometown, as David White seems to suggest, describing the people as Christian's "cannibal cousins"?[57] If so, why do they remark on Christian's dogheaded appearance, since cynocephaly seems here to be a necessary condition for cannibalism? And, if they are of the same race as Christian, how do they manage to communicate with the apostles, when Christian required divine help for the same project? And if they are of the same city, then Christian is practicing a savage endocannibalism, rendering him more one of the "*sylfaetan*," as the text of *Andreas* terms the cannibals, than his previously exclusively exocannibalistic brethren.[58] While there are obviously difficulties and ambiguities here that elude a straightforward explanation, the bulk of the evidence seems to suggest that this particular version does not intend that Christian devour humans, even with apostolic permission. Since such a horror is not perpetrated upon the city of Bartos, it is not necessary for the purposes of ironic justice that the citizens of that city be identified as Christian's brethren, but merely as run-of-the-mill evildoers. However, it seems probable that this text, with its confusion and conflicting information, is dependent upon an earlier version, not necessarily textual, in which Christian reverts to his cannibalistic nature and slaughters and devours the men of his own city in the name of God. Such a cruelly just narrative obviously spawns much larger questions about the Christian morality of such utilitarian cannibalism, suggesting that one can, if temporarily Abominable, kill and cannibalize human flesh for ultimately "Christian" purposes—hence the bowdlerized and somewhat confused text that remains extant. And yet, if one is to avoid the trap of dualism, this manifestation of God's permission for such a barbarous act must be merely a difference of degree. Andrew's cannibal evangelical version of the incredible hulk serves God merely more directly, and with purer intent, than the monstrous races behind Alexander's Gate, or even the cannibalistic mother at the siege of Jerusalem, whom I discuss at some length in chapter four.

In direct contrast, the versions of a slightly later English text that has been named *The Wonders of the East* is interesting in this context largely because of the fact that both the translator(s) and the illustrator(s) appear to have foregone any attempt at Christian didacticism. The versions include three illustrated English manuscripts in Old English and/or Latin, dated between 970 and 1150, as well as eight continental versions, seven of which are Latin.[59] All three of the English manuscripts appear to be based, in varying degrees of directness, on the fanciful catalog of monstrosity known as the *Letter of Pharamenes to the Emperor Hadrian*,[60] and speak to an intense and palpably dynamic interest in the anatomy of monstrosity.[61]

These races are monstrous by virtue of their transgression of normally rigid categories—by their hybridity, their physical excess or lack, or their moral and behavioral characteristics.[62] One of the prime moral transgressions is that of consuming human flesh, the illustration of which occupies a disproportionately large number of the monstrous miniatures. The most well known of the man-eaters, and certainly the ones that have received the most critical attention, are the Donestre, who inhabit holy geographic space, in this case, an island in the Red Sea. They are anthropophages in the sense that they beguile and eat tourists, and they are indeed described as "*moncynn*," but they are hybrid creatures: "*Tha syndon geweaxene saw frihteras fram than heafde oth thone nafelan, and se other dael byd mannes lice gelic*"—They are shaped like *frihteras* from the head down to the navel, and the rest resembles a man's body.[63] Gibb glosses "*frihteras*" as meaning "soothsayer," or "divine" in his standard glossary,[64] but describes "Donestre" in his glossary of proper names as "race of men who are half-soothsayer or half-lion and half-man."[65]

The former is difficult to imagine—what does it mean to be a soothsayer to the navel, but otherwise human?—while the latter gloss puts their humanity, and therefore their status as true cannibals, into question. The Tiberius manuscript does, however, help resolve, if not the meaning of "*frihteras*," at least a contemporary understanding of it, since it contains illustrations of the Donestre with flowing leonine manes.[66] Despite their bestial nature, the Donestre's humanity is reaffirmed by their two primary characteristics. Unlike the other monstrous cannibals encountered so far, the Donestre have the gift of human speech—indeed, they surpass mere humans in knowing "*eall mennisc gereord*"—and of human emotion. They use the former attribute as a hunting device to lure in victims, and the latter as a sign of mourning for their actions: "*And thaenne, aefter than, hi hine fretath ealne butan his heafde, and thonne sittath and wepath ofer than heafde.*"[67] The contemporary analogy for this might be crocodile tears, but the crocodile does not appear weeping or as a symbol of either hypocrisy or compassion in medieval bestiaries. In fact, the Donestre bear a closer resemblance to the hyena, which eats the bodies of men and mimics their voices, making "sounds like a man being sick to lure out dogs."[68] This animal, it is said, represents the children of Israel, perhaps in the sense of mimicking Christian prayerfulness and spirituality, but eating not the living Christ, but only the rejected and the dead.

The other cannibals in the *Wonders* texts are the enormous black "Hostes" from across the Brixontis River, a mythical Nile tributary. Despite the appellations "men" and "*homines*," their humanity is in fact highly dubious, as they seem to fall rather into the category of giants: "*Tha habbad fet and sceancan twelf fota lange, sidan mid breostum seofan fota lange.*"[69] John Block Friedman identifies the given name as the result of a misreading of the Latin "*hostes*"—enemy—in an Old French translation of the fictive *Letter to Hadrian* on which the *Wonders* is based,[70] but the possibilities of verbal confusion also bring to mind the linguistic interplay of host, with its triple meaning of enemy, hospitaller/guest and eucharist.[71] The Hostes also find a home in the illustrations, costumed in black up to the chin[72] and munching on a limb in Vitellius fol. 102r, and too huge to fit upright in the frame as they devour terrified humans headfirst in Tiberius fol. 81v and Bodley 614 fol. 40v.

However, the fear of consumption and incorporation was not limited to possible encounters with the marvelous at the fringes of civilization. Death itself, inescapable and terrifying, involves a process of decline, decay, and the eventual union of the body with the earth—a process for which the metaphor of physical incorporation has proven particularly apposite, as the well-known etymology of "sarcophagus" illustrates. Indeed, the thirteenth-century anthologist Caesarius of Heisterbach is following a fairly standard etymology in deriving "*mors*" from "*morsus*": death from bite, and medieval hells, as we shall see, were envisioned as voracious pits of anthropophagy.[73] But early Christians also found ways to express salvation in terms of digestion, although here the digestion is divine. Tertullian uses a word for "martyrdom" which literally means "devouring," explaining that if God wants martyrdom, "we must count happy the man whom God has eaten."[74]

Neither did the early theologians neglect the elegant symmetry of the incorporation of Christ's body into a human and that of the human into the body of Christ. Irenaeus argued as early as the beginning of the third century that our only defense against the relentless maceration and digestion of the earth is our own consumption of the flesh of Jesus. As we eat Christ, we are incorporated into him, instead of vice versa, ensuring that we cannot be wholly consumed by death or the grave.[75] Augustine describes the paradox similarly, his God explaining, "Grow, and you shall feed on me, but you shall not change me into your own substance, as you do with the food of your flesh. Instead you shall be changed into me."[76]

Moreover, the sacraments, particularly that of the eucharist, specifically worked to pry open the masticating jaws of the underworld. The twelfth-century *Hortus Deliciarum* envisions Jesus using the tree of life to penetrate the throat of Leviathan, inducing the vomiting forth of those souls the monster had swallowed unfairly,[77] while the roughly contemporary Peter of Celle envisioned death biting ravenously at the body of Jesus, only to shatter its teeth on Christ's hidden divinity.[78]

The metaphor of the monstrous jaws of hell closing over their victims, trapping tormented souls and consigning them to the belly of the beast, appears as early as 3 Baruch, and can be seen in operation in the appearances of the great fish and the leviathan in the books of Jonah and Job respectively.[79] The very fact that it is possible to discuss the "mouth" of hell without glossing—or even noticing—the metaphor is indicative of the tenacity and omnipresence of such imagery. Once behind the teeth of hell, however, the damned soul is often said to experience a further rending, devouring and consumption, tortures which Jacques Le Goff has linked with the Jewish tradition of a verminous bed of punishment in Sheol,[80] Some of the most colorful and dramatic imagery is early, occurring, for instance, in the second-century apocalypses of Peter and Paul, where vipers, dragons, and worms gnaw ceaselessly at guilty souls, and those who sinned verbally—blasphemers and bearers of false witness, and disrespectful slaves—are condemned to chew their own tongues or bite through their own lips.[81]

The same motif of souls suffering a harrowingly appropriate punishment manifests itself consistently in the punishments allotted to sinful mothers (women who have had abortions, or committed infanticide, or refused to nurse, or exposed their offspring), where, instead of nursing their babies, they are forced to breastfeed hideous carnivorous beasts. In the *Apocalypse of Peter*, this is particularly graphic and apposite, as the women are perpetually eaten by monsters that emerge from their curdled breastmilk: "the milk of their mothers flows from their breasts and congeals and smells foul, and from it come forth [tiny] beasts that devour flesh, which turn and torture them forever, with their husbands."[82] These women's sinful bodies have been made to revolt against them, as they exude the means to the agony of their souls. Similarly, in the *Vision of Ezra*, infanticidal mothers have serpents attached to their nipples, and in the *Apocalypse of Baruch* widows who have had abortions are eaten by flaming serpents and dogs, as are priests, who are presumably the secret impregnators of the women.[83] The Greek version of the *Apocalypse of Mary* describes abortion as "eating human flesh,"[84] while the Ethiopian version features nuns being devoured by flaming beasts of prey for abortion and infanticide while fetuses or children accuse them of throwing them to wild beasts.[85]

Some of the later texts also include this kind of imagery: the knightly protagonist in *St. Patrick's Purgatory* encounters successive fields of devouring torture, one in which people lie prone or supine, attacked by flaming dragons, toads, and snakes, and finally reaches what Jacques Le Goff calls "a real chamber of horrors of the most diverse kinds," featuring "men and women suspended by iron hooks stuck in the sockets of their eyes or in their ears, throats, hands, breasts, or genitals, while others have fallen victim to hell's kitchen and are being baked in ovens, roasted over open fires, or turned on spits..."[86] It becomes clearer that the authors are drawing on a strong tradition of demonic consumption when the images become inconsistent or contradictory, such as in the *Vision of Alberic*, c. 1120, which envisions a thorny valley in which rejecting mothers who refused to breastfeed their infants seem to be hung up by their nipples, which at the same time are being sucked by snakes.[87]

One of the most persistently alimentary of the visions of hell is the *Visio Tnugdali*, which bears close examination, not only for this reason, but also due to its unusually widespread provenance, with almost two hundred extant manuscripts, and evidence of translation into fifteen medieval vernaculars since 1149,[88] in addition to virtually wholesale incorporation into Vincent of Beauvais's thirteenth-century *Speculum Historiale*. Almost all of the perverse punishments of this hell are alimentary. It features a vast iron cooking vessel in which murderous souls are simmered to the point of liquefaction, then regathered and cooked again.[89] The tools of the fiends are cooking implements; they have "forkes & tonges in hande./ And grete krokes of yren brennande"[90] for lifting sinners from fire to ice and back. Actual consumption and digestion also appear. The beast Acheron swallows "coueytous menne,"[91] and in its flaming belly the English covetous soul suffers "kene howndys that on hym gnewe, / And dragones that hym all todrewe. / Wyth edderes and snakes & other vermyne / He was gnawen in ylke a lyme,"[92] while his Latin counterpart faces the bites and rendings of "*canum, vrsorum, leonem, serpencium et animalium aliorum innumerabiliem in cognitorum*"— dogs, bears, lions, serpents, and other innumerable unknown animals.[93] Thieves must cross a lake of "hydwes bestes & felle" where "on eche a syde they waytede ay / To swolewe [souls] that wore hare pray."[94] Indulgers in bodily excess, the fornicators and gluttons, are enclosed in an enormous oven, where the gluttons are carved "in gobbetys smale"[95] by devilish butchers, only to be immediately reassembled and chopped up again, while the clerical sinners are eaten inside and out by vermin in their entrails. Other fornicators of both sexes appear to have had their genitalia chewed away— "payned were in her priuetese and all tognawen betwene her these"[96]— although in the Latin, in addition to worms gushing from within, there are implications of disease and decay, whether literal or metaphorical, which are lacking in the Middle English version: "*pudenda vero ipsa putredine corrupta videbantur scaturire vermibus*"—the genitalia, corrupt with rottenness, appeared to be gushing forth worms.[97]

The alimentary theme continues yet further with the punishment devised for lecherous and disobedient priests. They are consumed and digested in the fiery belly of a monstrous beast, which then casts them forth pregnant with demonic iron-headed vipers, which chew through their intestines. Since, due to the genders of the *gravidi*, the vipers cannot be delivered in the normal manner, they erupt though the skin, where they are anchored by the spikes in their tails, and turn again on their unfortunate "mothers," plunging their heads back in "thorow ych a ioynte, senwe & vayne."[98] Not unexpectedly, the deepest and most foul part of Tondal's vision of the otherworld contains a cannibalistic Lucifer, bound on a "gredyll" rather than by ice, and sucking in a thousand souls with each breath, which are then exhaled and reinhaled, until they are defecated forth in with a sulphurous reek and fall into the fire to begin the endless process anew.[99]

The most famous medieval underworld vision is of course that of Dante. After the ubiquity of digestion in Tondal, the breadth of punishment available to Dante's sinners seems astonishing, but Dante too returns to alimentary themes. Spendthrifts are pursued and ripped to pieces by savage dogs in Canto XIII, but most of the digestion in Dante is more complex than mere consumption by beasts.[100] Perhaps Dante avoids this imagery because his hell itself is a gigantic gullet, the very bowels of which contain his triple-mouthed Satan, punishing the treacherous even as he himself is punished: "In each mouth he crushed a sinner with his teeth as with a heckle and thus he kept three of them in pain."[101] Two of Lucifer's victims, of course, are upright, with their heads protruding from his jaws, while Judas is head down with his legs protruding. Bynum's analysis of images of regurgitation and resurrection suggests that the consumed and resurrected body is disgorged headfirst; Judas, then, is beyond all hope of resurrection.[102]

Other sinners in Dante's hell are prepared for the table in overtly culinary terms; the demon cooks force the damned back into the boiling pitch in Canto XXI: "Just so cooks make their scullions plunge the meat down into the cauldrons with their forks that it may not float."[103] At the end of this episode, of course, the cooks themselves fall into the pitch and are cooked "within their crust."[104]

Given the intimate confusion here and elsewhere in *Inferno* between eater and eaten, punisher and punished, Maggie Kilgour would seem to be right when she points out that consumption in Dante's hell must necessarily be a form of autocannibalism, citing characters such as Filippo Argenti, and Minos and his creature, who bite at their own bodies in passion and fury.[105] There is self-cannibalism, too, in the story of Ugolino, who "bit both hands for grief" during his imprisonment,[106] whose sons offered him their own flesh, and who, Dante intimates, may have resorted to cannibalizing them in his extremity: "then fasting had more power than grief."[107] Ugolino, blind to the spiritual possibilities of his sons' words, can commune only physically, and his misinterpretation ultimately damns him to lock his teeth eternally on the skull of his jailer: "and, as bread is devoured for hunger, the one above set his teeth in the other at the place where the brain joins the nape."[108]

The digestive imagery of these hells is a clear contrast to the lack of physicality associated with heaven. In *St. Patrick's Purgatory*, for instance, after Sir Owen passes safely through purgatory, he reaches first earthly paradise, where his sustenance is the fragrance of the meadows, and finally experiences heavenly nutrients—a divine flame.[109] Food is perfume and light—a far cry from the brutally alimentary nature of purgatory and hell. Yet Christ, the church taught, descended to the very bowels of such an alimentary hell, which Piero Camporesi, in typically purple prose, describes as "this machine which devoured, this mouth which swallowed and sucked, this horrible, swollen and labyrinthine intestine, this amoebean place, like a gut in perpetual peristalsic motion . . . absorbed and destroyed this repellent human fauna with its diseased and putrefying adiposity."[110]

It seems inevitable then, that the body of Christ, swallowed at mass, should travel through the esophagus and into the stomach, and thence the bowels, of the believer. As Camporesi points out, "[t]he descent of the body of Christ into the *antrum*, into the wet and foul-smelling guts, is followed by theologians with a worried gaze and with thoughtful anxiety."[111] It is alarming enough that the literal physical body of God be swallowed, and perhaps even masticated, let alone be digested and excreted. Clearly, a god in the bowels is hardly a god at all—a speculation picked up by, among others, the Lollard Margery Baxter in 1429, in her concern for gods being entirely consumed, and, then, colorfully, "*emittunt per posteriora in sepibus turpiter fetentibus.*"[112] The orthodox response called for a denial of the digestive process, such as that contained in Roland Bandinelli's story of the heretic who tried to prove that he could digest Christ by living on nothing but the host. After fourteen days, he died, proving only that testing God is a bad idea, and that he had been excreting and digesting only himself, not the eucharist.[113] God may be eaten, but he cannot be consumed.[114]

But the concept of cannibalism, as Peggy Reeves Sanday reminds us, is never just about eating.[115] It is a powerfully complex and divisive symbol that channels communal and individual anxieties about incorporation, ultimately functioning to reinforce critical social and cultural taxonomies. This brief survey of the background of medieval cannibalism reveals some telling clues as to what is ultimately at stake. Certainly, it seems that at one level, it tells us what it means to be human. An intrinsic property of late medieval concepts of humanity appears to be the verbal—language itself. Again and again, those who eat human flesh are or become sublinguistic: Lycaon, become a wordless werewolf; Tereus, become a hoopoe, known for its mournful but incommunicative cry; the barbarians at the gate of Alexander, mumbling incomprehensibly, or worse, in Hebrew, or barking like the dogs they resemble; Hasum, unable to communicate with Christians until his cannibalistic nature is suspended; Ugolino, unable to appropriately interpret his sons' language. Instead of using the mouth to pronounce the word of God, both the act of speaking and the knowledge of the divine separating the human from the bestial, the anthropophage uses it to rend and to devour. Perhaps it is for this reason that the Donestre stand out from among their co-cannibals, since they know all human speech—and yet they are visibly inhuman, and use their speech to diabolic ends, luring men to death with "*leaslicum wordum*"—lying words.

Cannibalism, then, suggests a prelinguistic lawlessness—a return to the Lacanian Imaginary, of being literally *infants*. This is the domain of the mother, and it is not surprising, then, to note the associations between cannibalism and the relationship of mother and child that manifest themselves throughout the episodes of consumption that I trace in this project. They are discussed particularly in chapter four, which focuses on the medieval and early modern redactions of the legend of the starving mother who consumes her baby at the siege of Jerusalem in 70 C.E., but also appear in my discussions of the blood libel, of sacramental heresy, of witchcraft allegations, of the phantasy of the New World, and of course, of the eucharist itself. It is the maternal body which Bakhtin points to as illustrative of the transgressive grotesque, outgrowing its own boundaries, open, proliferating, double-bodied. Similarly, the act of eating distorts limits, opening the body to an ambivalence in which eater and eaten "are interwoven and begin to be fused in one grotesque image of a devoured and devouring world."[116] The cannibalistic woman is the Bakhtinian grotesque body par excellence. Interestingly, although Bakhtin identifies the fifteenth and sixteenth centuries as marking a highly significant shift in ways of looking at the bounded body, and even though he deals with Protestant satire specifically targeting Catholic ritual, he does not link the grotesque eating body with the divine body of the eaten Christ.

Throughout these narratives, it has been with the child victim, the eaten body, the contents of the (usually) female and maternal belly, that identification has normally been assumed.[117] Peggy Phelan makes an analogous argument in her discussion of the contemporary anti-abortion movement, suggesting that the erosion of male control over the reproductive process manifests itself in an anxious nostalgia played out in the theater of organizations like Operation Rescue, which attempt 'to hide the fact that the baby it wants so desperately to rescue is that mythically innocent white man, still caught in the silent womb of the maternal body."[118] It is the same "mythically innocent white man," adult or child, who is envisioned as endangered by the voracity of the consuming ma(w). The archetypal is always also the political.

The victims of the cannibalism are, with the exception of those women who are subjected to righteous hellish punishments, young male innocents, whether the sacrificed infant of the eucharistic *exempla*, the prepubescent Christian boy drained of blood at Passover, the tiny baby devoured by his Jewish mother, the castrated Arawak boys destined for the pot, or the unwitting Italian sailor dismembered by cunning Carib women. The body that is desired and therefore endangered is ultimately the male body, and whereas the cannibal perpetrators are not always woman, the masculinity of the male cannibals is often opened to doubt. Mutilated or sodomitical men, they are collapsed back into the feminine threat.[119]

Clearly, there is a symbolic relationship between the anxious metaphors of engulfment and female, particularly maternal, sexuality, and more specifically, between cannibalism and incest. Levi-Strauss called cannibalism "an alimentary form of incest," and William Arens points out that cannibalism and incest are linked as markers of lack of civilization, and that "the ultimate horror" in the mythology of cannibalism takes the form of a doubly incestuous transgression—"one member of the family devouring another."[120] There is evidence, too, that a medieval audience would have such a metaphorical slippage available to them—Gower describes incest in *Confessio Amantis* as an auto-cannibalism: a "wylde fader thus devoureth / His oghne fleisshe,"[121] and Antiochus's famous Oedipal riddle revolves around the decoding of such a metaphor: "I ete and have it noght forbore / Mi modres fleissh . . ."[122]

Both incest and cannibalism are acts that invoke the bestial, allowing for the drawing of convenient boundaries between culture and non-culture, inside and out. The existence, or even potential existence, of such a fearsome Other allows for the construction of civilized identity, always superior, but always endangered, and the frontier between the two must therefore be policed with an absolute vigilance, including oppression, enslavement, and extermination. Yet the body politic is essentially vulnerable—to piercing, infiltration, or engulfment—and metaphors of incorporation are strategies that point to potential dangers, from Jews, heretics, and witches, poisoning the body and Christendom and draining it of its vital fluids, as well as whole continents of hungry aliens to the east and west.

Yet paradoxically, as allegations of cannibalism function to place the accused outside the borders of civilization, they simultaneously work against themselves, reaffirming the humanity of the accused. Like Solinus's bird, which had a human face and would, if it preyed upon a man too much like itself, shrivel with remorse,[123] the cannibal can be cannibal only by dint of his/her own human face, or body, or tongue. The accusations logically fail, then, collapsing under the weight of their own internal contradictions, and yet the power of the allegation remains, yielding a spectacular impact in social, historical, and human terms. In the next four chapters, I examine some of these allegations and their role in policing the borders of a body politic always already under threat.

Chapter Two

Corpus Christi: The Eucharist and Late Medieval Cultural Identity

Therfor the Jewis chidden togidere, and seiden, Hou may this gyue to vs his fleisch to ete? Therfor Jhesus seith to hem, Treuli, treuli, Y seie to you, but ye eten the fleisch of mannus sone, and drenken his blood, ye schulen not haue lijf in you. He that etith my fleisch, and drynkith my blood, hath euerlastynge lijf, and Y schal agen reise hym in the laste dai. For my fleisch is veri mete, and my blood is very drynk. He that etith my fleisch, and drynkith my blood, dwellith in me, and Y in hym.[1]

T LEAST ONCE A YEAR, THE VAST MAJORITY OF CHRISTIANS IN THE Middle Ages had an immediate and personal experience of anthropophagy. In swallowing a consecrated wafer that did not merely represent the body of Christ, but *was* the body of Christ, the medieval believer not only partook of human and divine flesh, but was incorporated into a community of theophagists for whom theophagy was a central and fundamental aspect of the church. The ritual eating of the sacrificed body of the god is a remarkable symbol that gains much of its charge from the juxtaposition of the sacred and the taboo, but the very power of this combination cannot be contained within the ritual itself; once implemented, such a ritual gathers its own meanings and valences that manifest themselves in narrative and practice. For this reason, a number of complex late medieval narratives that explore the possible implications of the eucharist cluster around that sacrament, some of which accept and elaborate upon the possibilities inherent in the mass to the point of a grotesque realism, others of which project such participatory anthropophagy onto communities outside the Christian body, and still others of which reconfigure the cannibalism in the eucharist to arrive at a carefully negotiated and unexceptionable position. In this chapter, I examine some of the ways in which the underlying fantasy of the mass, the cannibalism that communion mimics and transcends, appears in these manifestations, first in the eucharistic miracles and visions of the literalizing of the host, and secondly in the appearance of narratives of cannibalistic beliefs and rituals about non-Christians. Not only do these narratives overlap, but both function to divide heretic and believer, Christian and infidel, underscoring the importance of communion to a church struggling to define orthodoxy and to overcome regional and doctrinal variations of belief and ritual in order to establish what Miri Rubin has called a "sacramental world view."[2] Finally, I would like to address the impact of sacramentalism on popular secular narratives, specifically, the eruption of eucharistic symbolism into the profoundly secular space of the fabliaux, marking a negotiation of sexuality, cannibalism, and communion. The richness and density of eucharistic symbolism place the mass in a unique position within late medieval religiosity, as an assurance of salvation, as a means of direct and intimate access to the divine, and as a metaphor for the body of the faithful and for the church itself. More practically, communion functioned to define and reinscribe the authority of the priesthood, to reify church teaching, and to police the increasingly permeable frontier separating orthodoxy and heresy. Remarkably, then, the mass helped maintain clerical hierarchy at the same time as it offered an individual experience of God.

Yet the eucharist did not take on such critical importance until the High Middle Ages, with the eleventh century onward being marked by such developments as the coining of the term "transubstantiation," the declaration of the doctrinal status of transubstantiation at the Fourth Lateran Council, the establishment and rapid growth in popularity of a feast of Corpus Christi, and the trend toward identifying personal religiosity with the suffering humanity of Christ, manifested in the dedication of cults as well as in bodily practices. At the same time, as Maggie Kilgour points out, the church negotiated a slippage of terms that elided distinctions among the three holy "bodies"; originally the historically physical body of Christ had been referred to as "*proprium et verum corpus*," the body of Christ in the host referred to as "*corpus mysticum*," and the body of the church and its members referred to as "*corpus Christi*." At some point during the twelfth century, the increased insistence on the real presence necessitated the use of the term "*corpus verum*" to refer to the host. "*Corpus mysticum*" would come to be used to refer to the body of the church, while "*corpus Christi*" would come to refer to part or all of a system of meaning that included host, community, and identity.[3]

Thus it was that the vision of Jesus received by Colette of Corbie in the early fifteenth century, while startling to twenty-first-century perceptions, was far from unique, or even unusual, during the later Middle Ages. The Franciscan nun saw her Savior in the form of a serving dish filled with the body of a child, dismembered into fragments of bloody meat, while the voice of God the Father explained that the sin of the world was responsible for carving up His son.[4] This extraordinarily potent image of the Christ child fragmented and destined to be eaten is, of course, the logical and literalized extension of the doctrine of transubstantiation—the miracle whereby the real presence of the body and blood of Christ replaces the consecrated bread of the eucharist. Such direct and divinely sanctioned evidence proves the truth of transubstantiation, heretical objections notwithstanding, in a much more accessible, immediate, and concrete way than any number of papal bulls, conciliar teachings, or theological debates. Consequently, such eyewitness evidence of the truth of church doctrine seems to have been found in abundance, and in many cases it was tied even more directly to the sacrament of the mass than was the vision of Colette of Corbie.

One such case is that of the monk Gotteschalk of Volmarstein, whose vision during his own celebration of mass is recorded by Caesarius of Heisterbach in his *Dialogus Miraculorum,* a collection of *exempla* with a strong emphasis on eucharistic miracles, as follows:

> [w]hen he was before a certain altar on Christmas Day filled with devotion and shedding many tears, as he was wont, and had begun as usual, to wit, "Unto us a son is born," and the transubstantiation had taken place, forthwith he found in his hands and saw with his eyes no longer the appearance of bread, but a most glorious infant, indeed Him who is most beautiful in form compared with the sons of men on whom also angels desire to look. Kindled with His love and transported with His wondrous beauty, he embraced Him and kissed Him. Being afraid that any delay might upset the others who were there, he laid the Beloved on a corporal and he[5] took again the sacramental form in order that the mass might be accomplished. So long as that blessed saint saw the appearance of the child, he saw there no species of bread and vice versa.[6]

Here the vision of the Christ child is evidently granted as a blessing and a reward for unusual faith and devotion, just as the more alarming vision of Colette of Corbie marks her as a moral nonparticipant in the dismembering sins of the rest of the world. But while in some cases the vision or miracle is a reward for especial devotion to *imitatio Christi,* in others it shores up a faith shaken by the intangibility of the real presence, or converts or reveals non-Christian or heretical or sinful participants. As Caesarius points out, "[t]he Saviour condescends, as I said at the beginning, to show the reality of His body in this sacrament to good priests in order that they may be comforted;

to those who are wavering in their faith that they may be strengthened; to those who are living ill that they may be warned."[7]

Such a divine warning appeared to a particularly sinful priest named Adolphus:

> [o]ne day when this Adolphus was celebrating mass and before the "Agnus Dei" had lifted up the host to break it, he saw the Virgin in the host itself sitting upon a throne and holding the infant to her breast. Wishing to know what was on the other side, as soon as he turned to the host he saw a lamb in it, and when he again turned he saw in it, as if through a glass, Christ hanging on the cross with bent head.[8]

This is a dense passage extraordinarily rich in food/flesh imagery. Not only is the broken body of Jesus interchangeable with both the paschal lamb, described by St. Catherine of Siena as "roasted not boiled" on the "spit of the cross"[9] and the wheaten bread of the host, but the lactating body of Mary is similarly represented as becoming and providing food. Unlike the pious Goddeschalk, Adolphus is terrified rather than blessed by the vision, since he has been in the practice of celebrating and receiving the body of Christ while living with a concubine.[10] However, the fact that a corrupt priest could receive ocular proof of transubstantiation spoke also to the truth of the church's position on the celebratory power of all priests, even the wicked, and directly against the heretical position of Donatism.[11] However, sometimes it is not entirely obvious whether a eucharistic vision is intended as a blessing or a rebuke, so that Daniel, Abbot of Schönau, received an ambivalent vision of human blood in the communion chalice: "[a]nd as at the time he knew himself free from mortal sin, he did not think it was granted him for his condemnation, but hoped it was sent for his consolation."[12]

In some eucharistic *exempla*, the focus is on the miracle of the appearance of an adorable (and whole) infant Jesus in the host; in others, the emphasis is on the much more gruesome torn flesh of the sacrificial Christ, sometimes as child and sometimes as adult, literally envisioned as bleeding meat. There seems to be little distinction to be made between these two forms of eucharistic miracle. While the former appears much less macabre and sadistic than the latter, both appear to the impious, the doubtful, and the saintly alike, both reinforce the doctrine of transubstantiation, and since in both kinds the Savior—whether adult or child, whole or dismembered—will ultimately be eaten, both endorse the discourse of eucharistic cannibalism.

Recipients of visions of the smiling infant Jesus in the consecrated bread are frequently holy women, such as the beguine Mary of Oignies, and sometimes even whole houses of nuns, such as those at Helfta, Engenthal, and

Töss.[13] Indeed, Caroline Bynum has suggested that devotion to the cult of the eucharist is a peculiarly female development in medieval piety, endorsed, or sometimes merely tolerated, by a masculine clerical machinery that realized the uses of eucharistic piety as a weapon against heresy.[14] Certainly, the initial impetus for a feast of Corpus Christi is generally ascribed to a nun, Sister Juliana of Cornillon, and its success was due in no small part to the recluse Eve of St. Martin.[15] Moreover, women were more likely to change houses or orders, as Agnes Blannbekin did, to enable them to avoid rules against communing more frequently.[16]

Small children are also often the naïve recipients of the vision of the child in the bread, such as the young son of Geoffrey le Despenser who was appalled and frightened for his own safety when he saw Brother Peter of Tewkesbury devour a child on the altar,[17] or the little Jewish boy who chattered eagerly to his father about the sweet little boy he had been given to eat in church, only to be thrown into a glassblower's furnace by his furious father.[18] Clearly, the motif of the visionary child allows for contrasts to be drawn between the pure faith of the innocent or ignorant and the jaded hairsplitting of the educated, too caught up in fastidious debate to experience the reality of Christ's sacrifice.[19] Indeed, the frequent appearance of eucharistic *exempla* in female hagiography may serve a similar contrasting function.[20]

More common than visions of the undamaged baby or the innocent sacrificial lamb to the pure in heart, however, are the appearances to heretics, or unbelievers in various states of doubt, such as the vision of Christina of Stommeln, whose uncertainty about transubstantiation was miraculously resolved when she saw a child in the hands of the priest celebrating mass.[21] Other doubters received visions of a whole and beautiful Christ child whose body was broken and divided during the course of a mass, such as that in the *Vitae Patrum* of the very old and holy Egyptian monk whose faith could not extend to the literal presence of Christ in the eucharist. Two of his colleagues prayed for divine help, and at mass all three witnessed a small boy lying on the altar. As the priest reached for the bread, an angel descended from heaven, stabbing the child and catching His blood in a chalice, and as the bread was broken, so the child was cut up into bleeding chunks for the recipients. When the doubting monk was given his piece of flesh, he cried out his renewed faith in the presence, and the bloody meat miraculously assumed the form of bread again.[22]

Although one might be tempted to dismiss the concept of a horrified response to such a revelation as an anachronism, it should be noted that, in each case, if it is the officiating priest who witnesses the miracle, the ceremony cannot proceed until the bread has again returned to its former appearance—a clear indication of the powerful ambivalence of the miracle.

Certainly the fact that Christ ordinarily did not allow his body and blood to be seen in the wafer and chalice could be viewed as further evidence of his mercy in sparing the feelings of His congregation—as Berthold von Regensburg asks, "[w]er möchte einem kindelin sin houbetlin oder sinin hendelin oder sinin füezelin abegebizen?" "Who would like a little child to have his little head, or his little hands, or his little feet bitten off?"[23] Indeed, the idea is found as early as Paschasius Radbertus (c. 785–860) that Christ's appearance as bread is a cloak to avoid the effect that having to swallow His raw and bloody flesh would have on the members of the church,[24] and Honorius Augustodunensis in his *Elucidarium* (c. 1100) also pointed out that such exposure to the reality of the eucharist would leave us "horrified to touch it with our lips."[25] According to a fourteenth-century Latin sermon, the reasons that the consecrated host remains perceptible as bread despite the reality of the miraculous transformation of its substance are threefold—to test faith, to avoid abhorrence of raw human flesh, and to save the body of Christ from the ridicule of heretics.[26]

Clearly, then, the doctrine of real presence entailed an awareness on the behalf of a medieval congregation that, on its most literal level, Holy Communion was a form of participatory and often infanticidal anthropophagy. Moreover, this participation was fundamental to medieval Christian identity formation, delineating a rigid boundary between inside and outside, and even providing a means of purging the body politic of undesirable infiltrators. For this reason, eucharistic visions of the child in the bread were not always limited to Christians; in the account of the attempted host desecration by the "Jew of Cologne" reported in an early sixteenth-century sermon, the Jew spat out the host to find that it had turned into a small child smiling at him.[27] During the Passau host desecration trial of 1478, the supposed stabbing of the eucharist by hostile Jews was said to have turned the bread into a young boy, and the lurid broadsheet that appeared two years later claimed that the host turned into a beatific Christ child after the Jews had thrust it into an oven, testifying, beyond all doubt, to the truth of transubstantiation, acknowledged and proven here even by the mortal enemies of Christ.[28]

The appearance in both of the latter miracles of a wicked Jew is not coincidental, since Jewish characters figure prominently in eucharistic *exempla*, just as they do in responses to Holy Communion that deal with its implications by projecting them outward rather than accepting them. Moreover, Jews figure especially in those eucharistic *exempla* that feature bloody and dismembered Christ figures, such as that in the English "Sermo de corpore Christi," where a Jew looking for his Christian traveling companion enters a church only to see the priest lifting above his head a "ffeir child, I-wounded sore/In foot, in hond." As the child is divided, the congregation receives not fragments, but individual replicas of the child, and the horrified Jew watches them devour the babies. This gory sacramental vision is explained, not as a blessing, but as the Jew's inheritance of the sins of his ancestors: "And thy kun made hym dye / Therfore al blodi thou hym seye."[29]

However, the physical evidence of Christ's blood in the host certainly manifests itself in order to correct the sins and doubts of Christian believers, as the *Vita* of Hugh of Lincoln says it did to the priest who celebrated mass in a state of mortal sin, so that when he broke the bread blood began to flow and part of the host itself "took on the appearance of flesh and became blood-red,"[30] or as in John Mirk's version of the miracle of St. Gregory's Mass, in which a woman laughed in church at the idea of the bread she had baked herself containing God. Gregory prayed for a sign, and "the ost turnet into raw flesch bledyng."[31]

Finally, gory miracles of literalized communion were also granted to those, like Colette, whose holiness made them pleasing to God. Among the most unpleasantly literal of these is the vision of Adelheid of Katharinental, whose Christ ripped flesh from his palm for her communion,[32] yet among the holy, the especially gory and gruesome visions and miracles were received not with horror and disgust, but with joy and desire. The cannibalistic implications of feeding on the body of a sacrificed god are embraced and elaborated on in this series of miracles, so that although both ordinary and miraculous communion seem to have produced a taste of honeycomb sweetness in the particularly devoted, an especial blessing was to experience the literalness of Christ's presence in the consecrated bread in tasting or feeling Him on the tongue as meat, as Ida of Louvain felt flesh in her mouth whenever she recited John 1:14.[33]

However, the acceptance of feeding from and with the body was certainly not limited to the eucharist itself in the later Middle Ages. The body, especially both the female body and the body of Christ, was a highly charged symbol of suffering generativity, and this age of eucharistic piety extended the metaphor of bodily feeding and salvation beyond the eaten Christ on the altar through visions and images of nursing from the wounds of the crucified to literal feeding from the body of self or others.[34] Caroline Walker Bynum has convincingly demonstrated that medieval images of the nurturing crucified Christ parallel those of the lactating Virgin, His wounds and blood providing the same spiritual sustenance as Her breasts and milk. Whereas some medieval mystics, like Henry Suso and Lukardis of Oberweimar, were suckled in visions by the breasts of the Virgin Mary, others, like Mechtild of Magdeburg, refused the milk in favor of blood from the wounds of Christ.[35] Lutgard of Aywieres's biographer, Thomas, describes her vision of Christ crucified "with His wound all bleeding. And she sucked such sweetness with her mouth at His breast that she could feel no tribulation."[36] Moreover, it is difficult to interpret the popularity among mystics of the specifically taboo habit of drinking at the wounds of the diseased as anything other than an opportunity to combine physical abasement with an externalization of the promise of salvation through consumption of the body. The fact that the unlikely habit of kissing or drinking from other people's sores should need to be illegal suggests that the occurrence of the practice was not infrequent. Angela of Foligno, for example, literalized communion in her daily life, kissing and swallowing the scabs from the sores of lepers and pronouncing them to taste as sweet as communion, while she found the eucharist itself to taste like "especially delicious meat," while Catherine of Siena drank pus from a woman's diseased breast, declaring that "never in my life have I tasted any food and drink sweeter or more exquisite."[37] In addition, these women's own bodies also fed others and themselves—several of them restored breast milk to dry women, Lidwina of Schiedam miraculously nursed a woman on Christmas Eve, and Christina the Astonishing sustained herself for nine weeks on her own breast milk.[38]

Certainly the connection between theophagy and anthropophagy seems to have been well enough established for such an eating of the human body to have been able to stand in for communion as a pathway to the divine and to salvation—a communion, moreover, that bypassed and even flouted male authority. Indeed, part of the appeal for medieval women of the suffering, generative Christ may well have been that He, like them, fed others with His body. As Bynum has neatly summarized, "[m]edieval women fed others. They abstained in order to feed others. They fed others with their own bodies, which, as milk or oil, became food. They ate and drank the suffering of their fellow creatures by putting their mouths to putrefying sores."[39] It seems, then, that not only were the cannibalistic underpinnings of the eucharist recognized by these holy women, but that the eucharist itself resonated so profoundly for them precisely *because* of its implications of cannibalism, which were fundamental to the development of a specifically female piety in the later Middle Ages.

However, despite these examples of what seems to twenty-first-century readers to be a macabre. albeit joyful, literalizing of the cannibalistic undertones of the mass, the tremendously powerful eating of God present in the symbol of the eucharist also produced responses that were profoundly ambivalent. Some theologians accepted the implications of the theology and were consequently unable to accept the theology itself, arguing forthrightly, like Berengar of Tours, (c. 999–1088) that the real presence would "entail the faithful in a kind of cannibalism,"[40] and while, in the eucharistic *exem-*

pla discussed so far, the transgression was embraced, there were also medieval responses to the eucharist that functioned to deny the implications of Christian participatory cannibalism, tending instead to project such behaviors onto non-Christian or nonorthodox Christian subgroups.

The problem of literalism has dogged Christianity since its very beginnings. As early as a hundred years after Christ there is evidence from both the enemies of Christianity and apologists for the nascent religion that rumors of Christianity as a cannibalistic cult were firmly established. Pliny the Younger, Governor of Bithynia under Trajan c. 112 C.E., reported to the emperor that while Christian prisoners admitted to communal meals, they steadfastly denied that these meals were unusual or suspicious in any way, and, given the context, the implications of cannibalism here are evident. Forty years later, Tatian felt obliged to render an explicit defense, stating plainly, "There is no cannibalism amongst us,"[41] and toward the end of the second century Christian writers Tertullian and Minucius Felix produced scathing parodies of the elaborate cannibalistic rituals, culminating in anonymous and incestuous orgies, that Christian worship was alleged to involve. The words of Minucius, based probably on a lost anti-Christian oration, by Marcus Cornelius Fronto,[42] are illustrative of how the same accusations that were originally targeted against fledgling Christianity would eventually reappear as tools of its own officers:

> As for the initiation of new members, the details are as disgusting as they are well known. A child, covered in dough to deceive the unwary, is set before the would-be novice. The novice stabs the child to death with invisible blows; indeed he himself, deceived by the coating dough, thinks his stabs harmless. Then—it's horrible!—they hungrily drink the child's blood, and compete with one another as they divide his limbs. Through this victim they are bound together; and the fact that they all share the knowledge of the crime pledges then all to silence.[43]

But despite both the denials and the implausibility of the alleged accounts,[44] accusations of Christian cannibalism continued to abound, and may have prompted, or at the very least provided ammunition for, the horrific persecutions of the Christians of Lyons under Marcus Aurelius in 177 C.E. [45]

However, despite the obvious possibilities for a literal reading of communion that Christianity provided, other religions had even earlier been accused of practicing ritual forms of eating human flesh. Posidonius is credited with the earliest almost contemporary version of the story of Antiochus Epiphanes, who desecrated the Temple of Jerusalem in 168 B.C.E. Inside the temple he is said to have found a Greek captive being fattened for consumption by the Jews, who ritually slew and ate a Greek prisoner every seven years to reinforce their antagonism toward the nation. The tale is repeated by Molon and Damocritus, and further elaborated by Apion in the first half of the first century B.C.E. Flavius Josephus both described and refuted the charges in *Contra Apionem*, and it seems clear that by this point the alleged ceremony had mutated into an annual occasion.[46] Moreover, in the war against Trajan of 115–117 C.E., the Jews were again accused of cannibalizing the enemy, this time by Dio Cassius, who wrote: ". . . the Jews are said to have killed 220,000 persons in Cyrene, to have sawn their enemies asunder, besmeared themselves with their blood, and eaten of their flesh."[47] It should be noted that Dio Cassius seems to have been particularly prone to the romance of enmity cannibalism, alleging the identical offense by both Egyptian warriors and the Catiline conspirators.[48]

Much more effective and longer-lasting than suggestions of brutal battlefield behavior were the allegations that religious minorities, whether orthodox Christian, heretical, or Jewish, indulge in a domestic ritual cannibalism involving babies and small children—the same allegation that Tertullian and Minucius Felix refuted in the second century. However, while the allegations against other minorities seem to have taken a path linked much more to a general discourse of bestial monstrosity, which will be addressed more fully in chapter three, those against Jews seem to have developed in a somewhat different direction—one that leads to an absolutely literal parallel of eucharistic cannibalism projected almost wholesale onto a convenient non-Christian scapegoat.

Later medieval accusations of cannibalism against the Jews, drawing perhaps on the rituals described by Apion, or even, ironically, on Josephus's denial of such ceremonies,[49] seem to have fused with high medieval charges against Christian heretics to produce a discourse of deliberately horrific infanticidal cannibalism that specifically echoed and parodied the mass. Although the earlier accusations of enmity cannibalism against the Jews were reinforced by Christian theologians like John Chrysostom (347–407), who accused them of almost every possible offense, including the charge that they killed and ate their own children,[50] the ritual murder accusation and its corollary, the blood libel fantasy, did not emerge until well after the discourse of heretical cannibalism had been established. Once these charges appeared, however, they proliferated wildly, indicating the depth of the medieval need for scapegoats.[51]

Although the first accusations of domestic ritual murder against the Jews did not involve allegations of blood use or consumption, initially merely involving narratives of Jewish repetition of the crucifixion, like that alleged after the death of William of Norwich, or of diabolical Jewish hatred for the purity and innocence of Christian children, like that of Chaucer's Prioress's Tale, within a century of the development of the medieval discourse of ritual murder that of the blood libel had been born, merging gradually but graphically with the former. In Fulda in 1235, the bodies of five Christian children, all siblings, were found on Christmas Day, when their parents returned from church. Suspicion immediately fell upon the Jewish community, and under torture several individuals confessed not only to killing the children, but to having collected their blood in bags coated with wax, supposedly to use the blood for medicinal purposes.[52] Thirty-four Jews were executed, and although the Emperor Frederick II began an enquiry which would ultimately exonerate them, this case caught the imagination, proving an unpleasantly fruitful precedent for later anti-Jewish fantasies. As Gavin Langmuir points out:

> A new fantasy, the medieval libel of Jewish ritual cannibalism, was created by some people at Fulda in 1235. It caused the death of thirty-four Jews immediately; it attracted the attention of the highest authorities throughout Europe immediately after; it was soon responsible for the death of more Jews; and, directly or indirectly, it was responsible for the death of many more in the centuries to come.[53]

Once a notion of a Jewish ritual involving the blood of a Christian child had been established, however tenuously, it was a small but helpful psychological step to imagine that the ritual was a grotesque and brutal parody of Christian mass. By March of 1247, the Jews of French Valréas could be accused of crucifying a Christian child and of taking his blood to use for communion on the Saturday of Passion week; torture resulted in a number of confessions and executions.[54] An appeal by the Jewish community to Innocent IV led to a papal condemnation of the persecutions on May 28, but by early July of the same year he had to respond to an appeal by German Jews to charges that they communicated with the heart of a murdered child not at Easter, but at Passover.[55] Several days later he reissued the general papal bull for the protection of Jews, with the additional stipulation that accusations of ritual blood use were not to be given credence.

Papal disavowals notwithstanding, however, the development after 1247 of the identification of ritual murder and tragically literal communion with a genuine Jewish holy day and feast proved particularly effective in spreading the discourse of ritual Jewish cannibalism. In 1329 in Savoy, a Jew admitted under torture to a confused fantasy, presumably that of his interrogators, of selling several Christian children to his coreligionists, who killed them in order to make "a salve or food" to be distributed among the Jewish community, who "eat of this food at every Passover instead of a sacrifice."[56]

The combination of such a community meal, celebrated close to Easter with red wine and flat bread, and Gentile ignorance and suspicion of Jewish ritual practice proved lethal, although it seems to have taken some time for a direct correlation between the bread and wine of Passover and that of Christian communion to have become established. As Joshua Trachtenberg points out, "[t]he notion that Jews use Christian blood in baking their Passover unleavened bread, or mix it with their Passover wine, seems to be no older than the fourteenth century, and became a fixed element of the charge only in the fifteenth century."[57] However, when in 1422 Martin V issued the by-then conventional papal denunciation of ritual murder charges, his version was specifically directed against the vicious rumor, spread, he noted, by preachers, that the Jews mixed human blood into their unleavened bread,[58] and a case near Regensburg in 1476 produced confessions that the Jews made a habit of mixing Christian blood into wine and of smearing it on unleavened bread, the reason given here being that such sustenance helped them prevent leprosy.[59]

The connection between ritual murder accusations and the Christian eucharist, gradually becoming more transparent as accusations focused more specifically on the Seder, becomes firmer still with the development of the parallel accusation of host desecration, in which offenders are said to physically attack or otherwise attempt to humiliate the consecrated host. Although host desecration merged with the discourse of ritual murder, the former acknowledges the cannibalistic underpinnings of the mass, proving, like the other eucharistic miracles, that even the unenlightened Jews understand at heart that Christ is really in the consecrated bread, while the latter demonstrates the denial of ritual Christian cannibalism, instead projecting it onto the Jews. The idea that Jews could represent a threat to the body of Christ was, of course, not a new one—after all, if they were ultimately responsible for torturing and crucifying the living Christ, how could they be trusted with the miracle, however frequently repeated, of His reappearance? In 1267 the Council of Vienna decreed that the "murderers of Christ" were no longer to witness the carrying of the consecrated host through the streets, and must instead withdraw to their homes, locking their doors and windows, on hearing the processional bell—a step deemed necessary to protect the body of Jesus from His killers.[60] This decree postdated by some twenty-four years the first accusation of host desecration, which occurred at Belitz, near Berlin, and although the alleged crime had no human victim, such a sacrilegious assault on the divine resulted in the wholesale burning of the entire Jewish population of the city.[61]

Although the connection between the narratives of host desecration and the blood libel/ritual murder are not immediately obvious, the link can be seen in the legend of the 1337 host desecration at Deckendorf, during which a host desecration metamorphoses into both a singular ritual murder and a baby-in-host tale. The host is stolen at Easter by a Christian woman at the request of the Jews, who then take the bread and torture it. It bleeds miraculous blood and then turns into an infant Jesus, who, despite the best efforts of the panic-stricken Jews, proves indestructible. They are then caught and punished when the Virgin Mary is overheard lamenting the repetition of the torture and murder of her son.[62] The assault on the host and the blood libel are also closely linked in the parallelism of two tales from the late thirteenth century, one of the supposed ritual murder in Weissenburg in 1270, when Jews were accused of hanging a Christian child by the feet and cutting open every artery in the body to ensure that they collected all of the blood, and another of the ritual murder/host desecration charge that in Oberwesel in 1286 the Jews hanged a boy by the legs in order to retrieve the sacrament he had just swallowed, then opened his arteries with scissors in order to collect his blood.[63] John Mirk's *Festial*, c. 1495, contains a parallel story that merges the two themes even more explicitly, as a Christian cleric is cut open by Jews who intend to steal the recently consumed consecrated wafer. Miraculously the host, swallowed but not digested, in accordance with doctrine, shines so brilliantly that the wicked Jews are blinded, and the injured cleric is immediately healed.[64] Hsia reports a similar merging in the previously mentioned Passau host desecration trial of 1478. Although in this case the charge for which a number of Jews and a Christian thief and traitor were executed was one of desecration alone, by 1490 a popular broadsheet charged that one of the suspects, tortured and executed for stabbing the host until it turned into a young boy, had previously bought a child for the Jews to murder.[65] In other cases, such as that of Brandenberg in 1510, post-desecration torture extracted confessions of ritual murder as spurious and unlikely as those of desecrating the host. Trachtenberg describes a peculiarly apt, if gruesome, footnote to a host desecration case in Bohemia in 1338; after the purported offenders had been executed, it was noted that no blood flowed from their mutilated bodies.[66] The consecrated bread, which bleeds, is therefore proven more human than the Jews, who cannot.

Evidently, one of the functions of the discourse of eucharistic miracles, such as the host desecrations and the other visions of Jesus in the wafer, is to prove the reality of transubstantiation, binding popular miracles to official church doctrine. However, popular eucharistic piety also led to the development of unofficial uses for the body of Christ, rare before the thirteenth century,[67] such as its application in agriculture, or use in love charms, so that, as I discuss in chapter three, the host played a significant role in continental witchcraft accusations. Moreover, Jews were not exempt from accusations of this form of sacrilege either; they appear again as alleged participants in conspiracies to poison or otherwise destroy Christendom with bizarre mixtures that included such ingredients as spiders, lizards and either a human heart, entrails, blood or urine, or a sacred host, which seems in this instance to stand in for or compound the use of human remains.[68]

It seems, then, in the blood libel, and specifically in its later manifestation as a form of Seder "communion," there is a projection onto a vulnerable and culturally marked subgroup of Christian anxieties about the implications of their most fundamental and sacred ritual. This is particularly clear in those narratives that link the blood libel and host desecration allegations, since the latter are, at base, highly politicized and spectacular eucharistic *exempla*. The concurrent appearance of narratives of the flesh-in-the-host and of discourses of denial and projection reflects the rich symbolism and dissonant complexity of the late medieval eucharist.

Although the doctrinal equivalence of the eucharist and literal body and blood had been officially recognized at the Fourth Lateran Council, called by Innocent III in 1215 largely in response to the increasing threat of dualism, the significance of this in the development of sacramentalism has perhaps been exaggerated. Certainly this concept did not originate with Lateran IV, but had arisen considerably earlier, and had even earned the neologism of "transubstantiation" as early as the eleventh century.[69] In fact, Lateran IV is interesting here chiefly in terms of its response to the threat of heterodoxy. This response not only focused on the eucharist as a site of primary symbolic importance, but also addressed the problem of a minority subgroup that resisted incorporation into Christian society. Moreover, it did so in a way that linked the eucharist with the visible markers of Judaism—it was Lateran IV that implemented the wearing of distinctive Jewish clothing, including a compulsory wafer-shaped yellow felt patch. As Joshua Trachtenberg points out, since the Jews refused to accept the eucharist privately in their hearts, they were condemned to wear it publicly on their clothes.[70]

The focus on the eucharist as a locus of anxiety in response to heresy identifiable in the proceedings of Lateran IV will be discussed more fully in chapter three, but is clearly indicative of the importance attached to the sacraments in general, and the eucharist in particular, by the developing bureaucracy of the medieval church. However, although the texts I have examined so far have been specifically contextual theological and political discourses in which the strength and centrality of eucharistic symbolism might not be entirely unexpected, a more general concern with the symbolism of the host also erupted into popular secular texts. In at least one case, the link between communion and cannibalism manifests itself in a peculiarly priapic form which speaks, perhaps, to the feminizing of the discourse of cannibalism discussed in chapter one.

The motif of the eaten heart is a staple of medieval romance. Structurally, it features a forbidden love discovered by an authority figure, who reveals his knowledge of the dalliance by the rather dramatic device of producing the heart of the male partner, which is then wholly or partially consumed, either wittingly or unwittingly, by the female partner.[71] A good example of this is the late thirteenth- or early fourteenth-century French tale, "Le Roman du Chatelain de Coucilet et la Dame de Fayel," by a Jakemon Sakesep, which passed into English as "The Knight of Curtesey and the Lady of Faguell." In this romance, the knight is fatally wounded in battle, but arranges to have his heart cut out and sent to his married love, together with a letter that plays on the metaphor of his heart belonging to her for eternity. The heart and letter are intercepted by her jealous husband, who has the organ made into a meal for his wife. When she realizes what she has eaten, she refuses all other food and dies shortly thereafter.

A version of this romance was likely familiar to Boccaccio, who includes two similar tales on Day Four of the *Decameron*, itself a series of variations on the dangers of the body. In the first, IV:1, Fiammetta tells the tale of a king who opposes his daughter's love for a commoner to the extent that he not only condemns her suitor to death, but has his heart cut out and presented to her in a chalice of gold. But her father's triumphant gesture backfires, and she appropriates the heart and chalice, using her tears of mourning to help distill a poison that she pours over the heart and drinks, prompting her father's repentance. In Filostrato's more macabre tale, IV:9, a jealous husband discovers his wife's betrayal of him with his best friend, and kills him, tearing out the heart, which he then has chopped and served to his wife as a stew. After ensuring that she has thoroughly enjoyed the dish, he gleefully tells her what she has eaten, and she throws herself out of a window, smashing her own body to pieces below.

The "Lai d'Ignaure," on the other hand, composed about 1200 by a poet known only as "Renaut," differs from the above romances in that it is a lay—in point of fact, more fabliaux than romance. The eponymous hero has wooed and won not one courtly lady, but twelve, and sworn exclusive fidelity to each one: "He carried on with all twelve; to each he promised that if she wanted it she could have his love entirely and he would consider himself served as a count. Each believed he was hers and behaved most tenderly and graciously."[72] Each of the twelve ladies discovers the universality of her experience during a game in which one of them plays a priest and hears the amorous "confession" of the other eleven. Furious that they are sharing the same deceptive lover, they ambush Ignaure, who escapes their knives only by assuring them of the absolute equality of his love and by promising to limit himself to only one of their number. Unfortunately, the concentration of his efforts on a single mistress alerts her husband, leading to the discovery by the other eleven husbands of their own wives' infidelity: "A mouse which has only one hole does not live long."[73] The men imprison Ignaure and debate his fate for a period of days, during which time the wives attempt to take collective action on his behalf, undertaking a hunger strike. They are, however, persuaded by their husbands to take a little nourishment, and when they again inquire about Ignaure, they are assured that he is closer to them than ever, for they have just partaken of a meal consisting of his heart and penis: "You have eaten the great desire that you used to hold to be such pleasure, for you desired no other. In the end you were served [by] it! I have killed and destroyed your lover; you will all have shared the pleasure that women desire so much."[74] The women then insist that, having eaten of such food, they will never consume anything else, and they die from starvation, mourning the loss of their lover in an elegiac blazon that concludes: "And another regretted his sweet heart, of which none would ever be the equal."[75]

What is most interesting about the "Lai d'Ignaure" is the sacramental nature of the tale, what Milad Doueihi has called "a clear and somewhat facile parody of the Christian founding narrative."[76] But in interpreting the text as simply blasphemous parody, Doueihi misses the ambivalence of the tale, and particularly the way in which it marks the eruption of cultural and religious bodily practices into secular social space. The women are discovered to have taken Ignaure's body into their own, both sexually and romantically—both penis and heart. Their bodily boundaries are no longer impermeable. The husbands plot a punishment that will appropriate the power of their rival, but do not consider the ultimate transgression of ingesting his organs themselves. Thus, as Doueihi points out, "the husband's assimilation of his rival is necessarily mediated, imaginary, and phantasmagoric."[77] In their violent and gruesome attempt to punish transgression by transgressing, they achieve not a reversal or mitigation of the original transgression, but an invocation of a shared sense of the sacred.

The effect of this is to rob the husbands' crude and violent gesture of its intent. Their language is not at all sacramental, but sexualized, punning on "*servie*" as both sexual service and a serving of food, and envisioning their punishment as a literal perversion of the metaphors of love and of sexual intercourse. But in consuming Ignaure, his lovers incorporate his strength and that of the religious symbol their meal invokes. They appropriate the meaning of their husbands' act so that their consumption of the body is not horrific, but becomes a funerary feast. The women regain, then, a final dignity, which includes the power to punish their husbands doubly in choosing to die rather than to dishonor Ignaure's memory by eating profane food.

The casual parody that marks the treatment of the sacrament of confession earlier in the poem is replaced by a more complex negotiation of eucharistic territory. The hunger strike is reconfigured as a time of precommunion fasting, the twelve women at their cannibal meal as apostles at a Last Supper, the heart and genitals of a playboy as the body and blood of Christ, upon which they will exist exclusively for the rest of their lives. Even Ignaure's early promise to love each wholly, despite the diffusion of his attentions, reflects the doctrine of the nonfragmentation of Christ in the divided host. As Mark Burde has pointed out, the "Lay d' Ignaure" cannot be dismissed as simple parody, but its dexterity with eucharistic symbolism must be recognized as being "tightly interwoven with strands of contemporary social intertext," and he adds that, while the poem certainly exaggerates popular notions about religious rites, it does so "in a manner more consonant with than opposed to actual practice."[78] The poem, then, "digests" the sacrament, producing a new scope of interpretation.

The incorporation of such a fundamental transgression of taboo as the eating of human flesh into Christianity's most sacred ritual produced a highly charged symbolic system, erupting into popular secular culture as well as political and theological exchange, and it might be argued that the power of this system is sustained by its openness to interpretation, by its own uncontainability, by the ranges and scopes of meaning it conceivably supports. In acknowledging the transgression of taboo in the mass, Miri Rubin has argued that "[t]his area of the symbolic gave the occasion for playing with things dangerous and going away unscathed,"[79] but this suggestion of the eucharist's ultimate easy digestibility elides some of the practical and politicized manifestations of late medieval and early modern unease about the meaning of a ritual at the heart of Christian social and cultural identity.

Chapter Three

Mass Hysteria: Heresy, Witchcraft, and Host Desecration

S INCE THE AUTHORITY OF THE MEDIEVAL CHURCH DEPENDED LARGELY
on its own cultural and economic monopoly of the channel to salvation, the ability to pronounce the words that would produce God from
a piece of bread was of fundamental importance.[1] The eucharist was considered an arch-sacrament, and unlike baptism, marriage, and extreme unction,
could not be performed by the laity, even when the recipient was at the point
of death.[2] In fact, it has been suggested that the interdependence of
Christian clergy and Holy Communion goes so deep that the former cannot
exist without the latter:

> Thus, far from the conception of Christ reconciling God and man by His sac-
> rificial death as priest and victim, the Christian priesthood was established in
> the Church especially for the perpetuation of the eucharistic memorial of His
> self-offering. As the idea of priesthood developed in relation to the episcopal
> *sacerdotium* it acquired an ecclesiastical jurisdiction with the growth of the
> Church and eventually became a rallying force and consolidating centre in an
> age of imperial disruption.[3]

Moreover, beyond the theological and political necessity of the mass, it
served an important economic function by the late Middle Ages, with votive
masses for the dead bringing in a significant financial return. By the end of
the fifteenth century, there existed a large order of priests whose duty
entailed only the saying of the private masses that provided their income.[4] A
metonymic symbol for the church itself, the eucharist rapidly became the
emblem of political orthodoxy or its opposite, so that as heretical possibilities proliferated, so did increasingly vigorous papal and conciliar restate-
ments of the doctrinal truth of transubstantiation. As Miri Rubin notes:

"[t]he eucharist was the hinge on which the symbolic world turned. In the words of the Bishop of Vienne to Pope Paul III in 1536, before convening the Council of Trent, 'There indeed is the hinge around which things revolve.'"[5] As the bishop advised, the Council of Trent, like those before and after it, vigorously endorsed the doctrine of transubstantiation, and just as vigorously denounced its challengers. In fact, the appearance of antisacramentalism, and eucharistic abuse in particular, stirred up the most vehement of antiheretical responses, both popular and learned, one of the results of which proved to be a lurid series of fantastic allegations that linked unorthodoxy with antisacramentalism, and antisacramentalism with bizarre eucharistic parodies in which the expected murder and cannibalism are almost eclipsed by incest, *coitus interruptus*, homoeroticism, and masturbation.

The twelfth-century chronicler and defender of orthodoxy Guibert of Nogent describes, in horrified tones, such an occasion:

> In a certain famous monastery, a monk had been brought up from childhood and had attained some knowledge in letters. Directed by his abbot to live in an outlying cell of the abbey, while he was staying there he fell ill of a disease. Because of this, to his sorrow, he had occasion for talking to a Jew skilled in medicine. Gathering boldness from their intimacy, they began to reveal their secrets to one another. Being curious about the black arts and aware that the Jew understood magic, the monk pressed him hard. The Jew consented, and promised to be his mediator with the Devil. They agreed upon the time and place for a meeting. At last he was brought by his intermediary into the presence of the Devil, and through the other he asked to have a share in the teaching. That abominable ruler said it could by no means be done unless he denied his Christianity and offered sacrifice to him. The man asked what sacrifice. 'That which is most desirable in a man.' 'What is that?' 'You shall make a libation of your seed,' said he. 'When you have poured it out for me, you shall taste it first as a celebrant ought to do.' What a crime! What a shameful act! And he of whom this was demanded was a priest! The ancient enemy did this, O Lord, to cast the dishonor of sacrilege on Thy Priesthood and Thy Blessed Host![6]

Some of the anxiety in this account may stem from a (mis)understanding that whatever is consecrated by a priest becomes the actual body and blood of Christ. However, the orthodox view of eucharistic specifications was in fact fairly narrow; as James of Vitry pointed out, "Only that which is of grain will be transubstantiated."[7]

Despite Guibert's horror, whether at such blasphemy or at the homoerotic subtext he had produced, allegations of seminal communion had both a strong history and a promising future. In a tome conceived as a first-aid kit against the poison of heresy, the fourth-century Bishop Epiphanius of Salamis accused both the Simonians and the Gnostics of similar atrocities, claiming that Simon Magus "instituted mysteries consisting of dirt and—to put it more politely—the fluids generated from men's bodies through the seminal emission and women's through the menstrual flux, which are collected for mysteries by a most indecent method,"[8] and goes into more detail in his discussion of the Gnostics:

> [T]o extend their blasphemy to heaven after making love in a state of fornication, the woman and man receive the male emission on their own hands. And they stand with their eyes raised heavenward but the filth on their hands, and pray, if you please . . . and offer that stuff on their hands to the actual Father of all, and say, "We offer thee this gift, the body of Christ." And then they eat it, and partake of their own dirt, and they say, 'This is the body of Christ; and this is the Pascha, because of which our bodies suffer and are made to acknowledge the passion of Christ.' And so with the woman's emission when she happens to be having her period—they likewise take the menstrual blood they gather from her, and eat it in common. And 'This,' they say, 'is the blood of Christ.'[9]

A final case of seminal communion comes from the literature, not of heresy, but of witchcraft, almost a millennium and a half after Epiphanius. In his 1599 *Disquisitionum Magicarum Libri Sex*, Martin Del Rio insists that

> they [witches] offer up two children to the Devil. In former years this had been done by mothers-frequently, according to Binsfeld—and in 1458 a mother sacrificed three of her children, according to Jacquier in the seventh chapter of his book. Other authorities say that they make a sordid sacrifice to the idol Moloch; offering to the Devil and killing in his honour with great cruelty and malice both their own children and those of strangers. Even ejaculated semen is offered up, as in the case of the sorcerer who had sexual intercourse with a woman in church and mingled his semen with the holy oil, as Jacquier relates in the 58th Folio of his *Scourge of Fascinators*. Finally, when they communicate they keep the Host in their mouths and afterwards remove it and offer it to the Devil, subsequently to be trampled on by the company.[10]

Certainly one could make an argument for a kind of autocannibalism in the consumption of one's own blood, and even of semen, as the parodic "*hoc est corpus Christi*" implies. It would be interesting, though, to examine to what extent the ritual consumption of semen or of menstrual blood could be seen as the more traditional form of infanticidal cannibalism imputed to heretics. Certainly these cases existed long before homunculus theory suggested the presence of rudimentary people in spermatozoa. Nevertheless, although they were without the backing of canon law on this issue, a number of church fathers asserted that wastage of human sperm could be equated with homicide, as early as Augustine in condemnation of onanism,[11] and as late as Peter Cantor in his twelfth-century allegation that "homicides and sodomites" both destroy men.[12] Note that Chaucer's Parson, perhaps following the thirteenth-century Paraldus,[13] goes so far as to consider unnatural intercourse a form of manslaughter, placed under the category of sins of wrath rather than lust:

> Eek whan man destourbeth concepcioun of a child, and maketh a womman outher bareyne by drynkinge venemouse herbes, thurgh which she may nat conceyve, or sleeth a child by drynkes wilfully, / or elles putteth certeine material thynges in hire secree places to slee the child, or elles doth unkyndely synne by which man or womman shedeth hire nature in manere or in place ther as a child may nat be conceived, or elles if a womman have conceyved, and hurt hirself and sleeth the child, yet it is it homicide. . . . Also, whan they treten unreverently the sacrement of the auter, thilke synne is so greet that unnethe may it been releessed, but that the mercy of God passeth alle his werkes; it is so greet, and he so benigne.[14]

Perhaps the most outspoken voice on this issue is, as it is so often, that of St. John Chrysostom, who equated castration with murder,[15] and contraception with worse: "Indeed it is worse than murder, and I do not know what to call it; for she does not kill what is formed but prevents its formation."[16]

Moreover, contemporary competing theories of reproduction were alike in attributing an almost independently generative power to sperm. Even the Hippocratic two-seed theory, which necessitated the contribution of "sperm" by both parties, was fundamentally weakened by Galen's emphasis on the feebleness of the female seed, while the Aristotelian single-seed theory held that sperm comes from the male, and contributes form, while menstrual blood comes from the female, and contributes matter.[17] Chrysostom mentions mixing of seeds, suggesting that he is an advocate of the Hippocratic theory.[18] A third classical position, typified by Soranos, who attributed reproduction to "the prolonged hold on the seed or an embryo or embryos in the uterus"[19] viewed the female contribution to reproduction as little more than incubation. Augustine, John Baldwin has suggested, appeared to "favor the single-seed theory because his preferred metaphor was that of the farmer sowing seed by hand,"[20] and indeed Augustine did attribute the transmission of original sin to Adam's semen.[21] The apparent ritual equivalence in Epiphanius of semen and menstrual blood seems to suggest a similarly Aristotelian bent.

However, John Noonan, although conceding the importance attached to sperm by each theory,[22] is at great pains to make it clear that the equation of misusing sperm with homicide is "neither biological nor legal, but moral,"[23] pointing out that "under no theory was the male seed itself equal to a 'man,' for under no theory was it maintained that the seed already had a soul."[24] However, elsewhere he concedes that "[t]here is the apparent assumption that each seed is a man in potency,"[25] and his moral explanation seems unable to accommodate the phenomenon of *amplexus reservatus,* or *coitus reservatus*—a form of *coitus interruptus* lacking only ejaculation. This is mentioned without condemnation by Huguccio in the twelfth century, and discussed briefly by Peter de Palude in the fourteenth as unlikely to be a mortal sin like *coitus interruptus.*[26] Noonan finds this puzzling, particularly as he associates the practice with both Catharism and courtly love,[27] but it is quite in keeping with anxieties about the nature of semen.

The behavior of those who supposedly communed with semen, then, was at least morally an act of cannibalism. The accounts differ in their details; for instance, the account of Guibert of Nogent is of merely a single aberration, or to be exact, the suggestion of an aberration, albeit under the instruction of a Jew who could be assumed to have in mind a more general subversion of the Christian faith, whereas those of Epiphanius are intended to illustrate a pervasive doctrinal abomination, and that of Martin del Rio a ritual both subversive and conspiratorial. However, the connection is strengthened when it is considered that each report of autocannibalism and morally infanticidal cannibalism is linked, more or less explicitly, with a full-fledged cannibalistic infanticide. For instance, the somewhat faulty reasoning Epiphanius gives for this bizarre form of communion is that the dualism of the Gnostics forbids procreation.[28] He goes on to explain what occurs when their habits of *coitus interruptus* fail:

> But even though one of them gets caught and implants the start of the normal emission, and the woman becomes pregnant, let me tell you what more dreadful thing such people venture to do. They extract the fetus at the stage appropriate for their enterprise, take this aborted infant, and cut it up in a trough shaped like a pestle. And they mix honey, pepper, and certain other perfumes and spices with it to keep from getting sick and then all the revellers in this <herd> of swine and dogs assemble, and each eats a piece of the child with his fingers. And now, after this cannibalism, they pray to God and say, 'We were not mocked by the archon of lust, but have gathered the brother's blunder up!' And this, if you please, is their idea of the 'perfect Passover.'[29]

The sheer implausibility of this scenario has not prevented even contemporary critics from manifesting credulity about the rites of heretics. John Noonan, for instance, apparently concluding that smoke is evidence of fire, says of Epiphanius's description of Gnostic cannibalistic and seminal communion that "[i]t is difficult to conclude that he is completely imagining what he describes."[30] One wonders if he would have a similar response to the roughly contemporary allegations by Mandeans that Christians communed with both semen and human flesh.[31]

That medieval chroniclers should be similarly credulous about possible abuses of communion is less surprising. In fact, Guibert of Nogent's account of the priest being encouraged to celebrate with semen is not unique in its link between liturgy and sexuality, even within the corpus of his own work. His *De Vita Sua* contains the story of a pilgrim to Compostella who masturbates during mass, and is convinced by the devil, disguised as St. James, that the only expurgation for this sin is emasculation and suicide. After committing both, he is pardoned by the Virgin and restored to life with his wounds healed, but his genitals and sexuality are not restored.[32] Guibert demonstrates a particularly vexed relationship to the mass and to images of consumption in general. He manifests a real reluctance to dwell on the bloodier implications of the eucharist, insisting that the consecrated host be seen as the body of resurrection, not crucifixion.[33] Caroline Bynum has suggested that his squeamishness "may stem partly from Guibert's horrified fascination with details of bodily torture,"[34] and indeed, his memoirs recount a vivid and terrifying vision of the postmortem consumption and decay experienced by his beloved mother, in which dead men appeared with "their hair seemingly eaten by worms" and tried to drag her into the abyss.[35] Furthermore, his description of the consumption habits of the heretics at Soissons, whom he identifies as Manicheans, is both bizarre and derivative. They are said to meet in underground vaults, where

> some loose woman lies down for all to watch, and, so it is said, uncovers her buttocks, and they present their candles at her from behind; and as soon as the candles are put out, they shout 'Chaos' from all sides, and everyone fornicates with whatever woman comes first to hand. If a woman becomes pregnant there, after the delivery the infant is taken back to the place. They light a great fire and those sitting around it toss the child from hand to hand through the flames until it is dead. Then it is reduced to ashes and the ashes made into bread. To each person a portion is given as a sacrament, and once it has been received, hardly anyone recovers from that heresy.[36]

Benton suggests that this is based on the report of the heresy discovered in Orleans in 1022,[37] but although there are similarities in the two accounts, the tradition Guibert is drawing upon is far older than Benton supposes. In chapter two, I discussed the refutation of Minucius Felix of the second-century charge that Christians indulged in wild orgies of sex and cannibalism; although the infanticidal communion is presented there as a prelude to the orgy rather than as an epilogue nine months later, the accounts are suspiciously close, even to equally outlandish means of extinguishing the light:

As for the initiation of new members, the details are as disgusting as they are well-known. A child, covered in dough to deceive the unwary, is set before the would-be novice. The novice stabs the child to death with invisible blows; indeed he himself, deceived by the coating dough, thinks his stabs harmless. Then—it's horrible!—they hungrily drink the child's blood, and compete with one another as they divide his limbs. Through this victim they are bound together; and the fact that they all share the knowledge of the crime pledges then all to silence. . . . On the feast-day they foregather with all their children, sisters, mothers, people of either sex and all ages. When the company is all aglow from feasting, and impure lust has been set afire by drunkenness, pieces of meat are thrown to a dog fastened to a lamp. The dog springs forward, beyond the length of its chain. The light, which would have been a betraying witness, is overturned and goes out. Now in the dark, so favourable to shameless behaviour, they twine the bonds of unnameable passion, as chance decides. And so all alike are incestuous, if not always in deed at least by complicity; for everything that is performed by one of them corresponds to the wishes of them all.[38]

Norman Cohn has collected a number of these accusations, revealing a distinct pattern in their subject matter and rhetoric. The fourth-century bishop Philastrius of Brescia accused the Montanists of mixing a child's blood into the Easter offering, and sending pieces of it to their "erring and pernicious supporters everywhere."[39] According to St. John IV of Ojun in 719, the Paulicians practiced secret incestuous orgies: "If a child is born, they throw it from one to another until it dies; and he in whose hands it dies is promoted to the leadership of the sect. The blood of these infants is mixed with flour to make the Eucharist; and so these people surpass the gluttony of pigs who devour their own brood."[40] Likewise, the melodramatic report of Michael Constantine Psellos on Bogomiles c.1050 indicates that, after the now familiar incestuous orgy, the heretics are content to wait nine months,

until the time has come for the unnatural children of such unnatural seed to be born, they come together again at the same place. Then, on the third day after birth, they tear the miserable babies from their mothers' arms. They cut their tender flesh all over with sharp knives and catch the stream of blood in basins. They throw the babies, still breathing and gasping, on to the fire, to be burned to ashes. After which, they mix the ashes with the blood in the basins, and so make an abominable drink, with which they secretly pollute their food and drink; like those who poison with hippocras or other sweet drinks. Finally they partake together of these foodstuffs; and not they alone but others also, who know nothing of their hidden proceedings.[41]

Clearly, the accusations are derivative and interdependent. They imply the existence of a dangerously secretive and conspiratorial society, battening ruthlessly on the most vulnerable members of society and performing the most inhuman, repellent, and sacrilegious acts. Cohn argues that "[i]t was only to be expected" that, for the purposes of discrediting a theologically unorthodox fringe group, "monks would draw on this traditional stock of defamatory clichés," adding that "by the fourteenth century, certain chroniclers deliberately inserted such stories into their narratives in order to provide preachers with materials for their sermons against heresy."[42] Yet the righteous indignation of, for instance, Michael Constantine Psellos, sounds as if the author himself is convinced, if not that the Bogomiles have been performing such acts, at least that they were thoroughly capable of doing so.

But why does heresy lead to such bizarre and specific charges? And why only certain kinds of heresies? As John Noonan has said about accusations of sexual deviance against heretics, "[i]t has sometimes been supposed that the accusation of sexual crimes was a stock charge against heretics. On the contrary, nothing like the charges made against the Manichees was advanced against the theologically more dangerous Arians."[43] Similarly, of the multitude of medieval heresies, only a small proportion accrued the dubious honor of accusations of cannibalism, and I would like to argue here that the common denominator in each of these cases was a perceived threat to the eucharist. For instance, the Paulicians accused of communing with the blood of a child conceived during an orgy by the Armenian John of Ojun rejected the sacraments as well as the recognized institution of the priesthood, interpreted the Last Supper as symbolic, and were adherents of Docetism.[44] The heretics of Orleans in 1022 were said to have rejected the efficacy of the eucharist, and their teachings have been associated with Bogomil influence.[45] The Bogomiles themselves, accused of stabbing babies conceived during orgies and of using their blood and ashes in a ritual drink, were also opposed to the clerical establishment, and "like the Paulicians they interpreted Christ's words at the Last Supper as a commendation of his teachings—the body and blood were the Gospels and the writings of the Apostles—and therefore held the bread and wine of communion to be a meal like any other."[46] The heretics Guibert of Nogent describes as communing with the ashes of a dead child conceived at an orgy at Soissons are also described as being violently opposed to the eucharist: "They so abominate the mystery which is enacted on our altar that they call the mouths of all priests the mouth of hell. If they ever receive our sacrament to hide their heresy, they arrange their meals so as to eat nothing more that day."[47] Indeed, whereas Miri Rubin has argued that it was the later Middle Ages that saw the development of the sacrament of the eucharist into "a central symbol or test of orthodoxy and dissent,"[48] it seems that, even earlier, the eucharist was in use as a literal test of orthodoxy: Guibert's heretics were given mass, with the words "Let the body and blood of the Lord try you this day."[49] They were then made to swear to their orthodoxy, and were thrown into a vat of water, where one of the leaders "floated like a stick," much to the "unbounded joy" of the congregation, which later, concerned about the possibility of clerical mercy, dragged the heretics from the prison and burned them in what Guibert calls "a righteous zeal."[50]

However, the eucharistic dispute that spawned suggestions of cannibalistic ritual practices did not necessarily appear in the form of direct doctrinal challenge, and indeed, may have lain primarily in the eye of the beholder. The most frequent attack on the eucharist in the later Middle Ages came in the form of a movement toward apostolic reform that was named after the fourth-century schismatics known as the Donatists. Although historical Donatism had been stamped out by the early fifth century, the fundamental questions raised by the movement enjoyed a revival that began in the eleventh century and flourished for hundreds of years;[51] if priests, and only priests, have the awesome yet invisible capacity to produce God from a piece of bread, what requirements are there to be a priest in the true sense of the word? If members of the clergy embrace worldliness in the form of wealth, power, or immorality, can they still channel the divine grace necessary to complete the transformation? Clearly the suggestion that unworthy priests forfeited the ability to say mass must have been enormously threatening, since, for one thing, it brought into question the possibility of anyone ever achieving the state of grace necessary for consecration, and consequently, the mystery of consecration itself. As William the Monk pointed out in his dispute with the heretic Henry of Le Mans, c. 1135–36:

> 'The body of Christ,' so you say, 'cannot be consecrated by an unworthy minister.' In this I see your wickedness explicitly, for you wish to make this a means of weakening the basis of a great sacrament and of depriving the Church of that by which the body of man is strengthened and the spirit sustained. For you say, 'Mass may be sung and Christ's body consecrated, provided anyone can be found worthy to do so'; thus enjoining us to discover an imaginary person who never can be found, because no one is without sin, not even a day-old child. You ask the impossible, seeking to shatter the ordinances of our faith.[52]

Further, the charge was frequently made by followers of apostolic poverty that all clergy, whether or not in personal mortal sin, were inherently corrupted by the wealth of the Church and its involvement in secular matters. The letter of Everinus to St. Bernard of Clairvaux, documenting the appearance of heresy in the Rhineland in 1143, illustrates the connection between eucharistic reservations and clerical abuses at the institutional level: "There are also some other heretics in our country. . . . These deny that the body of

Christ is made on the altar, because all the priests of the Church are not consecrated. For the apostolic dignity say they, is corrupted, by engaging itself
in secular affairs . . ."[53]

Moreover, even if the Church itself were not indicted for its worldliness,
Donatism could lead to a blurring of priestly authority: if sinlessness rather
than office is the touchstone for performing mass, then a moral layman is at
least as effective, if not more so, than an immoral priest; the most radical
Donatists, such as particular branches of the Waldensians, were even said to
have accepted the efficacy of a mass said by a woman in a state of grace:
"They say that the sacrament of the Eucharist may not be conferred by a
priest in the state of mortal sin. . . . They say that a good layman, and even
a woman, may consecrate the Eucharist, if they know the words. They say
that transubstantiation is in the mouth of him who takes the host worthily,
and not in the hand conferring it . . ."[54] Notice, however, that, Donatism
apart, this statement of faith is in fact remarkably orthodox, accepting not
just the truth of transubstantiation, but also the necessity for certain powerful incantational words.[55]

The popularity of Donatism from the early eleventh century on was evidently a response to manifestations of clerical corruption and abuse—
indeed, it may have been that a wide range of grievances against the clergy
was subsumed under the heading of Donatism, since repressing heresy was
ultimately easier than undertaking fundamental church reform.[56]
Hierarchical responses to Donatism included the imposition of penances for
those who doubted the value of sacraments administered by unworthy
priests[57] as well as the development of sermons and *exempla* that stressed the
appearance to concubinary or otherwise sinful priests of the infant Jesus or
his flesh in the host, illustrating that transubstantiation occurs independent
of the status of the soul of the officiating priest. In some cases, ostentatious
rejections of Donatism seemed called for. Despite the commitment of St.
Francis to apostolic poverty and clerical reform, he was careful to avoid the
imputation of Donatism, as Lambert points out: "Etienne de Bourbon
records a meeting with a heretic who complained to him of the misdeeds of
a concubinary priest. Francis's response was simply to kiss the priest's hand
in token of reverence for his office."[58]

In addition to Donatism, eucharistic heresy also embraced specific tech-
nical considerations that had little to do with a wholesale rejection of the
eucharist. One such consideration was the emphasis on communion in both
kinds of the moderate Hussites, to whom frequent and even daily communion was seen as a lantern of faith that would guide them through the human-
ly inspired formalities of religion. "Just as the return to the Bible enables the
faithful to find their way through the suffocating mass (sic) of regulations of

human invention, so the practice of frequent, and preferably daily, communion, enables them to avoid the distractions of needless formalism in worship, of false relics and miracles."[59]

However, eucharistic heresy also entailed outright rejection of the fundamentals of the divinely inspired service during which the congregation receives and consumes the actual body and blood of Jesus in the guise of a disk of bread. The Hussite supporters of Tabor, for instance, agreed on a eucharistic doctrine that involved only a "sacramental or figurative" presence of Christ, and reconfigured their mass into a communal vernacular ritual invoked over simple vessels on an unconsecrated altar.[60] Moreover, even outright rejection of transubstantiation could be couched in more or less defiant terms: as early as 1218, for instance, Pierre des Vaux de Cernay argued in his *Historia Albigensis* that the Cathars

> so far annulled the sacraments of the Church as publicly to teach that the water of holy baptism was just the same as river water, and that the Host of the most holy body of Christ did not differ from common bread, instilling into the ears of the simple this blasphemy, that the body of Christ, even though it had been as great as the Alps, would have been long ago been consumed and annihilated by those who had eaten of it.[61]

Later Lollards were similarly bitter in their condemnations of orthodox masses, as the 1394 Conclusions reveal; the fourth conclusion is

> That the pretended miracle of the sacrament of bread drives all men but a few to idolatry, because they think that the Body of Christ which is never away from heaven could by power of the priests' word be enclosed essentially in a little bread which they show the people. . . . A final corollary is that although the Body of Christ has been granted eternal joy, the service of Corpus Christi, instituted by Brother Thomas [Aquinas], is not true but is fictitious and full of false miracles. It is no wonder; because Brother Thomas, at that time holding with the pope, would have been willing to perform a miracle with a hen's egg.[62]

Of course, skepticism about orgies and cannibalism cannot consistently be followed by credulity about eucharistic beliefs, and the veracity of some eucharistic allegations remains in doubt. Popular support for the mass meant that accusations of eucharistic unorthodoxy alone resulted in widespread suspicion, and such unwholesome viewpoints may well have been attributed to relatively orthodox groups, such as the Leicester Lollards, for instance.[63] Much of the surviving information about earlier heretical groups, moreover, comes from the point of view of ecclesiastical authority rather than from the groups themselves; at the same time, agreement with a particular set of unorthodox beliefs may not have implied endorsement of a particular eucharistic doctrine.[64]

Although the common denominator of eucharistic suspicion seems a likely catalyst for the firm but specific association between certain forms of heresy and cannibalism, other factors may also have contributed, including that of dietary asceticism.[65] Many heterodox groups seem to have renounced flesh-eating, some even equating the eating of animal flesh with cannibalism. Epiphanius, for instance, links a number of his heretical groups with vegetarianism, or pretended vegetarianism. These range from those whom, he claims, merely pretended to renounce meat for the appearance of discipline, such as the Satornilians,[66] through those, such as the Ebionites and Valesians, who considered meat to be too carnal, inflaming the body to lust,[67] to those who, like the Marcionites and Manichees, considered meat-eating a soul-destroying sin for which one would answer in the afterlife.[68]

As Malcolm Lambert has pointed out, such asceticism might seem to require a dramatic explanation, such as that cited by Peter Martyr for Cathar vegetarianism: "Beasts and birds, it were said, were of human flesh—the foetuses of pregnant women which fell from heaven on to the earth after they had miscarried during the battle between the forces of God and Satan. The prohibition of eating their flesh thus amounted to a prohibition of cannibalism."[69] Such an association between heretics and cannibalism, even couched in oppositional terms, may indeed have contributed to the plausibility of tales of heretical cannibalism, especially since many of the accusations of libertinism were thrown at particularly sexually ascetic sects, and the reformist Waldensians, living and campaigning for lives of apostolic poverty, were dogged by the slander that they possessed huge and hidden wealth.[70]

On the other hand, Caroline Bynum has suggested that accusations of cannibalism stem from the perception that heretics equated the body with putrefaction, thereby linking the allegations with contemporary controversy over the resurrection rather than over the eucharist. "Heretics (say the orthodox) think the body is filth. They equate fertility with decay. They think therefore that nothing important can happen to the body; they deny that body is self."[71] However, it seems to me that it is *precisely* the conflation of body and self that occurs in orthodox resurrection theology that accounts for both anxiety about the eucharist and heretical antisacramentalism.

Moreover, it was not resurrection theology that led to the most bitter vituperation against heretics (except possibly in the case of Origen), but eucharistic dispute, whether direct, or couched in terms of popular Donatism. Lambert's quantitative assessment of medieval heresy concludes that most common among the heresies of the twelfth century was that of priestly unworthiness invalidating the sacraments.[72] Furthermore, eucharistic dispute is repeatedly singled out as a doctrinal breaking point, whether between heresy and orthodoxy, as in the symbol of the lay chalice in the breach between the Hussites and the Church,[73] or between divided factions within a heretical group, such as between the Lyonist and Lombard factions of the Waldensians in the early thirteenth century.[74] Lambert even goes so far as to identify John Wyclif's moderate rejection of transubstantiation as his crossing of a doctrinal Rubicon.[75] Furthermore, soon after Wyclif died, his death began to be linked with his rejection of the eucharist, as his Lutterworth curate, John Horne, spread the story that Wyclif's fatal stroke had struck him down at exactly the moment of the elevation of the host on the Feast of the Holy Innocents, 1384.[76]

Finally, it would be the nature of the eucharist that would symbolize the fissure between Catholic orthodoxy and a newly emerging Protestantism in the sixteenth century—as Rubin says, it would become "the hinge on which the symbolic world turned."[77] Pure eucharistic belief demanded either a full acceptance of the daily miracle of the returning Christ, or an outraged rejection of priestly chicanery, and neither approach allowed for the possibility of reform. Therefore, "when a crisis about its use and meaning emerged, Europe was thrown into turmoil for 150 years over it."[78] As the doctrinal challenge of the new Protestantism increased in strength and in vituperation, so did Catholic commitment to transubstantiation, as laid out at Constance in 1415 and Trent in 1562. Each camp condemned the other in the strongest possible terms, each ascribed the other's power to the work of the Devil, and, ironically, each condemned the other in the rhetoric of witchcraft.[79]

This is superbly ironic, since the theology of demonolatry that underlay the sixteenth- and seventeenth-century witchcraze, whether utilized by the newly emerged Protestantism or the Counter-Reformation Catholic Church, would link the spiritual rebellion of witchcraft to both purported cannibalism and eucharistic desecration. Although witches were never accused of the host stabbings and burnings characteristic of late medieval attacks against Jews, some of the earliest manifestations of witchcraft materials linked witches with similar forms of eucharistic profanation. Indeed, a number of early anti-Semitic host desecration allegations attribute the source of the abused host to a wicked Christian woman concealing the host in her mouth during communion in order to steal it from the church and sell it. The *exempla* that feature women stealing the host for their own quasi-magical purposes—to make bees fruitful,[80] for instance, or to fertilize cabbages[81]—are milder, but provide evidence of an interest in narratives that feature women abusing the eucharist for their own wicked purposes. For a time, such acts by otherwise Christian women remain linked with anti-Semitism—for instance, the widow of Mainz who buried a consecrated host with a toad in the 1380s, only to have her deed revealed by the crying of a child from underground, was alleged to have done so at the suggestion of a Jew.[82] The later development of demonolatry, however, while allowing for women to have acted alone in these matters, as in the account of the woman of Annecy in 1477 who confessed to trampling and frying the host, not to mention eating children and having bestialsex,[83] did not signal an end to the interdependence of anti-Semitism and witchcraft allegations.

This interdependence exists not only in sermons and *exempla*, but also in anti-witchcraft manifestoes and in conciliar rulings, which overflowed into areas as diverse as clothing and etymology. The same council that adopted the doctrine of transubstantiation in 1215 also instituted obligatory distinctive clothing for Jews, including the wearing of a round yellow felt patch, which was also compulsory for those found guilty of magical abuse of the host.[84] The word "sabbat" for the imagined sexual and alimentary orgies, used first by Nicholâs Jacquer about 1458 and part of standard witchcraft vocabulary by the early sixteenth century, is, despite the demurs of such writers as Aldous Huxley and Pennethorne Hughes,[85] derived from Judaism, "traditionally regarded as the quintessence of anti-Christianity, indeed, as a form of devil- worship," as is the word it replaced for the witches' revels, "synagogue."[86] Ironically, the first printed book on witchcraft, the 1467 *Fortalicium Fidei*, was written by a Franciscan convert from Judaism, Alphonsus de Spina, but is nevertheless vehemently anti-Semitic, featuring tales of Jewish as well as female opprobrium toward the eucharist.[87]

Although the pogrom would eventually prove more enduring than the witch-hunt, the latter temporarily eclipsed the former in most parts of sixteenth- and seventeenth-century continental Europe. While Jews had also been accused of a variety of abusive eucharistic practices, including boiling, baking, and stabbing the host, as well as communing with the blood of a Christian child, either as a ceremonial drink or mixed into matzah, the witch trials offered an almost infinite variety of possible blasphemous or obscene abuses for the host. For instance, the witches' hatred of holy objects supposedly led to attacks on the host during their meetings, either for pure unholy pleasure, or as an ordeal to prove the commitment of the initiate or the continued fortitude of the seasoned witch. The 1587 trial of Walpurga Hausmanin of Dillingen led to a confession that she had not only stamped on a consecrated communion wafer until it bled, but also given a host to her personal demon.[88] Other witches were alleged to express their hostility to Christianity by spitting or excreting on the host.[89]

The potential uses of the host for magic must have been almost unlimited, although, according to the *exempla*, they apparently carried a similar potential for backfiring on the user. Caesarius of Heisterbach writes of a wicked priest who tried to use the host for love magic by kissing a woman with it in his mouth. Unfortunately for him, "[w]hen he desired to go out of the door of the church he seemed to have grown in such a way that he knocked against the ceiling of the church with his head." In a guilty panic, he removes the wafer and tries to bury it in a corner of the church, only to have another priest discover instead a tiny flesh and blood man on a cross.[90] Witches seem to have been more fortunate in this regard, succeeding at least in getting the host out of church, since, according to some authors, the notorious flying ointment was sometimes made of consecrated wafer, "fed to a toad that was subsequently burned and its ashes mixed with the blood of a child, unbaptized if possible, and kneaded into a paste."[91]

Other trials allege that the ceremony of holy communion was attacked at sabbats by repellent parody, such as the consumption of analogous but abhorrent substances, so that, for instance, witches communed with a fluid like blood or "black moss water" in a late trial in Scotland.[92] Alternatively, the devil might manufacture his own wafers for the purpose—one of the most damning indictments against Dame Alice Kyteler in Ireland in 1324 was that there had been discovered in her possession "a Wafer of sacramental bread, hauing the diuels name stamped theron instead of Jesus Christ."[93]

However, the most consistent form of eucharistic parody attributed to continental witches was actual cannibalism, principally of babies and small children. This appears both alone and in tandem with other forms of eucharistic abuse. In many cases, the charges are described in lurid and remarkable details, such as in the following excerpt from the lengthy finding of a Dominican Inquisitor in Avignon in 1582:

> You . . . did murder many newborn children. . . . And your own children, many of them with your own knowledge and consent, you did by the said maleficia suffocate, pierce, kill, and finally you dug them up secretly by night in the cemetery, and so carried them to the aforesaid synagogue and college of witches. Then you did offer them to the prince of devils sitting on his throne, and did draw off their fat to be kept for your use, and cut off their heads, hands, and feet, and did cook and stew the trunk, and sometimes roast them, [*assari curastis*], and at the bidding and hest of your aforesaid evil father did eat and damnably devour them. Then adding sin to sin, you the men did copulate with sucubi, and you the women did fornicate with incubi; by most icy coitus with demons you did commit the unspeakable crime of sodomy. And, most hateful of all, at the bidding of the aforesaid serpent thrust forth from paradise, you did keep in your mouths the most holy sacrament of the eucharist received by you in the sacred church of God, and did nefariously spit it out on the ground with the greatest contumely, impiety and contempt.[94]

The tremendously complicated cannibalistic process demonstrated in the account seems to be indicative of the competing discourses of infanticide circulating around the witchcraft trials. They murder newborn children, theirs and others, by piercing them and/or suffocating them, but also retrieve bodies of (the same?) children by robbing graves, then offer the already dead children to the devil at a sabbat, and then thriftily reserve usable parts, apparently including fat, heads, and limbs, before roasting or stewing the trunk for ceremonial consumption. The infanticide therefore not only offended god and man, but also conveniently provided a variety of byproducts useful in magic. For instance, the infant fat was alleged to be made into an ointment with a variety of uses, including the achievement of transvection.[95]

Moreover, certain supernatural powers, primarily taciturnity under torture, were also said to be directly accessible via the consumption of human flesh of a certain quality and prepared in a certain fashion. The *Malleus Maleficarum* refers twice to a Hagenau witch named Walpurgis, who "was notorious for her power of preserving silence, and used to teach other women how to achieve a like quality of silence by cooking their first-born sons in an oven."[96] The later reference makes it clearer that the victim did not necessarily have to be the firstborn child of the student-witch herself, but merely "a newly born first-born male child who had not been baptized," who was roasted, and ground into powder, the resulting substance ensuring, when carried by "any witch or criminal," that the bearer would never confess.[97] This tradition occurs as late as the seventeenth century, and in areas as geographically, theologically, and politically disparate as France, where in 1611 witches were accused of consuming a postsabbatical cake made from black millet and the flesh of unbaptized babies in order to prevent confession under torture, and Forfar, Scotland, where in 1661 a number of women confessed to making a "pye," from bodies retrieved from the cemetery to ensure their silence.[98] Of course, an act as socially unacceptable as infant cannibalism was, like the stabbing of the child in the dough charged to unwary Christian initiates and refuted by Minucius Felix, likely to ensure the continued silence and complicity of any initiate who had partaken of it, but such a concept also had the advantage of explaining both the remarkable ability of women to hide their huge diabolic conspiracy at a time when women were believed to talk uncontrollably, and the fact that some alleged witches neither revealed their accomplices nor confessed to their own crimes, even under severe torture.

The alleged cannibalism of the nonexistent sabbat has puzzled critics, some of whom have attributed it to either an ancient theophagic ritual à la Margaret Murray, or a parody of Christianity's most sacred ceremony, indulged in by an aggressively oppositional cult, or like Pennethorne Hughes, to both: "This must, in the early times, have been the culmination of the witch sabbat—the eating of the god. Yet, as has been said, the tradition was a muddled one by the time of the recorded trials, when a palimpsest of early rituals was overlaid by the desire to parody the Christian Mass."[99] For Joseph Klaits, the cannibalism is the only aspect of the witchtrials that does not fit neatly into sublimated sexual fantasy: "The powerfully sexual nature of the dominant imagery begins with the broomstick ride, continues with excited whippings, the fascinating close-up look at devilishly huge sexual organs, the baby-eating (possibly sublimated incest or infanticide?), and finally, the frenzied orgy itself."[100]

However, infanticidal cannibalism has a sexual connotation when it is linked with abortion and contraception as a means of hiding illicit sexual activity from paternal authority, and this link has been made by writers as diverse as the fifteenth-century Dominicans Kramer and Sprenger and 1970s critic-activist Arthur Evans. Evans, apparently undeterred by the absence of evidence to back him up, claims that "Women accused later of witchcraft were often abortionists,"[101] while the *Malleus Maleficarum* contains headings such as "Question XI: That Witches who are Midwives in Various Ways Kill the Child Conceived in the Womb, and Procure an Abortion; or if they do not this Offer NewBorn Children to Devils," and "Chapter XIII. How Witch Midwives commit most Horrid Crimes when they either Kill Children or Offer them to Devils in Most Accursed Wise," and describes one particular midwife who was forced to confess "that she had killed more than forty children, by sticking a needle through the crowns of their heads into their brains, as they came out from the womb."[102]

Rhetorical strategies aside, there is strong evidence in Kramer and Sprenger's text, and in continental witchcraft trials as a whole, of a link between the allegations of cannibalism and both the vulnerability of fetuses or newborn infants and the perceived power of women, whether over the infants themselves or in the women-only mystery of the birthing process.[103] Modern critics have identified specific manifestations of this connections, as in Lyndal Roper's analysis of Augsburg witchcraft trials, which demonstrates that lying-in maids, intimately involved in the process of birth and of new motherhood, were particularly open to allegations of witchcraft,[104] or Deborah Willis's reading of early modern English witchcraft trials as products of infantile "fantasies of maternal persecution,"[105] internalized and projected outward: "Those misfortunes likely to be interpreted as the product of witchcraft affected those types of things over which the young child believes the mother to have 'omnipotent' control. Women in particular blamed the witch for disruptions of the birthing process and for the sickness and death of young children."[106]

Evidence for her argument includes the allegations against witches of the use of wax dolls or "mommets," suggesting "children over whom a controlling but monstrous mother holds the power of life and death," and the witch-hunter's search for supernumerary nipples, illustrative of a "fear of maternal power."[107] While the trials of continental Europe were more likely than those of England to focus on the monstrous sexuality of the witch, as she copulated with the devil or his incubi or interfered in male sexuality, either by forcing men to sin with her sexually, or preventing them from copulating with or impregnating their wives, even English witches were said to target reproduction, and English maleficium is aimed "almost always against domestic activities associated with feeding, nurture, or birth."[108] Similarly, Roper has noted that the fundamental motifs of the Augsburg allegations "concern suckling, giving birth, food, and feeding; the capacities of parturient women's bodies and the vulnerability of infants."[109] As for monstrous sexuality, Roper argues that what is at issue in the trials is not genital but pre-Oedipal sexuality.[110]

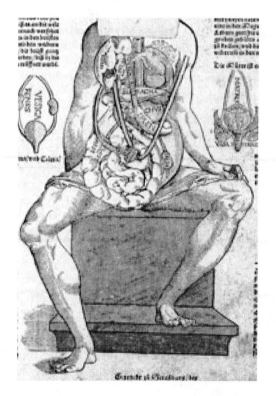

Like the embryo or fetus thought to be nourished in the womb by the blood of its mother, otherwise shed during menstruation, breastfeeding babies were thought to feed, vampire-like, upon their nurse's blood, which was channeled to the breast by means of a lacteal duct known as the *vasa menstrualis* and mercifully whitened in order to avoid the repugnant sight of a child sucking blood [figure 1].[111] Erich Neumann has

Figure 1. Sixteenth-century medical illustration showing the *vasa menstrualis*.

argued that it is this supposed transformation of blood that is at the root of all food transformation miracles, which would include that of the mass: "After childbirth the woman's third blood mystery occurs: the transformation of blood into milk, which is the foundation for the primordial mysteries of food transformation."[112] Caroline Bynum has demonstrated how the image of the lactating Madonna, particularly popular in early Renaissance Europe, parallels that of the bleeding Christ,"[113] and the image of the *Maria lactans* is often used to prefigure the crucifixion and the eucharistic sacrifice, as can be seen in Jan van Hemessen's 1544 Marian painting "Virgin and Child in a Landscape," in which the mother and child are depicted in a grape arbor.[114]

In keeping with the oppositional trope of witchcraft, witches exude for nourishment not mercifully whitened breastmilk, but unrepentantly crimson blood.[115] As Willis has noted, the services provided for the witch by her demonic imps or familiars were usually exchanged for food,[116] sometimes the kind of foods Valerie Fildes has identified as likely to be handfed to infants when breastfeeding was unacceptable or unavailable, such as beer, animal milk, or shredded pieces of bread or meat,[117] but most frequently in return for the witch's blood, sucked from a supernumerary nipple, or from any protuberance on her body that could vaguely resemble a teat. These could in theory be found anywhere on the body, but tended to be located around the armpits, genitals, and anus, perhaps because skin tags, hemorrhoids, and prolapses were ripe for misdiagnosis. As Roper points out, this proliferation of nipples indicates a disorganized diabolic body, in which bodily orifices and their functions have become confused and interchangeable.[118]

The witch, then, is a diabolically lactating mother who feeds only the demonic from her body, who can cause other nursing mothers to transmit poison to their infants through their own bodies,[119] and who actually feeds from the body of infants rather than vice versa, either in orgiastic and cannibalistic sabbat feasts or in surreptitious vampiric bloodsucking.[120] Lyndal Roper describes cases in which babies appeared to have been diabolically forced to lactate, producing milk from their nipples, or suddenly exhibiting a proliferation of tiny teats.[121] She suggests that "[t]hese beliefs rested on a whole economy of body fluids"—an economy within which a woman past childbearing age was assumed to be not just bereft of her own fluids, but ravenous for the liquid vitality of others, including not only blood and milk, but also the seminal fluid of young men, which she would greedily suck from their bodies, orally or vaginally.[122]

The image of witch as diabolically lactating mother can be observed in operation in the specific attacks on the breast peculiar to some continental witchcraft executions. A seventeenth-century torture manual notes the sensitivity of the female breasts, but mentions mastectomy only as a historical curiosity peculiar to the torture of Christian virgins.[123] During the 1600 public execution of Anna Pappenheimer and her family, Lutheran peasants in Catholic Bavaria under Duke Maximilian, however, the victims were stripped naked and their flesh torn by red-hot pincers. Fifty-nine-year-old Anna Pappenheimer was singled out for particularly violent attention; her breasts were cut off, and the severed nipples forced first into her mouth and then into the mouths of her two adult sons in a bloody parody of breast-feeding. While this execution was a singular as well as particularly ugly occurrence, breast removal being the exception rather than the rule, searing and mutilating the witch's naked breasts with hot tongs was a much more standard continental practice, perhaps an attack on, if not the source, at least the manifestation of both the witch's power and her vulnerability.[124] Ironically, the violent mastectomy of the stake is evocative of the lurid tortures of female saints—what Margaret Miles has termed the "religious pornography" of medieval hagiography, with its popular martyr-saints Barbara and Agnes perpetually suffering gladly the explicit and sadistic mutilation of their naked bosoms.[125] This form of torture, absent from much of Europe for many years, resurfaces in the New World, where it is used on Native American women, who, as I discuss in chapter five, were also peculiarly subject to accusations of cannibalism.

The appearance of the part of the female body associated with feeding as a site of social control is indicative of the ambivalence toward the breast discussed by Marilyn Yalom: "When the 'good' breast is in the ascendance, the accent falls on its power to nourish infants, or allegorically, an entire religious or political community. . . . When the 'bad' vision dominates, the breast is an agent of enticement and even aggression."[126] Yalom's division of the breast is significant in its relation to the work of Melanie Klein, who posits the existence of an oralsadistic or cannibalistic phase of infant development, marked by the psychological splitting of the mother's breast into "good" (feeding) and "bad" (devouring), and of Christiane Olivier in her diagnosis of masculine "breast envy."[127] Moreover, Yalom also cites identification of the "good" breast with young women and the "bad," devouring breast with the elderly, noting that "[m]en projected onto women's bodies not only their erotic longings, but also their fears of old age, decay and death," citing in particular "the contrast between the highperched breasts of youth and the hanging dugs of old age."[128]

As sources of food then, the bodies of women, whether transgressive by feeding and bleeding, or, worse, transgressive because beyond such phenomena, could become arenas for the contestation of social identity. As Mary Douglas has pointed out, "the body is a model which can stand for any bounded system,"[129] but she goes on to say that "the physical body is polarized conceptually against the social body." In other words, the site of contact between physical and social is always already a site of conflict, where a battle for meaning is engaged. As Sarah Beckwith has suggested, "we must look at Christ's body not simply as a social and communal rite, but as the site of a momentous and historically significant process of internalization, of social control through the formation of identity."[130] The late medieval eucharistic project—"to teach that a thin wheaten disk could become God through the words of the clergy"[131]—involved an ideological manipulation of an extraordinarily visceral and atavistic symbol. That the system such a symbol upheld should be one of hierarchical violence is scarcely remarkable.

Chapter Four

The Maternal Monstrous: Cannibalism at the Siege of Jerusalem

ONE OF GARY LARSON'S "FAR SIDE" CARTOONS FEATURES THREE female praying mantises in a traditionally genteel front parlor. The curtains are flowered, and the couch on which two of them sit is draped with lace antimacassars. The hostess insect is offering her guests a plate of snacks, and the caption gives the polite response of one of her guests in waving away the proffered food: "Oh, good heavens, no, Gladys—not for me. . . . I ate my young just an hour ago."[1]

The humor of the cartoon—and I find it particularly funny—lies in the perfectly evoked contrast between the stereotypically feminine and anthropomorphic environment (the coffee morning, the very proper furnishings, the guest's figure-conscious demur) and the insectile nature of its inhabitants. After all, what could be more insidiously nonhuman than a mother devouring her own young? Despite, or perhaps because of, its fundamentally disturbing qualities, the concept of such monstrous maternity has proved morbidly fascinating for at least the last two thousand years.[2] While a large number of variants of this motif exists,[3] the predominant European Christian version has crystallized in the story of Mary or Maria of Jerusalem, the woman who, trapped by the encroaching imperial army within the walls of Jerusalem during the Roman siege of 70 C.E., is said to have rehearsed the forthcoming violence in her domestic sphere, killing and eating her own child.[4] Although the figure of Maria appears intermittently in texts of the late classical period and the early Middle Ages, the eleventh to the sixteenth centuries witness a continuous upsurge in the popularity of this motif. In this chapter, I will sketch this proliferation and analyze the high and late medieval and early modem obsessive playing out of this trope in terms of its contribution to the growing discourse of cannibalistic monstrosity and of the negotiation of Christian masculine identity this discourse performs. In particular, I am interested in the relation of a figure of devouring maternity to the site of contestation that was the body of Christ.

The earliest reference to the devouring mother episode occurs in Flavius Josephus's *The Jewish Wars*, originally written in Aramaic around 77 C.E., and then translated into Greek. Indeed, it might be possible to credit Josephus with the creation of the character of Maria, although certainly the motif of the starving mother under siege existed long before him, even appearing in a context that would have been familiar to Josephus. This is the account in 2 Kings 6:28–29 of the woman of Samaria during the siege of that city by Ben-hadad, king of Syria. This woman complains to the king of Israel after she and her neighbor have, between them, eaten her son, not because of the state to which she has been reduced, but rather because of the dishonesty of her neighbor in reneging on an agreement to share her own child: "This woman said unto me, Give thy son, that we may eat him today, and we will eat my son tomorrow. So we boiled my son and did eat him; and I said unto her on the next day, Give thy son, that we may eat him; and she hath hid her son." The king rends his garments in sorrow and despair. While it is not impossible, or even all that improbable, given the exigencies of a siege, that an incident of the kind Josephus describes actually took place during the siege of Jerusalem, it seems more likely, then, that he included the melodramatic and ritualized scene as a traditional trope of desperation.

Both Jewish and a recent defector to the Roman side, Josephus provides a peculiarly ambivalent eyewitness account of the destruction of Jerusalem, and the historical validity of his version has spawned much debate.[5] In his text, the woman is named Mary the daughter of Eleazar, and she and her infant have fled to Jerusalem from the village of Bethezuba, or Beth-ezov, in the region of Peraea, east of the Jordan. Her property and food have been plundered by the rebels roaming the city, and in her fury and despair she has attempted to anger these men, so that she might be killed and thereby escape the continuing horrors of the siege, to say nothing of those to come with the eventual and inevitable fall of the city. Although the account is relatively lengthy, the specific detail Josephus provides justifies considerable quotation here:

> But no one, either out of resentment or pity, put her to death as she wished; weary of providing food for others—which it was impossible to find any-where—and while hunger ravaged her internal organs, and marrow and rage consumed her still further, she finally yielded to the promptings of fury and necessity and defied nature itself. Seizing her child, a babe at the breast, she cried, 'Poor baby, why should I keep you alive amid war, famine, and civil strife? We will only face slavery with the Romans, even if we survive until they

arrive, but famine will forestall slavery, and the rebels are more cruel than either. Come, be my food, and an avenging omen for the partisans, and to the world the only tale as yet untold of Jewish misery.' So saying she killed her son, roasted him, and ate one half, concealing and saving the rest. The partisans appeared at once, attracted by the unholy odor, and threatened that unless she produced what she prepared, she would be killed on the spot. She retorted that she had saved as fine a helping for them and disclosed the remnants of her child. Overcome with instant horror and stupefaction, they stood immobile at the sight. She said, 'This child is my own, and so is this deed. Come eat, I too have done so. Don't be softer than a woman, or more tender-hearted than a mother. But if you are pious and do not approve of my sacrifice, then I have eaten in your behalf and let me keep the rest.' At that they left trembling, cowards for once, though with some reluctance they left even this food to the mother. The whole city immediately talked of this abomination; everybody saw this tragedy before his eyes and shuddered as if the crime were his own.[6]

The news of this atrocity spreads to the Romans, and has the effect of increasing their detestation of the Jews. As a result, Titus plans to devastate the city entirely: "he would now cover the full abomination of the murder of that child with the ruins of their fatherland and would not leave standing on the earth for the sun to look upon a city where mothers ate such food."[7] According to Cornfeld, however "modem historians" agree that Titus had already decided to burn the Temple, and that his righteous anger merely provided a convenient excuse, or an after-the-fact justification, making this perhaps the earliest, but by no means the last, recorded example of the use of an alleged incidence of cannibalism to justify imperial military force. Moreover, the "food" to which Titus refers is evidently seen as even more horrific in that the devouring parent is female and thus militarily inactive, since Josephus has him add that "such food was less suited to the mothers than the fathers, who remained in arms after so many miseries" (219).[8] However, while Titus responds to this event with fury and disgust, identifying Maria with the rebels within the city and the treacherous Jews as a whole, Josephus himself goes to some length to justify her act, which is seen as one of necessity, compassion, and even political defiance.[9]

The popularity of the story of the siege in Latin Europe, however, is due primarily to a fourth-century Latin paraphrase of *The Jewish Wars*, attributed to one Hegesippus. Although the name of the translator has been identified as merely a corruption of Josephus, perhaps by confusion with the second-century historian and saint Hegesippus,[10] the *De Excidio Urbis Hierosolymitanae* has a clear anti-Judaic agenda. The destruction of Jerusalem is characterized as the fulfillment of Christ's prophecy during his entry into that city, recounted in Luke 19:43–44, in which Jesus forecasts both the siege and the final destruction of the city.

Given that the Lucan prophecy is probably a *vaticinium ex eventu*, a prophecy after the event,[11] the connection between Christ's "prophecy" and the eventual fall of Jerusalem fewer than forty years later is, of course, relatively standard in Christian exegesis, but only a small step from the position that "Hegesippus" takes up—viewing the siege as a form of divinely sanctioned vengeance against the Jews for their crucifixion of Christ. This paraphrase of *The Jewish Wars* is condensed, sensationalized, and thoroughly Christianized, and its emphasis on both the unnatural cruelty of the Jews and the righteous violence of the avenging Church Triumphant[12] leads to a correspondingly more prurient interest in the episode of the devouring mother.[13] Although "Hegesippus" does not name this woman within the description of her act, where she is merely "a woman from Peraea, which lies across the Jordan," the name Maria, even without the patronymic, is evidently familiar enough in this context to appear in the introduction to chapter 40, as he promises to relate "*factum Mariae, quod cuiusvis barbari atque impii mens perhorrescat*" [the deed of Maria, at which the mind of even the barbarian and the impious shuddered]. As this woman ritualistically consumes her son, she makes a lengthy speech replete with Christian irony, reversing and deconstructing the biblical *lex talionis*, as she addresses her child with "*reddite matri quod accepistis, redi fili in illud naturale secretum in quo domicilio sumsisti spiritum*" [return to your mother what you have received; return, son, to that secret place of nature, where you took up the spirit].[14]

Her injunction recalls the discussion between Jesus and Nicodemus in John 3:1–13. Jesus' direction that a man must be born again to see the kingdom of God provokes only the most literal interpretation from the Pharisee: "How can a man be born if he is old? Can he enter a second time into his mother's womb, and be born?" Nicodemus can read only on the most basic level—in fact, he is reading like a non-Christian: a pagan or a heretic. As Carolyn Dinshaw has illustrated in *Chaucer's Sexual Poetics*, late medieval Christian exegetes argued that to perform a literal reading of an allegorical text is to be seduced by the wantonness of the signifier, citing "the patristic association of the surface of the text (the letter) with carnality (the flesh, the body), and carnality with women."[15] Nicodemus, not just a Jew but also one of the Pharisees, regularly condemned by Jesus for their painstaking observation of the letter of the law, is oblivious to the spiritual signified, and on a nonspiritual level, Jesus' point can trigger only Oedipal associations, in which a return to the womb is literal, sexualized, and taboo.

Also manifested here is anxiety about the permeability of the female body, discussed in chapter one. The woman's capacity for holding a human body, especially a male one, inside her own, both sexually and, even more profoundly, in pregnancy, violates the classificatory system, blurring the outlines of individual and gendered identity. Pseudo-Hegesippus's astute conflation of stomach and uterus sheds, perhaps, some light on the feminizing of medieval and early modern accusations of cannibalism, which I addressed briefly in chapter three, and will discuss more fully in chapter five.[16]

However, although "Hegesippus" may have been the earliest Latin translator to embed the story of the desperate mother into a siege narrative that focused on the righteous punishment of the Jews, this ultimate horror of the Josephan siege also appears in two of the Greek works of ecclesiastical historian Eusebius Pamphilus (c. 265–340), bishop of Caesarea, one of which was translated into Latin by Rufinus of Aquileia (c. 345–411).[17] It appears again in the *De Subversione Jerusalem* of Walafrid Strabo (c. 807–849), which relies heavily on the more sensational incidents of "Hegesippus," including, predictably, the devouring of the child, which occupies a good tenth of his text. Yet perhaps the most widely known Latin redaction of this motif occurs in the context of Innocent III's *De Miseria Condicionis Humane*, a spiritual treatise written around 1195, when he was still the civil lawyer Lotario dei Segni.[18] It is particularly significant that the future Innocent III should express interest in this material, given the importance of the role he would play in crystallizing Church policy toward both the consumption of the body and blood of Christ and the status of Jews within the Christian community at the fourth Lateran Council in 1215.[19] The motif occurs here in isolation, without the surrounding context of the siege of Jerusalem, but Lotario follows Josephus quite closely.[20]

In both redactions, for instance, Maria's child is, specifically, a baby boy at the breast: "[*e*]*rat enim ei sub uberibus parvulus filius.*" The juxtaposition here of breastfeeding and cannibalism is interesting, given that, as I have pointed out in chapter one and elsewhere,[21] breastfeeding is a direct feeding on and from the female body, understood in medieval physiological terms as a lactation of transmuted blood. A large number of texts specify that Maria's baby is at the breast, and the ninth-century *Sacra Parallela* offers an iconographic representation of a breastfeeding Maria [figure 2]. In the first scene, she is nursing a child and displaying both breast and infant to the viewer in an image strongly reminiscent of the iconography of the nursing Madonna, which is found as early as the second century but proliferated in fourteenth-century Italy. The second image shows the dismembering of the boy, the third a highly disturbing combination of the consumption of a limb and a maternal gaze at the remainder of the child's body, while the fourth depicts

the revelation of her deed to two soldiers, whom Guy N. Deutsch tentatively identifies as allusions to Titus and Vespasian.[22]

Maria, then, eats the baby who eats of her. She is, like the classical Erysicthon, an autocannibal, or, more precisely, she is part of a closed cycle of consumption. From a more practical perspective, breastfeeding would be particularly resource-depleting during a time of famine, further justifying Maria's actions, while theologically, this image could be seen as a reference to Lamentations 4:4 and 4:10: "The tongue of the sucking child cleaveth to the roof of his mouth for thirst" and "[t]he hands of the pitiful women have sodden their own children: they were their meat in the destruction of the daughter of my people."

By the late thirteenth century, the story of Maria of Jerusalem was widely disseminated, entering into popular and even vernacular writing as well as into sermons, *exempla*, and homilies as the *sine qua non* of maternal depravity. Certainly, Dante's reference to the episode in *Purgatorio* is casual enough to

Figure 2. Ninth-century manuscript illustration of the devouring mother trope.

imply knowledge of the tale on the part of his readers: he compares the gluttons *to "la gente che perdé Ierusalemme, / quando Maria nel figlio diè di becco"*—the people who lost Jerusalem, when Maria struck her beak into her son.[23] Although Boccaccio's treatment of the theme occurs in the context of his Latin moral treatise *De Casibus Virorum Illustrium* rather than in his more popular vernacular texts, it was made available in a vernacular tongue when it was translated into French by Laurent de Premierfait as *Des Cas des Nobles Hommes et Femmes* in 1409.[24] It is probable, too, that Chaucer was familiar with the motif; in *The Legend of Good Women*, Alceste claims that the works Chaucer has translated include "the *Wreched Engendrynge of Mankynde* / As man may in Pope Innocent yfynde."[25] Robert E. Lewis, among others, has interpreted this reference to mean that Chaucer "intended to indicate that he had translated the whole *De Miseria* [including, of course, the episode of the devouring mother.] I think we can be almost certain about this."[26]

However, the earliest extant English versions seem to be the roughly contemporary poetic *Siege of Jerusalem*, written perhaps in the last decade of the fourteenth century, and John Trevisa's (d. 1402) translation of Ranulf Higden's mid-fourteenth-century *Polychronicon*.[27] The Maria episode in the Middle English *Siege* depends heavily on Josephus, but seems to owe something to "Hegesippus," particularly in Maria's suggestion that the child "yeld that I the yaf & agen tourne, / & entr ther thou cam out!"[28] This focus on the place of entry rather than that of gestation is clearly different from "Hegesippus's" "return . . . to that secret place of nature where you took up the spirit," in that this is not a womb/stomach conflation, but rather a vagina/mouth conflation, suggesting a connection between the motif of the devouring mother and castration anxiety.[29]

The Maria motif is disseminated both independently of other Josephan material and embedded within versions of *The Jewish Wars*. Even within the latter, reconfigured as *Vengeance of Our Lord* texts, the motif assumes a disproportionate importance. With the exception of the popular *Vindicta Salvatoris* sequence of texts,[30] every single version of the siege later than that of Walafrid Strabo focuses on, or at least features heavily, the episode of the devouring mother, even when this focus is at the expense of textual coherency. Since the enormous proliferation of vengeance texts from the twelfth century on prohibits extensive commentary on each one, I will confine my comments to those texts of significant interest in terms of the development of this episode.[31] For instance, a clear contrast in treatments of the Maria episode can be seen between the roughly contemporary French texts, the thirteenth-century *Legenda Aurea*, and the most prevalent version of *La Vengeance de Nostre-Seigneur*—the A/B text, or Japheth version, extant in some twenty-two manuscripts.[32] The former is clearly very influenced by either Josephus or Lotario—the mother is an unnamed wealthy noble-woman of the city who kills her newborn son when her home is invaded by pillagers, and both her act and her brief Josephan speech have the effect of repelling the robbers, who run away "in fear and trembling."[33] However, the text makes clear that the conquest and destruction of the city and subsequent dispersion of the Jews were a divine punishment for the death of Christ.[34] The symbolic inversion of the Crucifixion represented by the mother sacrificing her only son for physical life without the promise of salvation—note that the Maria of "Hegesippus" says "*ego consummabo sacrificium meum*"—is thus brought full circle.

La Vengeance de Nostre-Seigneur, on the other hand, tells a very different story. The woman here, although named Marie, is not a Jew from the environs of Jerusalem but the widow of the "king of Africa," and a Christian convert. She and her daughter are living with her companion, Clarice, also a new Christian, and Clarice's son, but the conditions of the siege lead to the deaths of both children from starvation. Both mothers grieve, but finally, and in desperation, Clarice suggests that they cook and eat a part of her son. The queen is horrified at the suggestion and faints, but is raised up by an angel who says, "Lady, God commands you by me that you eat of the child so that that which God said may be done. For he said on Palm Sunday, the day that he entered this city on an ass, that in this generation there would be in Jerusalem such great plague and famine so severe that a mother would eat her child."[35] Consequently, the two mothers, still in tears, prepare to roast a quarter of Clarice's son. The smell of the roasting meat attracts the attention of Pilate, an archetypal villain here playing the role of Josephus's Jewish rebels, to whose servant Maria and Clarice offer a piece of the child. Pilate is so distressed that he retires to bed for three days; he can now see no hope for the city. Having consumed Clarice's son, the two women now begin to eat the queen's daughter. After the fall of the city, the emperor is reminded that some have shown themselves to be friends of Christianity, including Joseph of Arimathea, Maria, Clarice, and their children,[36] and that these should therefore be spared the general punishment of the Jews. But Marie and Clarice cannot be found alive. Here, far from being a figure of anti-Christian animality, the woman echoes her namesake as a catalyst for the fulfillment of biblical prophecy. As both a gentile and a Christian, she is represented as humane enough to be appalled at the suggestion of infant cannibalism—which does not come from her—and agrees to the deed only at the urging of the angel. Finally, while she eats her child, a daughter, she is not responsible for killing her, since both children have perished from starvation as a result of the intransigence of the Jews. However, despite the divine permission for her acts and those of Clarice, neither mother survives—a sign, perhaps, of the psychological anxiety produced by even divinely sanctioned cannibalism. Perhaps even the women's Africanness, otherwise unaccounted for, is indicative of a linking of exoticism with the willingness to engage in cannibalism. Several later texts, including the fourteenth-century Middle English romance *Titus and Vespasian*, are influenced by this development of a divinely sanctioned tradition.

The story of the siege was also a popular subject for religious dramas, a medium that occupied a central place in European social, civic, and economic life: "like the Corpus Christi pageants with which they had much in common, the plays of the *Vengeance of Our Lord* became an important and abiding institution in European society."[37] The dramatic versions of the siege of Jerusalem, moreover, seem to have been especially popular and widespread,[38] especially in the sixteenth century, possibly, as Wright suggests, because they were relatively "theologically innocuous," in contrast to the doctrinally and politically controversial Corpus Christi plays.[39] In France, for instance, "no other kind of play in the vast repertory of the medieval Christian historical drama enjoyed such unrivaled preeminence over such a long period of time."[40] From the middle of the fourteenth century until well into the seventeenth century, plays with this theme were performed in Latin, French, English, Spanish, and Italian. Although only a remnant of the texts survives, the majority appear to deal with the Maria of Jerusalem episode at some length. One such play is *La Vengance Jhesucrist* of Eustache Marcadé, an early fifteenth-century text of immense influence[41] in which not only is the number of cannibalistic women multiplied, but the mothers go through a progressively more horrific and repetitive series of meals, including cats and dogs, until the ultimate horror of devouring their infants is reached.[42]

The two surviving manuscripts of Marcadé's *Vengance* are both illuminated, unusual for playbooks. Stephen Wright has emphasized the significance of the choice of illuminations for such a densely plotted narrative: "Clearly, the process of deciding which of the play's countless episodes to illustrate is an act of literary interpretation which reveals what elements of the text the artist (or his patron) considered to be most worthy of special attention and elaboration."[43] Among the twenty miniatures of the Chatsworth manuscript, painted by Loyset Liedet, is an illustration of a starving mother and her child before Josephus. Although the context is not spelled out, it seems likely that this moment represents the prologue to the consumption, especially as Liedet's miniatures tend, in general, to avoid the more gruesome aspects of the play. It seems clear that the episode of the desperate mother, or mothers, stood out in this regard. Moreover, another iconographic reference to a *Vengeance* drama, this one a series of sketches, apparently designed as blueprints for a specific dramatic production in Reims in 1531, also features this motif.[44] Commissioned by Cardinal Robert de Lenoncourt, bishop of Reims, one of the seven tableaux represents the grisly results of starvation during the siege—the besieged inhabitants are seen threatening one another, flaying a horse and catching and eating both pets and vermin, while to the right the episodes of the killing of the child, the roasting of it, and the displaying of the remnants to the appalled rebels occur in concurrent representation [figure 3]. The tableau of the killing of the child is particularly interesting: the naked child does not have its throat cut, but is pierced in the side by a large knife while cradled to its mother's clothed breast in a nursing posture, while the mother smiles beatifically. Again, the similarity to the conventional and by then contemporary representation of the lactating Madonna and her child is quite striking, especially given the piercing of the side of the sacrificial child, and the displaying of the dismembered body on a platter.[45] The linkage of Maria's act to contem-

Figure 3. Jerusalem under siege. Notice the progression from left to right that moves from eating household animals through the flaying of horses to Maria's display and consumption of her child.

Figure 4. Maria and Josephus on the battlements of a besieged Jerusalem.

porary eucharistic practices, under particular pressure in early sixteenth-century France, is thereby made overt.

Unfortunately, in no extant version of any of the dramatic texts is there a suggestion as to how the gruesome special effects may have been accomplished. The earliest visual representations of the episode tend to show Maria either nibbling on a whole, apparently raw, child or dismembering it and gnawing on a limb, such as in the illuminated initial of a twelfth-century *La Guerre des Juifs*, which features the attack on Jerusalem with Maria and Josephus standing on the battlements of the besieged city. Maria has her teeth fixed in the back of the intact child, while Josephus is clearly disapproving [figure 4].[46] Later illustrations, however, including those of Reims, focus more exclusively on the extent to which the child is like a joint of meat, frequently depicting its body being roasted on a spit.[47] This is particularly true of several French illustrations of Premierfait's translation of Boccaccio [figures 5 and 6] that are obviously interrelated, each depicting Maria on the left side of the image caught lifting a limb to her mouth, while the body of her child, variously mutilated, turns before a central fire.[48]

Obviously the staging demanded some theatrical skill. Beyond the cooking and eating of the child, Marcadé's play seems to call for, at minimum, large-scale battles, a shipwreck, a prophet being crushed by a heavenly rock, and a wondrous rain of fire. Performances of the *Vengance*, which runs

almost 15,000 lines, must have been elaborate and expensive undertakings. The immense popularity of the play may have suggested a way to recoup the expense, as private speculators were behind the 1531 Reims production, and crowds were said to have flocked to the show from thirty leagues away, despite an admission fee.[49]

Much shorter and less ambitious versions of the siege texts also existed. A Spanish version of the play, the *Aucto de la Destruicion de Jerusalen*, survives from the late sixteenth century, and despite the fact that it consists of only 697 lines,[50] the anonymous playwright, influenced probably by Marcadé, manages to squeeze in a predictable scene of two starving mothers consuming their dead babies. Much of the horror of this scene springs from the sheer accumulative banality of the stage direction "[*e*]*ntra otra Dueña con otro niño muerto*" [enter another woman with another dead baby].[51]

Similarly, the 1584 Coventry *Destruction of Jerusalem*, ascribed to a John Smith of Oxford, seems to emphasize the Marian episode at the expense of dramatic coherence.[52] Although the play is lost, its cast list indicates that it focused on three separate episodes of the siege—a battle, a mutiny, and the story of the devouring mother. However, this murderous mother is named not Maria but "Solome," suggesting that Smith may have felt it more appropriate to name his anthropophagous mother after a biblically wicked woman rather than an idealized and sacred one.

Biblical wickedness, moreover, manifests itself in familial siege cannibalism surprisingly often, particularly within the Old Testament.[53] John Boswell has suggested that the biblical tradition of starving parents devouring their children in times of disaster might well function to justify Christians resorting to such a desperate act;[54] it seems even more plausible that such accounts also function to characterize medieval Christian perceptions of the actual behavior of Jewish parents in such a position, particularly in the light of the apparently divinely sanctioned destruction of Jerusalem and its temple relatively soon after the crucifixion of Christ. Moreover, the association of Jews with cannibalism is both broader and more profound than that of scriptural example, including both historical allegations of martial enmity cannibalism and a discourse of a more subtle and domestic ritual cannibalism involving Christian babies and small children in the form of the blood libel, discussed at length in chapter two. Jews were also accused of more traditional forms of infanticidal cannibalism: a Warwickshire woman is said to have eaten "the mouth and ears" of her victim, and a fountain in

Figure 5. Devouring mother from Premierfait's translation of Boccaccio. *(opposite page, top)*

Figure 6. Devouring mother from Premierfait's translation of Boccaccio. *(opposite page, bottom)*

Berne, known as the fountain of the *Kindlifresser*, or child-devourer, boasts a statue of a Jew devouring one child while other small victims await their turn.[55]

However, the case of Maria at the siege of Jerusalem is not just another medieval anti-Semitic trope. Also operating here is an association of infanticidal cannibalism with women, specifically mothers, that includes resonances of anxiety over threatened family structure and unlicensed female sexuality. The most notorious, although largely postmedieval, association between women and infant cannibalism is, of course, the witchcraft trials, but the association also continued into sixteenth-century accounts of the New World. André Thevet's Amazons, for instance, are not quite cannibals, but they do roast their enemies, mate exclusively with cannibal men, and fail to return male babies to their cannibal fathers, instead preferring to kill them at birth.[56] Such a paroxysm of violence targeted specifically at infants by their mothers reinforced the perception of the society of the New World as the unspeakably barbaric antithesis of European Christian norms, where the ultimate familial bond disappeared into selfishness and cruelty. Vespucci, Hans Staden, and Jean de Léry all found peculiarly active cannibal women, and although, given the context, their victims were most likely to be European seamen, some of Vespucci's women, lacking in maternal instinct, also practiced malicious abortion and de Léry's mated with prisoners in order to produce future delicacies for the *boucan*.[57]

Moreover, Maria's geographic positioning within the city of Jerusalem locates her at a highly significant site in medieval cartographic and theological reasoning. The sense of freedom and fantasy associated with the monstrous further afield is unavailable to her; she does not have the license of the cannibalistic Plinian monstrosities said to inhabit the farthest comers of the world. Mary Campbell has likened the latter to grotesques frolicking unthreateningly at the margins of the medieval manuscript, pointing out that, "[o]nce firmly located in a margin, the grotesque poses little threat to the central order. It *need* not be integrated."[58] Instead, Maria is located squarely in the absolute center of the Christian world, within the very city that occupies the physical center of the medieval *mappae mundi*. In fact, one version of Maria's story, that in Higden's *Polychronicon*, appears in proximity to just such a Christocentric map. Her presence at the very center is ipso facto more fundamentally disturbing than if she had been relegated to the outer margins with the fantastic Cynocephali and Donestre.

What is particularly interesting about the accounts of Maria of Jerusalem is that she stands, very squarely, at the intersection of two linked discourses of medieval and voracious monstrosity—that of the Jew and that of the unnatural mother. In such a vulnerable position, Maria ben Eleazar is an ideal scapegoat for the violence that, in the context of the siege of Jerusalem, is neither Jewish nor female, and yet is identified as both. In short, the episode comprises a classic(al) subversion myth—a projection of the complicated problems of religious difference, violence, fear, and mortality onto an already marginalized victim. As Debbie Nathan and Michael Snedeker point out in their discussion of twentieth-century ritual abuse allegations,

> The crimes these culprits are charged with constitute the most evil, loathsome behavior imaginable, perpetrated against society's ultimate symbol of its own purity and self-renewal: its children. In many subversion myths the young victims are said to be destroyed by draining their blood, excising their vital organs, amputating their limbs, and cannibalizing their flesh. If all this were not terrible enough, the perpetrators in these stories often wreak their atrocities amid rituals of public promiscuity calculated to violate the culture's strongest sexual taboos, including incest.[59]

Especially significant in the Maria motif is the relegation of violence to the domestic sphere, in the bosom of the patriarchal family structure, the very privacy of which has proved so dangerous to women and children. In each variant it is the absence of a father figure that allows for Maria's brutal defiance—in Lacanian terms, without the protecting male, the nuclear family is Law-less, reincorporated by the dyadic/devouring mother, who, like the Jewish rebels with whom she is conflated, is in revolt against lawful patriarchy, refusing to release her child into the Symbolic.[60] The archetypal quality of the motif has been identified by Shulamith Shahar, who describes the Maria of Jerusalem figure as "deeply entrenched in the European collective consciousness." She goes on to say, "What seems to underlie this story is a fear of the 'great mother,' which is common to a large number of myths, of [the one] who bestows life but also devours and destroys in her rage. In the particular context of Christian culture, Maria of Azov represented the opposite pole to the Holy Mother. The cruelty of the former highlights the maternal compassion displayed by the latter."[61]

Certainly, Shahar is correct in pointing out that the figure of a Jewish Mary eating her only son has oppositional resonances in terms of Christian symbolism of the mother of Jesus. Mary, the mother of Jesus, Blessed Virgin and protector of little children, seems very different from Maria of Jerusalem. Yet the complexity of medieval mariology allowed for an understanding and acceptance of Mary's own complicity in the death of her son, as the fifteenth-century lyric "The firste day when Crist was born" demonstrates. In this poem, as in several other late medieval Marian lyrics, Mary is credited with responsibility not just for the birth of the Savior but also for his suffering: "A gerlond of thornes on his hed was set, / A sharp spere to his herte was smyt; / The Jewes seyde, 'Tak thou that!' / I thonke a mayden everydel."[62] More generally, Michael Carroll's study of Italian folk literature suggests that worship of the Virgin can and does manifest itself as propitiation of an angry deity,[63] and Marina Wamer has argued that the Virgin "belongs in the tradition of an all-devouring and savage goddess of myth who . . . sacrifices a substitute to the powers of darkness to save herself and then weeps for him."[64] A further medieval view of Mary's role in Christ's sacrifice is demonstrated by a fifteenth-century Swabian retable that shows the Virgin Mary pouring flour into the mill that produces the host [figure 7] She is complicit here in making the food that is her son. How far is she, then, from her mirror image, that other Jewish Mary, who made her son into food? Certainly, the need of the redactors of the A/B Old French versions of the *Vengeance* and the Middle English *Titus and Vespasian* to characterize Maria of Jerusalem as a Christian woman fulfilling prophecy is indicative of the anxiety-provoking closeness of the connection between the two mothers, especially in the later Middle Ages, with its increasing devotional focus on the suffering body of Christ and on communion as the most direct road to salvation.[65]

Anxieties about cannibalism can never be completely absent in the symbolic and literal act of eating the body and drinking the blood of a sacrificial victim, especially when that victim is frequently represented as a child. Alan Dundes sees the accusations of ritual murder against the Jews, particularly the cementing of the fantasy into the notion that Christian blood is used in matzoh and Passover wine, as a projection of anxieties about Christian consumption of the body and blood of a Jew.[66] This strategy, which he dubs "projective inversion," functions also to reify Christian virtue at the expense of Jewish depravity.

I submit that something similar is happening in the almost pathological proliferation of versions of the Maria story that appeared between the eleventh and sixteenth centuries. As Carroll reminds us, "Jung argues that the particular quaternity that will shape our conscious thoughts is one that predisposes us to think in terms of a balanced union of two specific contrasts, namely male vs. female and good vs. evil."[67] Maria of Jerusalem is the mirror image of the Blessed Virgin, the bad woman damned rather than redeemed by the body of her son, the Law-less Mary reproved rather than revered by the paternal Joseph, the Jew condemned through her own body rather than being saved by her avoidance of its pleasures. Maria's relationship to Eve, who was read by the medieval church as the mirror image of Mary, is not coincidental. Both women sin by breaking a fundamental patriarchal taboo on consumption.[68] However, just as Eve has been recuperated by fem-

Figure 7. Fifteenth-century retable of the mystical mill.

inist critics, it may be possible to do the same for Maria. Both infanticide and what Lilian Furst has called "disorderly eating" can be, for woman-as-sign, final gestures of both desperation and defiance.[69]

Representing both Jew and unnatural mother, Maria is demonized for blurring hierarchical boundaries in the most egregious manner, merging mother and son, male and female, human and animal, eater and eaten. She is the ultimate Other—the Other that threatens to assimilate the self. And yet she is also the flip side of the idealized medieval maternal figure, and her demonization absorbs anxieties, allowing the other Mary to remain firmly on the side of the Christian, the civilized, the cooked.

Chapter Five

Teratographies: Writing the American Colonial Monster

URING THE COURSE OF HIS DEFENSE OF THE INDIGENOUS PEOPLES OF the Americas from charges of a variety of barbaric and unspeakable practices, Bartolomé de las Casas refers to a confession he had occasion to take from "an old woman, Indian chief or lady, who had been married to a Spaniard, one of the first in the island" [Cuba]. In response to his questions about the possible existence of sodomy in Cuba before the arrival of the Europeans, his elderly source replies: "No father, because if it existed among the Indians, the women would eat them in bites, and no man could remain alive."[1] The suggestion that sodomitical practices among the Cuban men would necessarily culminate in a cannibalistic holocaust inflicted by their women resists a simple interpretation. It sets up a deadly rivalry between the sexes, implying the existence of a female vigilance about male relationships, and associates women deprived of men with unimaginably monstrous cannibal savagery. Furthermore, in its privileging of cannibalism above sodomy, it seems to reverse José de Acosta's schema of civilization, which theorized that the path out of barbarism would abandon cannibalism before sodomy,[2] and it also suggests that Las Casas himself may have found the idea of the consumption of male flesh less distressing than the idea of the penetration of it. The link here between sodomy and cannibalism, as well as the gendered implications of both, would reappear compulsively in proto-colonial narratives of the New World as the Europeans began to remake the newly discovered lands and peoples in their own image, and would prove a crucial factor in the larger colonial project, functioning as a convenient screen for European fears and phantasies and for the realities of colonial violence.

The earliest European texts of "discovery" and conquest of the New World inevitably both understood and represented the indigenous inhabitants in terms of the feared and fantasized expectations of their authors. It is partly for this reason that explorers like Columbus and Vespucci provide their readers with the exotic and erotic preoccupations of classical and medieval encyclopedists—mermaids, Amazons, sodomites, and cannibals. It is not especially perplexing that early explorers should have sensationalized their accounts with the stuff of medieval bestsellers, but what is interesting here is the way in which protocolonialist narratives of New World cannibalism return obsessively to the intersecting terrains of gender, of sexuality, and of monstrosity. In the New World, the vilification of the Other achieved by accusations of the ultimate inhuman monstrosity—cannibalism—paradoxically depends on both a hyperdelineation and a blurring of categories of gender, under which the indigenous women were represented as voracious and sadistic sexual aggressors and the men as sexually perverse and malformed monsters, each of whom practiced a bestial and bloodthirsty cannibalism deserving only of enslavement and extinction. At the same time as the allegation of cannibalism functions to divest the accused of their humanity, however, it invariably and ironically also functions to reaffirm it, since membership in the human species is a prerequisite for the eater of human flesh to be considered a cannibal. At one level, the accusation, then, will always fail, collapsing under the weight of its own logical contradictions, although in the case of the New World, it would not do so before fixing the European image of the Americas for centuries to come.

Although 1492 has been seen as a convenient point to mark the end of the Middle Ages and the beginning of the modern world, Columbus, in his dependence on medieval accounts of eastern travel, is an odd standard-bearer for the forces of modernity. He was evidently very familiar with Marco Polo and with Mandeville's *Travels*; some of his other influences included the *Imago Mundi* of Pierre d'Ailly, and perhaps the *Letter of Prester John*—texts that merge geographic practicalities and commonplaces with popular accounts of exotic marvels and terrifying monstrosities, including the practice of man-eating.[3] The idea of this practice moved Columbus strongly enough for him to add several editorial comments to the margins of these texts[4]

Columbus's familiarity with the longstanding traditions of medieval travelers, encyclopedists, and cartographers led him to expect not just anthropophagi, but also Amazons, mermaids, and cynocephali on the margins of the world. He saw the mermaids firsthand, on January 9, 1493, but they proved to be disappointingly androgynous in the flesh, providing an appropriate metaphor for the problematic issues of gender and species that would face the early European ethnographers of the New World. Since he was operating on the principle that he had reached Mandeville's sinful but almost exclusively heterosexual east, it does not seem to have occurred to Columbus to look for sodomy among the peoples of the Great Khan. He did, however, succeed in finding the anthropophagi, or at least, found that he could draw enticing descriptions of them from the people of neighboring communities. Unlike the frustrating mermaids, the anthropophagi, when he finally encountered them, were very satisfactory—bloodthirsty, resistant, and emasculating to boot, and at least dressed and made up to look fearsome, even if they were lacking the heads of dogs his informants had promised.[5]

Just how Columbus and his crew succeeded in understanding the accusations of man-eating and mutilation his informants seemed to be leveling against their neighbors is unclear, especially since his first contact with the accusations came as early in the voyage as November 4, 1492: "I also understood them to say that there are large ships and a trade in goods, all to the SE, and that a long way away there are men with one eye, and others with noses like dogs who eat human flesh; when they capture someone they cut his throat and drink his blood and cut off his private parts."[6] The only interpreter accompanying Columbus on the first voyage was a converso with a background in Arabic, whose usefulness would have been dubious even if Columbus had succeeded in reaching the country of the Great Khan, as he had intended.[7] As it stood, Columbus was forced to rely on the translation skills of captured natives, via whom communication was not merely difficult, but often frustratingly impossible: "Tuesday, 27 November. . . . I do not know the language; the people do not understand me, nor I them, nor any of my company."[8] The problem can only have been further exacerbated by the linguistic variation within the island groups. Despite Columbus's own facility in European languages, his attempts to bridge the cultural divide often failed miserably, leading to such near-disasters as that of Monday, December third:

> Before they came back a large number of Indians gathered and approached the boats, into which the men and I had withdrawn. One of them waded into the river as far as the stern of the boat and made a long speech which I did not understand, except that from time to time the rest of the Indians raised their hands high and gave a great shout. I thought they were reassuring us that they were pleased by our arrival, but then I saw that the Indian I had with me was turning as yellow as wax, and trembling, and he made signs to me that we should leave the river because they wanted to kill us.[9]

It seems, then, that Columbus must have been left with the options of demonstrating the medieval monsters he sought with the help of manuscripts or prints, as David Beers Quinn suggests,[10] or of depending upon an unreliable system of signs. Indeed, as Stephen Greenblatt dryly points out, the signing to which Columbus must have been forced to resort in order to convey his questions about the dog-faced, murderous, castrating man-eaters on Bohio "may help to explain why the natives, as he notes in the same entry, were 'very timid.'"[11]

Despite Columbus's training in the texts of Mandeville and Marco Polo and his obvious fascination with the notion of anthropophagy, he is at first reluctant to accept the accusations of man-eating at face value.

> Friday, November 23: I think they must have taken some captives, and when they did not return it was probably thought that they had been eaten. The Indians thought the same thing about me and the ship's company when some of them saw us for the first time.[12]

> Tuesday, 11 December: They must be right when they say they are harassed by a cunning people, for all these islands are in great fear of the Caniba people, and as I have said before, Caniba means simply the people of the Great Khan, who must live very near here and will have ships; they must come to capture these people, and when they do not return it is supposed that they have been eaten.[13]

This skepticism remains, even when he is confronted with supposed physical evidence of their predations. On Thursday, 29 November, the crew makes a gruesome discovery, but Columbus does not leap to conclusions about cannibalism: "In another house they found a man's head in a basket, covered by another basket, hanging on one of the posts, and another the same in a different village. They must be the heads of some important ancestor, for the houses are big enough for many people to live together in them, all probably descended from one man."[14]

Clearly, if Columbus had been determined to discover man-eaters at this point, he could easily have read man-eating into this funerary practice, as later explorers were to identify stripped bones or stewing meat as evidence of anthropophagy. In contrast, Columbus's companion on the second voyage, Dr. Diego Alvarez Chanca, not only noted the cleaned bones, but saw them as evidence of Indian rapacity: "They say that human flesh is so good that there is nothing like it in the world; and this must be true, for the human bones we found in their houses were so gnawed that no flesh was left on them except what was too tough to be eaten. In one house the neck of a man was found cooking in a pot."[15]

Although the human remains may just have easily have been prepared and preserved as funerary artifacts, as both Columbus and his son suggest,[16] it is just as likely that the remains may not even have been human at all. It seems doubtful that even a ship's doctor in the fifteenth century would have been able to distinguish disembodied human and animal remains with any reliability; hungry Spanish soldiers at Anzermo in 1553 supposedly made a meal of "a great pot full of cooked meat," assuming it to be the meat of guinea pigs before discovering a human hand at the bottom.[17]

In fact, to Columbus's credit, he seems to maintain his skepticism until Sunday, January 13, when he encounters a strange-looking emissary from the indigenous people:

> He came, and he was stranger to look at than anyone else we had seen. His face was all blackened with charcoal, although the people elsewhere also paint themselves with various colours. His hair was very long, gathered up and tied at the back of his head, and then put into a net made of parrot feathers. He was as naked as all the others. I believe he is one of the Caribs who eat other men's flesh, and that the bay I saw yesterday is a channel separating off a different island. . . . These Carib people must be fearless, for they go all over these islands and eat anyone they capture. . . . The people here are evilly disposed; I believe that these are the Caribs, and that they eat human flesh. . . . I should like to capture a few of them.[18]

Although the inhabitants of this island are unusually loath to trade and show (limited) signs of aggression, this is hardly the concrete evidence of anthropophagy needed to dissolve the admiral's skepticism so suddenly. Perhaps the unorthodox appearance of the "Carib" may have reminded Columbus of the notes he had taken from medieval travel texts—wild men who eat human flesh are expected to have faces "ugly and loathsome."[19] However, this Carib was, while odd-looking, not really ugly *enough*, since the strangeness in his appearance could be accounted for in terms of external cultural characteristics rather than physical malformation, leading Anthony Pagden to suggest that Columbus was "surprised to find that the Caribs had not been deformed by their foul diet."[20] However, the man-eaters would soon undergo a literary metamorphosis—as early as the second printed New World chronicle, Guillermo Coma of Aragon would establish the darkness of flesh and grimness of visage of the American anthropophagi.[21] Man-eaters, it would seem, were, or should be, immediately recognizable, as they would be for Columbus on his fourth voyage ten years later: "I found other tribes who ate human flesh, as their brutal appearance showed."[22]

However, there were factors that influenced Columbus's increasingly disenchanted view of the American people other than the incongruity of their appearance. By the time they encountered the "Caribs" on Española on

January 13, the crew had been making inroads along the coast of the Indies for some three months. The initial hopes of huge wealth for the taking had dwindled dramatically; although there were indications that the people of these islands were both familiar with gold and generous with the small amount they had, the crew had been unable to find the promised source. Moreover, Columbus's alternative cargoes of silver, pearls, spices, and finally even rhubarb and mastic, also proved either tantalizingly out of reach, or simply unidentifiable.[23] His frustration is palpable; as time progresses, he increasingly accused other crew members, especially Martin Alonso Pinzón, of greed, pride, insubordination, arrogance, and dishonesty.[24] The likelihood or unlikelihood of gold governs his attitude to the peoples he encounters; when and where gold seems possible, the emphasis in the journal is on the importance of treating the native people well: "Treating them thus can only be to Your Majesties' benefit, in all the islands but especially in this one, where you now have a settlement, for in an island with such a wealth of gold and spices and fine land the people must be treated honourably and generously."[25] Unfortunately, the corollary also held true: when and where gold seems less likely, the admiral, whose only previous focus on the landscape had been one of indescribable wonder at such a pastoral paradise, begins to cast an acquisitive eye on the financial possibilities of the fertile soil in terms of its potential for cultivation. At the same time, the land's inhabitants, previously considered only as potential Catholic converts and Spanish trading partners, begin to be viewed as sources of cheap labor:

> December 16: I assure your Majesties that these lands, especially this island of Española, are so rich and fertile that no man could describe them; no one would believe it all without seeing it. . . . [The Indians] are very timid; three men could put a thousand of them to flight, so they could easily be commanded and made to work, to sow and to do whatever might be needed, to build towns and be taught to wear clothes and adopt our ways.[26]

Less than a year later, in the "Memorial á Antonio de Torres" of January 1494, Columbus's plan to wring wealth from his discovery had reached its final stage: "The conveyors could be paid in cannibal slaves, fierce but well-made fellows of good understanding, which men, wrested from their inhumanity, will be, we believe, the best slaves that ever were."[27] Slavery, here, is the merciful route to humanity, and of course to salvation, for the Caribs.

But was it morally acceptable for a Christian nation to conquer the inhabitants of the New World by force of arms, even if it was ultimately for their own good? Did either the Church or individual Catholic monarchs have the authority to conquer and enslave a people who had never been evangelized, and were therefore not lapsed Christians, or even infidels?

Certainly, papal precedent seemed to indicate that they did: the 1454 bull *Romanus Pontifex*, written to address European expansion to the east and into Africa, established that non-Christian peoples did not have to be lapsed converts to be subject to colonization, but that non-Christians, by definition, held no rights to the land they inhabited, and that their failure to convert and pledge submission to Christian sovereignty meant that they could lawfully be killed.[28] Furthermore, the "discovery" that the inhabitants of the New World practiced such inhuman degeneracy as cannibalism meant that such intervention was not merely legal, but a religious obligation. By 1503, Queen Isabella's famous edict authorized a practice that must already have been underway for some years:

> . . . if such Cannibals continue to resist and do not wish to admit and receive my Captains and men who may be on such voyages by my orders nor to hear them in order to be taught our Sacred Catholic Faith and to be in my service and obedience, they may be captured and are to be taken to these my Kingdoms and Domains and to other parts and places and be sold.[29]

Here, the word "Cannibals" is clearly to be understood as referring to, or more precisely, inventing, a specific ethnic group, membership of which is dependent upon presumed social practices as much as upon national or territorial identity. Although any reference to anthropophagy is absent, resistance to the process of European colonization is implicit in the ethnic label. As Innocent IV argued, however, in the papal sanction of Christian interventionism in the New World in 1510, it was not cannibalism and human sacrifice alone that offended against God's law.[30] Indeed, the offenses of the Native Americans in general were assumed to be manifold, including sodomy and idolatry, and these acts, being *contra naturam*, provided a moral and spiritual justification for the atrocities of the colonial project.

Moreover, the men of the New World were not only assumed to be inveterate man-eaters, positioning them on the outer limits of humanity, but their position on the spectrum of masculinity was also called into question. As in other historical encounters, the well-established hierarchy male over female seemed to have provided a readymade topos upon which to map the new hierarchy, in this case, that of European over American. As Helen Carr has pointed out,

> in the language of colonialism, non-Europeans occupy the same symbolic space as women. Both are seen as part of nature, not culture, and with the same ambivalence: either they are ripe for government, passive, child-like, unsophisticated, needing leadership and guidance, described always in terms of lack—no initiative, no intellectual powers, no perseverance; or, on the other hand, they are outside society, dangerous, treacherous, emotional,

inconstant, wild, threatening, fickle, sexually aberrant, irrational, near animal, lascivious, disruptive, evil, unpredictable.[31]

The suspicious "femaleness" of the American men was not, then, manifested in specific behaviors so much as a function of the expectations of the colonizers, whether expressed in the rhetoric of the noble or of the brutal savage. America itself is female in protocolonial rhetoric and iconography, allegorized often as a sensually naked figure, but her erotic possibilities are complicated by the presence of weapons or even severed human heads and other remains.[32] An especially compelling image is that of Jan van de Straet's c. 1575 sketch of Vespucci's arrival in the New World in 1497, which achieved broad circulation via Theodor Galle's engraving a few years later [figure 8]. The sketch captures the moment when Vespucci, clothed in arms, finery, and European authority, and, in Anne McClintock's words, "erect and magisterial,"[33] grasping the tools of protocolonialism, encounters a native woman, clothed only in a feather headdress, who has been reclining in her hammock. Pushing herself up with her left hand, she extends her right hand toward the explorer in a gesture of wonder, or perhaps of recognition. Precisely above the gesturing index finger, in the background of the sketch yet exactly in the center, several naked figures are roasting a whole human leg, from haunch to foot, on a wooden spit over a blazing fire, while a second spitted leg rests a short distance away. The parallelism between the allegorical America and the feast is immediately apparent: "America's body pose is partially mirrored by both the apparently female figure who turns the spit and the clearly female figure who cradles an infant as she awaits the feast. Most strikingly, the form of the severed human leg and haunch turning upon the spit precisely inverts and miniaturizes America's own."[34] The implication is clear: even at the moment when the historical Amerigo encounters and claims his allegorical female namesake, she is already implicated in the savage yet strangely compelling horror that is cannibalism. More precisely, she is implicated both as cannibal and as victim—an unwitting symbol, perhaps, of the predatory intentions of the colonizers.

Despite, or perhaps even because of the possible dangers, the sexual possibilities of conquest played a significant role in early European reports of the New World, and descriptions of the fantasized sexual practices of the indigenous peoples, especially the women, were often distributed in the form of prurient entertainment for an lasciviously eager European public. Consider, in this context, the following extract, supposedly from Vespucci's first voyage:

> They are not very jealous, and are libidinous beyond measure, and the women far more than the men; for I refrain out of decency from telling you the trick

Figure 8. European representative Amerigo Vespucci encounters an allegorical representative of America.

which they play to satisfy their immoderate lust. . . . And although they go about utterly naked, they are fleshy women, and that part of their privies which he who has not seen them would think to see is invisible; for they cover all with their thighs, save that part [for] which nature made no provision, and which is modestly speaking the *mons veneris*. . . . Only exceptionally will you see a woman with drooping breasts, or with belly shrunken through frequent parturition, or with other wrinkles; for all look as though they had never given birth. They showed themselves very desirous of copulating with us Christians.[35]

Such is the stuff of heterosexual erotic fantasy, and yet the fantasy is an ambivalent one. Inevitably, the erotic promise of the naked women would bear a price—perhaps the specifically genital and nightmarish one said to be paid by the husbands of these women:

> Another custom among them is sufficiently shameful, and beyond all human
> credibility. Their women, being very libidinous, make the penis of their hus-
> bands swell to such a size as to appear deformed; and this is accomplished by
> a certain artifice, being the bite of some poisonous animal, and by reason of
> this bite many lose their virile organ and become eunuchs.[36]

Presumably this is the "trick" Vespucci is too modest to mention above. The
price paid by these women's husbands is reminiscent of that paid by the men
in Mandeville's *Travels* said to have copulated with women who had poison-
ous snakes hidden in their vaginas, and both protocolonial phantasies clearly feature the same crude anxieties about male sexual vulnerability that
appear in the signifying practices of cannibalism accusations. These anxieties
are again demonstrated by the island of voracious women said to have been
encountered by Vespucci on the third voyage. In an attempt to establish
friendly relations with the women, a European sailor is chosen to approach
them alone; picked for his appearance, liveliness, and assumed appeal to the
"desirous" women, the young man does not last very long:

> And he went among the women, and when he approached them, they made
> a great circle around him; and touching and gazing at him, they displayed
> their wonder. Meanwhile we saw a woman approaching from the hill, and she
> carried a big club in her hand. And when she reached the place where our
> Christian stood, she came up behind him, and, raising her club, struck him
> such a hard blow that she stretched him out dead on the ground. In a jiffy the
> other women seized him by the feet, and dragged him [by the feet] toward the
> hill; and the men sprang toward the beach, [and began] to shoot at us with
> their bows and arrows. And they filled with such consternation our people . .
> . nobody thought of laying hand on his weapons. Yet we did discharge at them
> four mortar shots, and they did not hit [anyone]; only, when the report [of
> these] was heard, all took flight toward the hill where the women were already
> cutting the Christian to pieces. And by a great fire which they had built they
> were roasting him before our eyes, exhibiting to us many pieces, and eating
> them.[37]

The unusually active and aggressive role of the native women in attacking,
dismembering, and roasting the European is a part of the cultural antithesis
expected in the New World, creating an anticulture that, as Louis Montrose
points out, "precisely inverts European norms of political authority, sexual
license, marriage and child-rearing practices and inheritance rules."[38] This
world upside-down topos, which, at least in the New World, seems to have
been utterly regardless of actual native practices, is frequently associated with
violation of European gender norms, ranging from the perception of androgynous or inverted social roles and appearance to phantasies of Amazonian
barbarity. The former include references as early as pseudo-Vespucci to unex-

pected female athletic, martial, and physical prowess, and culminate in the following bizarre comment from *The Chronicle of the Anonymous Conquistador*: "The men have a custom of urinating sitting down, like our women, and the women standing up."[39] Although editor Patricia Fuentes notes that this remark was "apparently intended as a witticism," its humor, if intentional, rather depends on an understanding of the topos of inversion.[40]

A paradigm for maximum inversion of gender norms, of course, already existed in the European imagination—the classical Amazons: beautiful, independent, lethal, single-breasted warrior women. In January of 1493, just two days before Columbus saw mermaids, he thought he had discovered an island of women living without men; a week later he had confirmation: "[t]he Indian told me that the island of Matenino is inhabited only by women, men visit them at a certain season; if they give birth to a girl, they keep her, and if it is a boy he is sent to the men's island."[41] By "the men's island," Columbus's informant seems to mean the "island" of the Caribs, although there is no further suggestion that the Caribs are exclusively male. The connection between the Carib men and the Mateninian women is maintained, however, in the fuller description of the women in Columbus's "Letter to the Sovereigns":

> Wherefore Your Highnesses should know that the island of the Indies, closest to Spain, is populated entirely by women, without a single man, and their comportment is not feminine, but rather they use weapons and other masculine practices. They carry bow and arrows and take their adornments from the copper mines, which metal they have in very large quantity. They call this island Matenino, the second Caribo, [blank] leagues out from this one. Here are found those people which all those of the other islands of the Indies fear; they eat human flesh . . . they go about naked like the others, except that they wear their hair very full, like women. . . . And when Your Highnesses give the order for me to send slaves, I hope to bring or send these for the most part; these are the ones who have intercourse with the women of Matenino, who if they bear a female child they keep her with them, and if it is a male child, they raise him until he can feed himself and them they send him to Cardo (sic).[42]

Despite the fact that no one ever actually lands on such an island, islands of independent women continue to appear in conquest narratives, such as Juan Diaz's chronicle of the Grijalva expedition to Mexico in 1518, which names the independent women as Amazons,[43] or even Francisco López de Gómara's biography of Cortés, which records the gullibility of Sandoval and his companions in believing in "an island of Amazons.[44] Despite López de Gómara's personal skepticism, Amazons appear again in André Thevet's *Singularitéz de la France Antarctique,* translated into English in 1568 as *The*

Newfound Worlde. Although Thevet was only in Brazil for some ten weeks, most of which he spent seriously ill, his publication of *Singularitéz* claimed the discovery of a fourth, Brazilian branch of Amazons to add to those of Asia, Africa, and Scythia.[45] Thevet's Amazons are not quite cannibals, which make an appearance in his 1577 *Cosmographie Universelle,* but they do attempt to broil their male captives by hanging them upside down and lighting a fire beneath them while using them for target practice, which Frank Lestringant calls an "excess of cooking."[46] Worse, they do not return male babies to their cannibal fathers, but kill them at birth. Such matriarchal violence, targeted specifically at infants by their mothers, reinforced the perception of the society of the New World as the unspeakably barbaric antithesis of European norms.

The lack of maternal feeling of Native American women appears repeatedly in the chronicles of the early explorers. The Soderini letter explains how the women are "so heartless and cruel that, if they become angry with their husbands, they immediately resort to a trick whereby they kill the child within the womb, and a miscarriage is brought about, and for this reason they kill a great many babies."[47] The women of Mexico are also said to have practiced abortion out of spite, and López de Gómara recounts a political revolt and fetal massacre by the one hundred and fifty pregnant wives of Moctezuma, which happened "they say," when the women, "persuaded by the devil, took exercises and medicines to get rid of the babies; or perhaps [they did so] because their children could not inherit."[48]

Moreover, native women were not only represented as practicing malicious abortion, a peculiarly and dangerously female power negating any suggestion of "natural" maternal instinct, but as breeding with captive prisoners specifically in order to produce children to be eaten. Both Hans Staden and Jean de Léry report this practice among the Tupinamba of Brazil, although Staden suggests that the children are not consumed until they reach adulthood: "[t]hey give him a woman who attends to him and has intercourse with him. If the woman conceives, the child is maintained until it is fully grown, then when the mood seizes them, they kill and eat it."[49] de Léry, on the other hand, reports that the children of captured enemies are often eaten right away:

> . . . if it happens that the women given to the prisoners are with child by them, the savages who have killed the fathers, claiming that such children have sprung from the seed of their enemies (a horrible thing to hear, and what follows is still worse to see). They will eat them immediately after they are born; or, if they prefer, they will let them get a little bigger before taking that step.[50]

Cieza de León reports a similar practice in parts of Mexico in 1553, although in this account, it is the mothers rather than the fathers who are the enemy:

> . . . the caciques of the valley of Nore collected all the women they could find from the land of their enemies, took them home, and used them if they had been their own. If any children were born, they were reared with much care until they reached the age of 12 or 13, and, being then plump and healthy, these caciques ate them with much appetite, not considering that they were their own flesh and blood. In this way they had many women solely to bring forth children, which were afterwards to be eaten; and this is the greatest of all sins that these people commit.[51]

In this case the practice seems to stress maternal lineage at the expense of paternity, a suggestion that has been scorned by Lestringant,[52] but either version may merely imply that, although the cannibals were in most cases credited with limiting their consumption to exogenous anthropophagy, the line between exophagy and endophagy was considered suspiciously blurred.

This is nowhere more stressed than in Vespucci's letter to Lorenzo di Medici in 1502, where the native women seem to become candidates for cannibalism merely by being married off to a captive male:

> If women sleep with a male prisoner and he is virile, they marry him with their daughters. At certain times, when a diabolical frenzy comes over them, they invite their kindred and the whole tribe, and they set before them a mother with all the children she has, and with certain ceremonies they kill them with arrow shots and eat them. They do the same thing to the above-mentioned slaves and to the children born of them. This is assuredly so, for we found in their houses human flesh hung up to smoke, and much of it.[53]

However, for the most part, women do not seem to have been the victims of cannibalism. Dr. Chanca's letter reports that "the flesh of boys and women is not good to eat,"[54] although Michele de Cuneo points out that "[t]he Caribs, whenever they catch these Indians, eat them as we would eat kids and they say that a boy's flesh tastes better than that of a woman,"[55] suggesting that both have been sampled, at least, although most commentators seem to agree that female captives were used primarily for breeding purposes. The threat of cannibalism, then, seems to have been aimed primarily at men, and, for the most part at adult men—not so coincidentally, the very subjects putting themselves in danger by conquering and chronicling such horror. As Jonathan Goldberg has pointed out: "[w]hat is good to eat in the Caribbean is what is most monstrously sacrificed on the mainland: the adult male body as the object of desire."[56] The role of women, as we shall see, is primarily that of devourer of the universal subject. According to Hans Staden's account of his captivity under the Tupinamba:

> The women seize the body at once and carry it to the fire where they scrape off the skin, making the flesh quite white, and stopping up the fundament with a piece of wood so that nothing may be lost. Then a man cuts up the body, removing the legs above the knee and the arms at the trunk, whereupon the four women seize the four limbs and run with them round the huts, making a joyful cry. After this they divide the trunk among themselves, and devour everything that can be eaten.[57]

The text of Calvinist missionary Jean de Léry is even more damning, stressing not just the role of women in general in enthusiastically preparing the victims, but also the particular role played by the older women, whom he describes as "covetous of eating human flesh," and as having "an amazing appetite for human flesh."[58] These elderly women, no longer conventionally sexually alluring or capable of reproduction, appear repeatedly as the chief culprits, addicted to the cannibal feast. In fact, de Léry is impressed enough by the motif of the greedy old woman to use it to link together his two alimentary histories—that of the Tupinamba in Brazil and that of the siege of Sancerre. In the latter, the appalling conditions of the Protestant community under siege lead to the dismemberment and consumption of a small girl by her parents and the elderly woman with whom they live. Based on his experience with the Tupinamba, de Léry suggests the extraordinary notion that the elderly woman may have been motivated less by advanced hunger, like the other culprits, than by her own "perverted appetite."[59]

The motif of the greedy old woman appears not just in de Léry, but also in Theodore de Bry's illustrations in *Great Voyages* at the close of the sixteenth century. Nine of De Bry's twenty-seven engravings of Hans Staden's experiences among the Tupinamba concern cannibalism, and they are distinctive not only for their lyrical classicalism, which is conspicuous in opposition to the crude woodcuts in Staden's original text, but in the primary role they allot to the naked women, some of whom are sumptuous Rubenesque nudes, while others are withered and elderly crones. Bernadette Bucher makes a complex structuralist argument for the significance of the pendulous-breasted old women in de Bry,[60] but while compelling, Bucher's argument passes quickly over some of the traditional European iconographic associations of the sagging breast—the associations, perhaps, that Vespucci was making when he expressed such surprise that the women he has already characterized as predatory, both sexually and gastronomically, should not possess sagging bosoms: "[i]t was to us a matter of astonishment that none was to be seen among them who had a flabby breast . . ."[61] While one context for this statement is the contemporary European fetishization of the firm, youthful bosom seen, for instance, in Clément Marot's apostrophes "Le Blazon du Tetin" and "Le Counterblazon du Tetin,"[62] another, related, context is that of European representations of the figure of the Wild Woman: uncivilized, libidinous, voracious, and often represented with pendulous breasts. Closely related to this figure, of course, is that of the witch, also represented, iconographically and textually, as a lascivious, anthropophagous hag.

Certainly de Léry had made this connection when, influenced by Jean Bodin's work on witchcraft, he appended his final conclusions on the Tupi women to the 1585 edition of his *History of a Voyage*: "I have concluded that they have the same master: that is, the Brazilian women and the witches over here were guided by the same spirit of Satan; neither the distance between the places nor the long passage over the sea keeps the father of lies from working both here and there on those who are handed over to him by the just judgment of God."[63] Columbus had, consciously or otherwise, made the same connection some years earlier, as Sara Castro-Klaren has pointed out, when he described the two small native girls, the older aged about eleven, who are sent on board the ship, Columbus fears, to bewitch them. He writes that "the older of the two old women (*la mas vieja*) must have been eleven." Castro-Klaren continues: "[h]ere, the feared figure of the European witch displaces the faint image of the two girls."[64]

However, Castro-Klaren does not go on to suggest why folkloric and anthropological fantasy so consistently link not just women but specifically, old women with anthropophagy—why, as Claude Rawson puts it, "grandmother and wolf should be one."[65] A partial answer might be suggested by one of Columbus's odder communiqués, which concluded that the earth was not, after all, round, as he had been led to believe. In fact, it was actually shaped like "a woman's teat on a round ball," with the unreachable Terrestrial Paradise at its summit.[66] Columbus's evident desire for origins reframes the imperial project as the impossible search for the nurturing pre-Oedipal mother, but since such an encounter is unattainable, the colonizers find only the castrating genital archetype, as in Thevet's later *Cosmographie Universelle*, which features cannibal women devouring the victims' "shameful parts."[67] The figure of the devouring mother is the negative side of the mother archetype, a conflation of not just womb and stomach, but also of mouth and vagina, connoted by that which "devours, seduces and poisons, that which is terrifying and inescapable"—the vagina dentata.[68] We return, inevitably, to the women who emasculate their husbands, albeit accidentally, through their own voracious lust, and the women who secrete deadly snakes inside their vaginas. de Léry's and de Bry's elderly matriarchs are the esthetically unappealing female principle—contemporary critic Michael Palencia-Roth goes so far as to call them "deformed"[69]—empty of womb and vagina, and hungry for white European men.

Heterosexual male anxiety about castration in these phantasies of cannibalism is even, although not always, explicit. Several of the early explorers agree that it was Carib practice to castrate and even entirely emasculate their male victims, although they did not always agree on the purported reason for this. Nicolo Syllacio's letter to the Duke of Milan, December 13, 1494, reads European agricultural techniques into this practice: "[t]hey customarily castrate their infant captives and boy slaves and fatten them like capons. The thin and the emaciated are carefully nurtured, like wethers. Soon, when plump and fat, they are devoured all the more avidly."[70] Peter Martyr, another armchair correspondent, also sees evidence of such farming: "[t]hose boys whom [the cannibals] capture they castrate, just as we do chickens or pigs we wish to raise fatter and more tender for food,"[71] while Michele de Cuneo postulates another possible reason: "[t]hese [captive boys] had the genital organ cut to the belly; and this we thought had been done in order to prevent them from meddling with their wives or maybe to fatten them up and later eat them."[72]

Francisco Guerra, on the other hand, offers an after-the-fact alternative possibility. His translation of Dr. Chanca's letter differs significantly from that used by J. M. Cohen: where Cohen has: "[t]hey castrate the boys that they capture and use them as servants until they are men,"[73] Guerra's translation, which is that of the 1825 edition, has: "the boys [the Caribs] made captive they cut them off the [virile] members and use them until they become men." Guerra goes on to add that:

> A young man thus emasculated [all the "male organ"] easily develops feminine characteristics and behaviour; therefore, the expression that the Caribs 'used them' must be understood as meaning that the castrated captives were used in the practice of sodomy, as eunuchs and *bardajes* were among Arabs. The expression 'to use' a young man is always found in that context later on in the chronicles.[74]

While Guerra's objectivity can be questioned here and throughout, the link between allegations of sodomy and of cannibalism is a historical commonplace. While Columbus found no sodomy in his oriental west, Dr. Chanca had his suspicions, and shortly thereafter it was discovered that sodomy was rife all over the New World: the first letter of Hernan Cortés from Vera Cruz on July 10, 1519—actually written by the elected town council of Vera Cruz—reads in part "we have learnt and been informed for sure that they are all sodomites and use that abominable sin."[75] From this point on, cannibalism and various acts interpreted as sodomy travel hand in hand in New World narratives, from *The Chronicle of the Anonymous Conquistador*, c. 1519, through that of Tomás Ortiz in 1525 and Fernándo de Oviedo in 1526. Oviedo was most disgusted by the apparent pride in sodomy exhibited by the Native Americans:

> Therefore what I have said of these people in this island [Hispaniola or Santo Domingo] and those neighbouring, is quite public, and even in Tierra Firme [Northern South America] where many of these Indian men and women were sodomites; and it is known that there are many of them over there. And look to what degree they boast of such a guilt, that, as other people used to wear some gold jewellery or precious stones around the neck so, in some parts of these Indies, they carried as a jewel a man mounted upon another in that diabolic and nefarious act of Sodom, made in gold relief.[76]

In 1514, he was so appalled by one such golden jewel that he personally smashed it with a hammer, although not so appalled that the gold was not smelted down and reused.

The implication is that sodomy was not only acceptable but habitual among the peoples of the New World, especially including those of Mesoamerica, despite the existence of Aztec, Maya, and Inca statutes which made unendorsed sexual acts illegal, and often even capital offenses.[77] In pre-Columbian Texcoco, for instance, passive sodomites were disemboweled through the anus, and then burned, while active sodomites were left to die under the ashes at the stake[78]—punishments not vastly different from those prescribed in parts of fifteenth-century Europe.[79] Oviedo's claim that it was due to the toleration of sodomy and like atrocities that the numbers of Indians were dwindling was angrily refuted by Las Casas, who denounced the suggestion as "vile, false, and ill-intentioned."[80] In fact, Las Casas's impassioned defense of the indigenous peoples involved an almost wholesale denial of sodomitical practices, while allowing for an occasional and often justifiable incident of cannibalism. For Las Casas, then, violence between men may have been preferable to intimacy.

Nevertheless, both accusations of sodomy and actions on that basis continued, the most notorious of which was that of Vasco Núñez de Balboa in 1513, reported by Peter Martyr and reproduced in a 1595 de Bry engraving. On his way through Panama, Balboa and his men entered the village of Quaraca on September 23, where they were appalled to find the cacique's brother and a number of young men "in womens apparel, smoth and effeminately decked, which by the report of such as dwelte abowte hym, he abused with preposterous Venus."[81] Here, standard European interpretation of such cultural markers as clothing, hair length, and the use of jewelry and cosmetics leave Balboa with no alternative but to read effeminacy. This, of course, is not intended to suggest that these victims of Balboa, who were ripped apart by the conquistador's dogs, did not practice what the Spaniards would have called sodomy, but actual sexual behaviors are less important here than how the idea of such behaviors functioned to reinforce heterosexual European concepts of the monstrous. These men are dangerous because they are suspected of being penetrable—and hence imply the penetrability of the male body in general.

While this incident is the most famous of Balboa's bloody executions of alleged sodomites, and indeed the first record of Spanish punishment for sodomy in the continental New World, it is by no means the only one. Just as illuminating is the execution of the renowned warrior cacique Poncra, who fled before the Spaniards, unfortunately leaving a collection of gold behind him. Despite his skepticism of Spanish overtures of friendship, he was finally induced to return and interrogated under torture, at which point he admitted engaging in sodomy. He was less forthcoming about the source of the gold:

> all Balboa could elicit from him regarding the gold was that vassals long dead had given it to his forefathers and that he, having no need for it, had not sought out its origin. The enraged Balboa, concluding that Poncra's three vassal chieftains as well as the cacique himself were the worst of sodomites, had them cast to the avidly awaiting dogs. After they had eaten their fill, Balboa consigned the remainder to the flames. Ironically, before he and his men left the province of Poncra, they themselves suffered such severe hunger that they were forced to eat some of these same mangy dogs.[82]

Sodomy, Michel Foucault's "utterly confused category,"[83] is here further confused with the offense of resistance to the Spanish agenda manifested as indifference to gold. Poncra, who is described as "grossly malformed," habitual sodomy apparently taking a toll on the body similar to that taken by habitual cannibalism, is seen as unnatural, and therefore a sodomite, because he neither possesses nor understands the Spanish craving for gold. Furthermore, such native indifference not only threatens the financing of the colonial agenda, but elicits uncomfortable questions about the unnaturalness of the hunger itself. On one level, this all-consuming desire for a decorative metal is the same kind of category mistake Balboa was projecting upon Poncra—in a famous engraving, Native Americans quench a Spaniard's unnatural thirst by pouring molten gold down his throat. For the conquistadors, however, the natives' failure to prize gold over beads or brass indicated a further confusion—inability to distinguish valuable from worthless, male from female, human from animal, spiritual from literal, right from wrong. Their failure to respect such categories manifests itself in unselective consumption—worms, lice, and human flesh—and unselective sex—sodomy, bestiality, and incest.

Like cannibalism, sodomy is a threat to social demarcations and hierarchies, and as such, a threat to the patriarchal male body. Even the body of the male cannibals is under threat—pierced and deformed by desirable golden earrings, noserings, and lip jewelry: "orifices have been opened and distended in ways they should not be. The male body is violated, pierced. . . . The pierced male body 'is' the sodomitical body, it appears."[84] Moreover, other orifices are also at risk; Staden's male victims are anally penetrated by the cannibalistic Tupinamba women under the guise of housewifely thrift,[85] and a bizarre passage from *The Chronicle of the Anonymous Conquistador* indicates another phantasy about Native American anal penetration: "In the province of Panuco the men are great sodomites, idlers and drunkards. When they have their fill of wine and can no longer drink it through the mouth they lie down and, raising their legs, have the wine introduced from beneath through a tube, until the body can stand no more."[86] In apparent confusion over this passage, the editor notes that "[u]ndoubtedly the author was pandering to readers' taste for sensationalism."[87] It seems possible, however, that the reference may be to the use of ritual enemas among the indigenous people; transformed through European eyes as one more native category mistake, and a remarkably invasive one, to boot, it seems to have caught the imagination of the Europeans.[88]

To the European explorers, colonizers, and missionaries, it was evident that such dangerously invasive practices as sodomy, which violates the sealed male body, must have a pathological, if not a demonic, root. Michele de Cuneo and his crew hypothesized such a genesis in contagion for the sodomy of the non-Carib Indians in 1494:

> According to what we have seen in all the islands where we have been, both the Indians and the Caribs are largely sodomites, not knowing (I believe) whether they are acting right or wrong. We have judged that this accursed vice has come to the Indians from those Caribs, because these, as I said before, are wilder men and when conquering and eating those Indians, for spite they may also have committed that extreme offence, which proceeding thence may have been transmitted from one to the other.[89]

While there is something of a logical problem in the idea that cannibals pass sodomitical habits to their victims, the suggestion that sodomy is a highly contagious and dangerous disease is an ancient one. The threat of both pollution and addiction is considered particularly dangerous for the passive partner, about whom it was believed, as Richard Trexler points out, that he "could not be turned away from such behavior once he had often enough received the penis."[90] Sodomy, then, is particularly to be feared because its contagious nature means that it cannot fully be resisted, and, once indulged in, it will prove too pleasurable to be ever resisted again, resulting in permanent and polluted emasculation. Likewise, since even a single taste of human flesh was believed to inspire insatiable cravings for more, taking such a taste marked the irrevocable loss of civilized and human self. Both impulsive and inappropriately pleasurable acts are imagined to have enormous and permanent consequences based on the phastasized superiority of the human male. The disgust for both cannibals and sodomites, then, incorporates a fear of "going native"—fear of passivity, fear of penetration, fear of plunder, fear of contamination, fear of emasculation, fear of absorption, fear of loss of control, fear of the forbidden and of the desired.

However, while the intersections of cannibalism, colonialism, and sexuality spoke to patriarchal European anxieties, they also served a practical function; sodomy, like cannibalism, functioned as a convenient justification for the oppression, enslavement, and slaughter of the alleged offenders. Trexler argues, citing López de Gómara, that sodomy alone was grounds for "just title of conquest": "[s]odomy or male homosexual behavior, however, did bestow right to conquer, if it could be demonstrated that it was widespread and tolerated by the indigenous civil authority"—hence, perhaps the repeated distortion of the cultural attitudes toward sodomy.[91] Certainly sodomy, along with cannibalism, was credited for enabling conquest: "the missionaries proclaimed to the Aztecs, the Maya, and the Incas that sodomy was their downfall: the wrathful Christian god had decided to send the Iberians to conquer the Americas because they had engaged in homosexual behavior."[92] Indeed, since the Europeans were merely facilitating a divine purge, their mercilessness was elevated to the status of divine purity: "And after they had populated this vast world, God tired of tolerating their abominations and evil doings and idolatries, so He brought alien people. Like an eagle that comes from the end of the earth, and with no respect for the old or the young, for the children or the women, without mercy He destroyed them."[93] Jonathan Goldberg suggests that it is as if the conquistadors are righting a wrong against the prerogatives of gender, citing the sixteenth-century texts, including the anecdote of Las Casas that opens this chapter, that portray Native American women as offended by the sodomitical usurpation of the female/feminine role,[94] but it seems clear that the emasculated, feminized, and sodomitical men are the counterpoint to the excess and inappropriate masculinity displayed by the Amazonian women. As Peter Mason has suggested, "[s]uch images could serve as European intervention to redress the balance, put matters right and restore a phallocentric order based on masculine men and feminine women."[95] Unlike the paternalist colonialism that Gayatri Spivak interprets as white men rescuing brown women from brown men, the protocolonialist literature of the New World, one might say, effectively represented itself as white men rescuing brown and white men from brown women, and from themselves.

However, as Van de Straet's *America* begins to suggest, the idea of cannibalism could also function not just as a metonym for the lack of civilization that led to conquest, but also as a metaphor for both protocolonialism and the colonialism to follow. And, perhaps inevitably, it becomes difficult to tell eater from eaten. The European conquerors were peculiarly vulnerable to the illicit temptations of both sodomy and cannibalism. Jonathan Goldberg has pointed out the "slippages around sodomy" in Peter Martyr, where thunder and lightning are associated both with sodomy and with the Spanish,[96] and more explicit accusations of Spanish sodomy were reported at Mexico City during the Noche Triste.[97]

Equally, occasional reports cite Spanish vulnerability to the temptations of cannibalism. Perhaps the best-known incident of Spanish anthropophagy is that recounted by Alvar Nuñez Cabeza de Vaca in 1542, the only cannibalism of any kind in his report. In November 1528, adverse weather conditions began to make food extremely scarce. As Francisco Guerra paraphrases the account, "five members of the Narvaez expedition to Florida survived by eating their companions as they were dying. The last one alive when he was found had already consumed the last of his comrades to die."[98] However, Guerra neglects to comment on the response of the Florida Indians to this occurrence: "[t]he Indians were so shocked at this cannibalism that, if they had seen it sometime earlier, they surely would have killed every one of us."

Another notorious occasion of Spanish cannibalism is recorded by Oviedo as having occurred during the expedition to Veragua under Felipe Gutierrez in 1536. After days without food, two Spaniards discovered an Indian killed by one of their comrades, and decided to "spend the night there and celebrate the funeral of that Indian and bury him in their own bellies. . . . The fact is that to satisfy their hunger and need they made a fire and satiated themselves with the flesh of that Indian, well or lightly roasted."[99] Shortly thereafter, the same two men killed a sick Sevillian Christian, and shared his flesh with a number of other Spaniards. A day later, they killed and ate a second Spaniard. "Those killers had disagreement about who among them should eat the brain, and one Juan de Ampudia, who was the worst and most cynical of them and he ate them, and they had the same debate about the liver." As a result of this event, the two initiators of the cannibalism were burned, while the others were enslaved and branded.[100]

Ironically, accounts of Spanish cannibalism proved as useful for English and French propaganda purposes as the Spanish accounts of native cannibalism had proved in Spain, and events like that on the Gutierrez expedition, utilized by Las Casas, among others, provided effective ballast for the development of the Black Legend of Spanish atrocities in the New World, so that, for instance, the illustrations for Schmidel's report of his expedition with Mendoza showed the Spanish in the act of cannibalism.[101] Other accounts of Europeans approaching the point of cannibalism include those of de Léry's *History of a Voyage*, when the return voyage leads to starvation and "evil thoughts,"[102] and Ferdinand Columbus's account of his father's return passage in 1496, when hunger on board ship led to the suggestion that the crew eat the Indians aboard. According to Ferdinand, his father opposed this, arguing that the Indians were "very like Christians."[103]

Although literal European cannibalism seems to have been both rare and as frowned upon as that imputed to the Native Americans, the harvesting of Indian bodily resources seems to have been much more frequent and acceptable. Bernal Díaz reports the killing of an Indian in order to make use of his fat for healing: "[w]e slept near a stream, and with the grease from a fat Indian whom we had killed and cut open, we dressed our wounds, for we had no oil,"[104] and de Léry reports the use of human unguents in an attempt to get rid of chiggers: [t]he surgeon of the ship on which we returned to France . . . brought back . . . an equal quantity of human fat that he had collected when the savages were cooking and roasting their prisoners of war, in the manner that I will describe in its place."[105] Francis MacNutt notes that human fat was used in New World shipbuilding,[106] and Tzvetan Todorov also points out the role of the Spanish invaders in promoting native cannibalism, in their use of human flesh to feed slaves, or to feed dogs, some of which were then consumed, as well as in the starvation rations fed to native slaves.[107]

There is evidence, too, that the Europeans were prepared to ignore the frequently conglomerated offenses of cannibalism and human sacrifice when it became politically advantageous so to do, such as during a particularly fraught period of Cortés's stay with Montezuma:

> There had already been sacrificed the night before four Indians, and in spite of what our Captain said and the dissuasions of the Padre de la Merced, he paid no heed but persisted in killing men and boys to accomplish his sacrifice, and we could do nothing at that time only pretend not to notice it, for Mexico and the other great cities were very ready to rebel under the nephews of Montezuma.[108]

In addition, the Spanish are prepared to ally themselves with the Tlaxcalans, despite the latter's alleged continued voracity. Cortés writes of the siege of Tacuba: "[i]n this ambush more than five hundred, all of the bravest and most valiant of their principal men were killed, and that night, our allies supped well, because they cut up all those who they had killed and captured to eat."[109] Moreover, the Spanish inability to persuade their Tlaxcalan allies to give up cannibalism does not seem to have been especially traumatic, and López de Gómara in particular sounds lighthearted on the matter: "Our Indian friends had a good dinner that night, for they could never be persuaded to give up the eating of human flesh,"[110] and "[b]oth sides lost many dead and wounded, upon whom all dined well!"[111]

It is of course, difficult to identify Native American attitudes to cannibalism through the European accounts. The chroniclers filter their linguistically limited observations through European eyes, ascribing their own motivations and even indulging in apparent mindreading.[112] However, the people of the New World are not reported as regarding cannibalism as the dreaded threat that the Europeans did. de Léry, for instance, notes that the prisoner-of-war slaves of Villegagnon in Brazil seemed to consider a cannibal death as preferable to a brutal slavery: "so these people would often say in their language: 'if we had thought that Paycolas (for so they called Villegagnon) would treat us this way, we would have let ourselves be eaten by our enemies rather than come to him.'"[113] Janet Whatley identifies Tupi cannibalism as "part of a code of honor,"[114] and notes that it "keeps categories of friend and enemy stable; it makes possible large, well-defined areas of trust that will, as we shall see, be the basis of [de Léry's] relationship with them."[115] Hans Staden's account of Tupi cannibalism suggests a high degree of mutual ritual between the prisoner and his killer. According to Staden, the executioner says, "'I am he that will kill you, since you and yours have slain and eaten many of my friends.' To which the prisoner replies, 'When I am dead I shall still have many to avenge my death.' Then the slayer strikes from behind and beats out his brains."[116] Indeed, it seems from de Léry's account that Tupi prisoners were given a certain amount of freedom, including wives, if not the run of the community. Certainly escape must have been possible— according to Staden, he only failed because a French crew returned him to his captors, and at times he was even armed and expected to help defend the village from its enemies.[117]

Moreover, at least in Mexico there appears to have been a link between cannibalism and divinity. Bernal Díaz, López de Gómara, and Andrés de Tapia all record a scene in which messengers from Tlaxcala approach the Spaniards in an attempt to appease them. Díaz has the messengers say: "If you are savage Teules, as the Cempoalans say you are, and if you wish for a sacrifice, take these four women and sacrifice them, and you can eat their flesh and hearts . . . but if you are men, eat the poultry and the bread and fruit, and if you are tame Teules we have brought you copal and parrots' feathers."[118] Gómara's account, in which the messengers specifically address Cortés, has: "[i]f you are fierce enough to eat flesh and blood, eat them and we shall bring you more. If you are a benevolent god, here are incense and feathers for you. If you are men, take these fowl and bread and cherries."[119] Similarly, the chronicle of Andrés de Tapia has, again addressed to Cortés: "[i]f you be a god that eats meat and blood, eat these Indians and we shall bring you more. And if you be a kind god, here are plumes and incense. And if you be a man, here are turkeys and bread and cherries."[120] The accounts are similar enough here to indicate either an interdependence, which Guerra has discounted,[121] or that this episode has been recorded relatively accurately, its repetition indicating, perhaps, how flattering it must have been to have been mistaken for a god. It seems odd, however, that the Tlaxcalans, a people represented repeatedly as inveterate cannibals, should associate human flesh only with the gods, and ordinary men with much more conventional food. Moreover, further inconsistencies in the Aztec view of cannibalism also arise. One is the example that William Arens identifies in Sahagun about legends accruing to a solar eclipse: "At the time, it was said that 'demons of darkness' would appear on earth and eat people."[122] A second is the account in Durán of the ill omen seen at a banquet before the Spanish arrive: "As soon as the people had sat down to eat, the delicacies in the dishes turned into human hands, arms, hearts, and vitals. In their terror the Xochimilca called their soothsayers and asked them what this meant. The soothsayers answered that it was an evil omen, since it meant the destruction of the city and the death of many."[123] All three of these examples suggest, as Arens argues, that

> in Aztec mythology the consumption of human flesh was associated with the unknown, feared and evil, not the mundane everyday world of humans. The activities of these two spheres are normally kept separate in any cosmology. The mention of cannibalism in the contrasting contexts of good and evil, natural and supernatural, myth and reality is an ethnographic oddity.[124]

Indeed, part of the problem in Spanish perception of the Aztec people as irredeemably steeped in cannibalism may have stemmed from a misunderstanding of the value of the threat of cannibalism as part of a Mexican insult tradition. Certainly the Spanish seem to have read these threats at face value, even in a situation where the Aztecs were at great disadvantage, such as at the siege of Tacuba:

At this point a Spaniard told them that they were surrounded and would die of hunger unless they yielded. They answered that they had plenty of bread and that, even if it should give out, they would have Spaniards and Tlaxcalans to eat. Whereupon they threw over some maize cakes and said: "Eat if you are hungry, for we are not, thanks be to our gods. And now get out, or you shall die."[125]

Even greater insult is evidently implied by the suggestion that the Spanish are not even worthy of cannibalism: "you are not fit to eat; we tried your flesh the other day and it tasted bitter, so we shall throw you to the eagles, lions, tigers, and snakes, which will eat you for us. Nevertheless, if you do not free Moctezuma and leave at once, you will soon be properly killed, cooked with *mole*, and eaten by the beasts, since you are not fit for a human stomach."[126]

Convinced, it is with some surprise that Cortés notes the reduced conditions of the inhabitants of Tacuba as the siege of the city drags on: "two poor creatures, who came out to our camp because they were starving, told us that during the night they came to hunt amongst the houses, looking for herbs and wood and roots to eat."[127] Clearly, starving Tacubans did not resort to cannibalism during the siege: "we found the gnawed roots and bark of trees in the streets." Gómara concludes from this that the Aztecs were strictly exogenous in their cannibalism: "[t]hus it is evident that, although the Mexicans did eat human flesh, they did not eat that of their own people, for, if they had done so, they would not have died of starvation."[128] However, the conclusion that they did not customarily practice cannibalism at all is equally or more compelling.

Whether the initial allegation that Native American peoples practised cannibalism was based on European misunderstandings of mortuary practices, ceremonial rituals, or battlefield rhetoric, on the desires of one native community to refocus Spanish attention on another, on literary and mythological expectations, on bare political expediency, or on a smattering of truth, the ideas of the New World and of cannibalism became inextricably linked. Certainly from the very beginning of the sixteenth century, the iconography and cartography of the New World began to feature man-eaters very heavily, to the extent that "the cannibal became the dominant image for Europeans of the people of the Indies, indeed eventually of the New World.[129] "*Illa de cannibales*" appear, in the approximate area of Dominica, on Juan de la Cosa's 1500 world map showing the New World discoveries.[130] In Johannes Ruysch's 1508 *Geographia* the "*canibalos*" are located somewhat further south, around Trinidad.[131] A Portuguese manuscript map of the coasts of South America, dating from about 1502–03, illustrates the coast of Brazil with a naked brown-skinned man turning a white man on a spit, possibly an allusion to Vespucci's account of the cannibalization of one of his crew. Martin Waldseemuller's 1516 world map labels an island just off the coast of South America with "*Cambales*," in addition to representing both Guiana and Brazil as cannibal, and by the time of Simon Grynaeus's world map in 1532, the "*cannibali*" have moved from the islands to the South American mainland.[132] Throughout the sixteenth century, atlases like the Huntington Library HM29 (1547), the Bibliothèque Minestere de la Guerre DI.Z.14 (1555), and the Diogo Homem atlases (1558 and 1568) feature naked men and women cooking, butchering, or devouring various human body parts.[133] From 1557 on, the accounts of Staden, Thevet, and de Léry, laden with ferocious cannibalistic imagery, proved immensely popular, Staden alone having three German reprints in the first year of publication.[134] Each of the latter situated his cannibals in the mainland, in Brazil or on the Columbian-Panamanian coast, and Myers argues that Iberian cartographers had succeeded in pushing the "cannibals" inland, to the remote South American interior.[135]

Certainly, as I discuss in chapter one, accusations of cannibalism function to accommodate strangeness and difference, but they also seem to work to accommodate an even more terrifying similarity. To the surprise of the earliest explorers and missionaries, a number of parallels could be observed between Native Americans and Judeo-Christian practices. Agustin de Zárate pointed out that the inhabitants of the southern hemisphere "have the looks of the Jews, they talk gutturally like the Moors,"[136] and Juan Díaz, noticing that infant circumcision was practiced by the Totomac and Olmec peoples, hypothesized that "Jews and Moors are to be found close by."[137] Indeed, the hypothesis that the Indians may be descendants of the lost tribe of Israel, based on historical analogies and alleged similarities in customs, circulated in Europe for some two centuries after Columbus, revealing itself in scribal errors whereby "*indio*" became "*judio*."[138] Among others, Diego Durán was a staunch defender of this thesis, returning especially to the theme in his book on Aztec history:

> Thus we can almost positively affirm that they are Jews and Hebrews, and I would not commit a great error if I were to state this as fact, considering their way of life, their ceremonies, their rites and superstitions, their omens and hypocrisies, so akin to and characteristic of those of the Jews; in no way do they seem to differ. . . . As proof of this, in order to make it clear, I wish to mention the rites, idolatries, and superstitions these people had. They made sacrifices in the mountains and under trees, in dark and gloomy caves, and in the caverns of the earth. They burned incense, killed their sons and daughters, sacrificed them, and offered them as victims to their gods. They sacrificed children, ate human flesh, killed prisoners and captives of war. All of these

were also Hebrew rites practiced by those ten tribes of Israel, and all were carried out with the greatest ceremony and superstitions one can imagine.[139]

However, it is the compelling parallels between Aztec and Christian rituals
and practices that seem at points to incapicitate some of the chroniclers
almost to the point of apoplexy. As Greenblatt has pointed out, the religion
Bernal Díaz believes he encounters in Mexico is, appallingly, "a displaced
version of his own system of belief: temple, high altar, cult of holy blood,
statue before which offerings are made, 'symbols like crosses.'"[140] For Diego
Durán, such parallels could only be accounted for as the work of God or of
the Devil—either incomparable divine grace in the wilderness, or "an especially perfidious diabolical ruse."[141] It must have been horrifying to be
unable to distinguish the work of God from that of the Devil, but one practice not only aped the most holy of all Christian mysteries, fiendishly paro-
dying its expiatory sacrifice and sacred symbolic consumption of body and
blood, but made it perfectly clear that it was diabolic rather than divine: the
alleged practice of human sacrifice and ritual cannibalism.

Durán and Díaz were not alone in seeing the diabolical analogies
between the eucharist and the alleged practices of cannibal tribes. The Swiss
reformer Zwingli argued that to believe that the bread and the wine literally
became the body and blood of Christ was "not only impious but also fool-
ish and monstrous, unless perhaps one is living amongst the
Anthropophagi."[142] Those who claimed to live among the Anthropophagi
made the same analogy: devoutly Calvinist missionary de Léry compared the
eucharistic theology of closet Catholics Villegagnon and Cointa with the
cannibalism of the Brazilian Ouetaca: "they wanted not only to eat the flesh
of Jesus Christ grossly rather than spiritually, but what was worse, like the
savages named *Ouetaca*, of whom I have already spoken, they wanted to
chew and swallow it raw."[143] Moreover, in an effective reversal of the same
argument, invoking Protestant scorn at Catholic ritual practices, he describes
the ritual chanting of the Tupi men as "like the muttering of someone recit-
ing his hours."[144]

As Ferdinand Cervantes has pointed out, the ritual indigenous practices
of the Native Americans were interpreted as an exact mimetic inversion of
those of Catholicism, worshipping Satan instead of God: "[i]t had its 'exacra-
ments' to counter the Church's sacraments: it had its ministers, who were
mostly women, as opposed to the predominance of male ministers in the
Church; and it had its human sacrifices which sought to imitate the supreme
sacrifice of Christ in the Eucharist."[145] Sara Castro-Klaren has also suggested that the alleged greater participation of women in cannibalistic rituals can
be seen as an inverted priesthood that both reinforces and eclipses the sym-

metries between cannibalism and the eucharist,[146] and other contemporary critics, who should know better, have suggested that the practice of communion allowed the bloodthirsty nature of "the pre-Columbian mind . . . to find an outlet in vicarious Catholic rituals which, therefore, became an intimate part of the behavioural patterns of contemporary Spanish-American people."[147] For Guerra, then, the bloody implications of the mass do not, as I am arguing, increase the likelihood that European colonizers, both Catholic and Protestant, will "see" cannibalism in the New World, but instead offer New World peoples a vicarious catharsis for an otherwise uncontrollable cannibalistic urge.

In a fitting historical irony, Columbus sailed for the New World twenty-four hours after the official expulsion of the Jews from Spain. Though the Catholic monarchs purged their realm of the undesirable, the inscrutable, and the alien, those who were said to threaten the eucharist and practice secret and bloody anthropophagous rites, they would immediately encounter another Other across the Atlantic, also, oddly enough, practicing the same bloody and abhorrent rituals, and, ironically, helping to rationalize the development of the Spanish agenda for the New World—what Stephen Greenblatt has called "the greatest experiment in political, economic, and cultural cannibalism in the history of the Western world."[148] The projection of European predatory intentions onto the victims of protocolonialism, written into the defining narratives as perverse and hypersexualized man-eaters, is indicative that the category of "cannibal" itself is a voracious one, consuming and subsuming its boundaries even as it is being utilized to draw them more clearly. Indeed, as Van de Straet's *America* suggests, cannibalism could function not just as a metonym for the lack of civilization that led to conquest, but also as a metaphor for the rapacious colonialism to come.

Notes

NOTES TO CHAPTER ONE

[1] Peter Hulme, *Colonial Encounters: Europe and the Native Caribbean, 1492–1797* (London: Methuen, 1986), p. 84.

[2] For the absolute centrality of the mass to the development of the early church, see E. O. James, *Sacrifice and Sacrament* (London: Thames and Hudson, 1962): "Thus, far from the conception of Christ reconciling God and man by His sacrificial death as priest and victim, the Christian priesthood was established in the church especially for the perpetuation of the Eucharistic memorial of his self-offering" (p. 59).

[3] Gary Macy, *The Theologies of the Eucharist in the Early Scholastic Period: A Study of the Salvific Function of the Sacrament according to the Theologians, c. 1080–c.1220* (Oxford: Clarendon, 1984), p. 32.

[4] Ibid., p. 119; Peter Browe, *Die Eucharistischen Wunder des Mittelalters* (Breslau: Verlag Muller & Seiffert, 1938).

[5] Hulme, *Colonial Encounters*, p. 85.

[6] This is not to suggest that the very real anxiety about food production in medieval Europe did not contribute to the social tension of the eucharist. On this, see Julia Marvin, "Cannibalism as an Aspect of Famine in Two English Chronicles," in *Food and Eating in Medieval Europe*, ed. Martha Carlin and Joel T. Rosenthal (London: Hambledon, 1998). Moreover, throughout this project I use the words "cannibal" and "cannibalism" as a convenient shorthand, but not uncritically, as I am well aware of both the anachronism and the historical loading of the terms, which I discuss in more detail in chapter five. For the most part, I agree with Peter Hulme, who argues that "[t]he logical step . . . is to leave 'anthropophagy' for those who want to talk—for whatever reason—about the eating of human flesh, and reserve 'cannibalism,' henceforth cannibalism, as a term meaning, say, 'the image of ferocious consumption of human flesh frequently used to mark the boundary between one community and its others'" (pp. 85–86), were it not for particular

occasions where either usage seems appropriate.

[7]I do not discuss here the long list of man-eating monstrosities in Greek mythology, including the Cyclopes and the Laestrygonians, or, later, monstrous figures such as the giants of insular romance, since they seem to be sufficiently non-human to be considered to be merely feeding outside their own species.

[8]"*Territus ipse fugit nactusque silentia ruris / exulalat frustraque loqui conatur.*" *Metamorphoses*, tr. Rolfe Humphries (Bloomington: Indiana University Press, 1955), Book I, ll. 232–33.

[9]The parallels to the story of Medea are plain here, but Medea, whose violence is, ironically, de-emphasized in late medieval redactions of the legend, such as *The Legend of Good Women*, is content with avenging herself on Jason with merely the death of his children, rather than ensuring his inadvertent consumption of them.

[10]James S. Romm, *The Edges of the Earth in Ancient Thought: Geography, Exploration, and Fiction* (Princeton, NJ: Princeton University Press, 1992), p. 47.

[11]Albert Mugrdich Wolohojian, *The Romance of Alexander the Great by Pseudo-Callisthenes* (New York: Columbia University Press, 1969), pp. 113–114.

[12]Ibid.

[13]Thomas of Kent, *The Anglo-Norman Alexander (Roman de Toute Chevalerie)* ed. Brian Foster (London: Anglo-Norman Text Society, 1976–1977), p. clxiii.

[14]Andrew Runni Anderson, *Alexander's Gate, Gog and Magog, and the Inclosed Nations* (The Mediaeval Academy of America: Cambridge, MA., 1932), p. 41.

[15]Ibid., p. 38.

[16]Gregory G. Guzman, "Reports of Mongol Cannibalism in the Thirteenth-Century Latin Sources: Oriental Fact or Western Fiction?" Scott D. Westrem, ed. *Discovering New Worlds: Essays on Medieval Exploration and Imagination* (New York: Garland, 1991), p. 46.

[17]Bernard McGinn, *Visions of the End: Apocalyptic Traditions in the Middle Ages* (New York: Columbia University Press, 1979), p. 75–76. McGinn's note says laconically, "The cuisine of the invading nations was never highly recommended" (p. 303). This theme of infanticidal cannibalism spans several centuries of Alexander romance—cf. here Solomon of Basra's roughly contemporary *Book of the Bee* in which the barbarians "never buried the bodies of their dead, and they ate as dainties the children which women aborted and the after-birth . . ." When they escape, "they will eat dead dogs and cats, and the abortions of women with the after-birth; they will give mothers the bodies of their children to cook, and they will eat them before them without shame" (Guzman, "Reports of Mongol Cannibalism," p. 47). Cf. also the thirteenth-century Ethiopian *History of Alexander*, which features the northern barbarians roasting a pregnant woman to concoct a magic potion from the fetus (ibid., p. 44). Guzman also points to eucharistic anxiety in the accounts of Mongol cannibalism: "[T]he six Western clerics may have responded by being unnecessarily harsh and even inaccurate when placed in the uncomfortable position of observing a religious and ritual custom conceptually similar to their own sacred practice" (p. 51), but his reasoning for the later lack of fetus-eating stories seems suspect: "It is

possible that the six celibate clergymen were so religiously oriented and so far removed from physical sexuality that such explicit sexual and medical references made them feel uncomfortable and possibly even sinful" (ibid.).

[18]"Sermo de fine extremo," cited in Guzman, "Reports of Mongol Cannibalism," p. 43.

[19]David White, *Myths of the Dog-Man* (Chicago: University of Chicago Press, 1991), p. 22.

[20]Anderson, *Alexander's Gate*, p. 58ff, and see also chapter five, below. "John Mandeville" goes further, asserting that the reason that contemporary Jews continue to learn and converse in Hebrew is that they wish to be able to identify themselves to these escaped barbarians when the coming of the antiChrist releases them to destroy Christians. See *Mandeville's Travels. Translated from the French of Jean d'Outremeuse, edited from MS. Cotton Titus CXVI in the British Library*, ed. Paul Hamelius (London: Oxford University Press, 1919), Chapter XXX, pp. 177–78.

[21]Both quotes cited without complete references in Reay Tannahill, *Flesh and Blood: A History of the Cannibal Complex* (New York: Stein and Day, 1975), p. 39.

[22]Guzman, "Reports of Mongol Cannibalism," p. 37.

[23]Matthew Paris, *Matthéi Parisiensis, Monachi Sancti Albani, Chronica Majiora* (London: Longman & co., 1872–83), tr. in Guzman, "Reports of Mongol Cannibalism," p. 38.

[24]The term is that of Margaret Miles in *Carnal Knowing: Female Nakedness and Religious Meaning in the Christian West* (Boston: Beacon, 1989), p. 56.

[25]White, *Myths*, p. 42. The thirteenth-century Ebstorf Map situates the island of Taracontum in the far north, and describes its inhabitants as "the Turci, part of the stock of Gog and Magog; a barbaric and morally unclean tribe, the most savage of all cannibals, who eat the flesh of youths and the premature offspring of men" (Guzman, "Reports of Mongol Cannibalism," p. 48).

[26]*Floovant: Chanson de Geste du XIIe Siecle* ed. Sven A. Andolf (Uppsala: Almqvist and Wiksells, 1941), ll.1839ff.

[27]*La Conquete de Jérusalem*, ed. Celestin Hippeau (Paris: A. Aubry, 1868), ll. 8043ff.

[28]Guibert of Nogent, *The Deeds of God through the Franks: A Translation of Guibert de Nogent's "Gesta Dei Per Francos,"* tr. and ed. Robert Levine (Rochester: Boydell Press, 1997).

[29]Norman Cohn, *The Pursuit of the Millennium: Revolutionary Millenarians and Mystical Anarchists of the Middle Ages* (New York: Oxford University Press, 1970), p. 337.

[30]Fulcher of Chartres, *A History of the Expedition to Jerusalem, 1095–1127*, tr. Frances R. Ryan, ed. Harold Fink (Knoxville: University of Tennessee Press, 1969), p. 179. Crusade cannibalism at Ma'arra and at Antioch is discussed at some length by Geraldine Heng in "Cannibalism, the First Crusade, and the Genesis of Medieval Romance," *Differences: A Journal of Feminist Cultural Studies* 10:1 (Spring, 1998).

[31]*Le "Liber" de Raymond d'Aguilers*, ed. John Hugh and Laurita Lyttleton Hill (Paris: P. Geuthner, 1969), p. 101. This text is also discussed by Jill Tattersall in

"Anthropophagi and Eaters of Raw Flesh in French Literature of the Crusade Period: Myth, Tradition, and Reality," *Medium Aevum* v. 57 no 2 (1988): pp. 240–53. A more sober account of siege cannibalism at Antioch can be found in Jonathan Riley-Smith's *The First Crusade and the Idea of Crusading* (London: Athlone, 1986).

[32]Lewis A. Sumberg, "The 'Tafurs' and the First Crusade," *Mediaeval Studies* XXI (1959): pp. 224–46.

[33]Riley-Smith, *The First Crusade*, p. 66; n. 45, p. 181.

[34]Karl Brunner, *Der Mittelenglische versroman über Richard Löwenherz*, Wiener Beitrage zur Englischen Philologie 42 (Vienna: Braunmüller, 1913).

[35]Stanley R. Hauer, "Richard Coeur de Lion: Cavalier or Cannibal?" *Mississippi Folklore Register* 14 (1980), p. 88–95. Hauer also notes that "a similar story had earlier been told of Richard's ancestress, the wife of Fulke the Black, Count of Anjou" (ibid.).

[36]It is not clear whether the "redemption" here is to be read as a sacrament for the forgiveness of the eaters, or as a form of sin-eating for the forgiveness of the dead. The former would obviously form a closer parallel with the Christian practice of communion.

[37]Vsevolod Slessarev, *Prester John: The Letter and the Legend* (Minneapolis: University of Minnesota Press, 1959), pp. 69–70.

[38]*Mandeville's Travels*, XXIII, p. 133.

[39]Josephine Waters Bennett, *The Rediscovery of Sir John Mandeville* (New York: MLA, 1954) passim. For Odoric, see Henry Yule, tr. and ed., *Cathay and the Way Thither: Being a Collection of Medieval Notices of China*, Series II; Volume II (London: The Hakluyt Society, 1913), pp. 174–76: "Departing from that island [Sillan = Ceylon] and going towards the south, I landed at a certain great island which is called Dondin, and this signifieth the same as 'Unclean.' They who dwell in that island are an evil generation, who devour raw flesh and every other kind of filth. They have also among them an abominable custom; for the father will eat the son, the wife will eat the husband, or the husband the wife. . . . [An idol decides if the sick will live or die; if the latter, the sick man is suffocated.] And when they have thus slain him, they cut him into pieces, and invite all their friends and relations and all the players of the country round about to come to the eating of him, and eat him they do, with singing of songs and great merrymaking. But they save his bones and bury them underground with great solemnity. . . . I rebuked these people sharply for so acting, saying to them:—'Why do ye act thus against all reason? Why, were a dog slain and put before another dog he would by no means eat thereof; and why should you do thus, who seem to be men endowed with reason?' And their answer was:— 'We do this lest the flesh of the dead should be eaten of worms; for if the worms should eat his flesh his soul would suffer grievous pains; we eat his flesh therefore that his soul suffer not.' And so, let me say what I would, they would not believe otherwise or quit that custom of theirs." Compare also the chronicle of Marco Polo: "Dragoian is a kingdom governed by its own prince, and having its peculiar language. Its inhabitants are uncivilized, worship idols, and acknowledge the authority

of the grand khan. They observe this horrible custom, in cases where any member of the family is afflicted with a disease. . . . [Magicians invoke a spirit who decides if the sick will live or die; if the latter, the sick man is suffocated.] . . . This being done, they cut the body in pieces, in order to prepare it as victuals; and when it has been so dressed, the relations assemble, and in a convivial manner eat the whole of it, not leaving so much as the marrow in the bones. Should any particle of the body be suffered to remain, it would breed vermin, as they observe; these vermin, for want of further sustenance, would perish, and their death would prove the occasion of grievous punishment to the soul of the deceased. They afterwards proceed to collect the bones, and having deposited them in a small, neat box, carry them to some cavern in the mountains, where they may be safe against the disturbance of wild animals. If they have it in their power to seize any person who does not belong to their own district, and who cannot pay for his ransom, they put him to death, and devour him." *The Travels of Marco Polo* (New York: Orion, 1958), pp.177–78. There is a suggestion in the concern for the worms of elements of Manichaeism; for further discussion, see chapter three.

[40]On this, see Stephen J. Greenblatt, *Marvelous Possessions: The Wonder of the New World* (Chicago: University of Chicago Press, 1991), p. 50.

[41]*Mandeville's Travels*, XXXV, p. 206.

[42]Yule, *Cathay*, p. 254.

[43]*Mandeville's Travels*, XXII, p. 129.

[44]Greenblatt, *Marvelous Possessions*, p. 45.

[45]Ibid., XXI, p. 119; XXXII, p. 189; XXII, p. 130; XXXII, p. 189. These criteria also form the basis for the savagery of Homer's cannibalistic Cyclopes.

[46]Yule, *Cathay*, n.3. pp. 148–49.

[47]Marco Polo, p. 103; p. 249.

[48]Ibid., p. 165–66.

[49]Ibid., p. 275–76.

[50]Ibid., p. 276. Marco Polo was apparently not interested in preaching, although he does emphasize the repugnance of some of his reports, primarily, it would seem, to underscore their novelty value. Tom Hahn has suggested that the apparent contradictions here may be due to conflict between Marco Polo's own "pragmatic facticity" and the romantic appeal of icons of otherness like cannibalism (personal correspondence). For the sensationalizing of late medieval and early modern protocolonial narratives, see chapter five.

[51]" *Naes thaer hlafes wist / werum on tham wonge, ne waeteres drync / to bruconne, ah hie blod and fel, / fira flaeschoman feorrancumenra*" (ll. 21–24), tr. Robert Boenig, *The Acts of Andrew in the Country of the Cannibals: Translations from the Greek, Latin, and Old English* (New York: Garland, 1991). "Mermedonia" is generally identified as Scythia, itself a generalized term for "the land of the tribes contiguous to the Black Sea," by association with Strabo's Myrmecium. See Kenneth R. Brooks, ed., *Andreas and the Fates of the Apostles* (Oxford: Clarendon, 1961), p. xxviii.

[52]Boenig, *Acts of Andrew*, p. iii.

[53]Here the narrative seems to borrow some of the elements of the story of St. Christopher, a cynocephalus converted and baptized after carrying Christ across a river—hence "*Christum ferres.*" For St. Christopher, see White, *Myths*, p. 34 and p. 41. White also points out that both St. Thomas and St. Nicholas have legendary cannibalistic characteristics (pp. 40–42).

[54]E. A. T. Wallis Budge, *The Contendings of the Apostles* (London: Oxford University Press, 1935), pp. 173–74.

[55]Ibid., p. 177.

[56]Ibid., p. 177–79.

[57]White, *Myths*, p. 197.

[58]*Andreas*, l. 175.

[59]Paul Allen Gibb, *Wonders of the East: A Critical Edition and Commentary* (Ph.D. thesis: Duke, 1977).

[60]John Block Friedman, "The Marvels-of-the-East Tradition in Anglo-Saxon Art." Paul E. Szarmach, ed. *Sources of Anglo-Saxon Culture* (Kalamazoo, MI: Medieval Institute, 1986), p. 320.

[61]Friedman points out that the earliest of the three, Cotton Vitellius A. XV, contains 29 miniatures, 15 of which depict monstrous races, while the second, Cotton Tiberius B. V has 38 miniatures, 18 of which feature monstrous races, and the latest, Bodley 614, has 39 colored drawings, 26 of which represent monstrous races (ibid., p. 338).

[62]Note that in this text, the gender transgression marked by the women in section 26 "*tha habbath beardas swa sithe oth heora breost*" is not a sign of spiritual monstrosity, as they are typified as a form of *imitatio Christi*, aggressive against sin (Gibb, *Wonders*, pp. 76 95, 108, 121). On the other hand, the women in the next section clearly cannot be interpreted so benignly: "Then there are other women who have boars' tusks and hair down to their heels and oxen's tails growing out of their loins [*feax oth helan side and on lendenum oxan taegl.*] These women are thirteen feet tall, and their bodies have the whiteness of marble, and they have camels' feet and donkeys' teeth. Because of their uncleanliness they were killed by the great Macedonian, Alexander. When he could not take them alive, he killed them because their bodies are foul and contemptible" (p. 109).

[63]Gibb, *Wonders*, p. 93.

[64]Ibid., p. 251.

[65]Ibid., p. 267.

[66]Fols 81b and 83v.

[67]"*Thonne is sum ealand on thaere Readan Sae thaer is moncynn thaet is mid us Donestre genemned. Tha syndon geweaxene saw frihteras fram than heafde oth thone nafelan, and se other dael byd mannes lice gelic, and hi cunnon eall mennisc gereord. Thonne hi fremdes kynnes mann geseod, thonne naemnath he hine and his magas, cuthra manna naman, and mis leaslicum wordus hine beswicath and hine onfoth. And thaenne, aefter than, hi hine fretath ealne butan his heafde, and thonne sittath and wepath ofer than heafde*" (Gibb, *Wonders*, p. 93). "Then there is an island in the Red

Sea where there is a race of men called by us Donestre. They are shaped like sooth-sayers from the head down to the navel, and the rest resembles a man's body. And they know all human languages. When they see a man of a foreign race, they address him and his relatives, the name of acquaintances, and with lying words they beguile him and seize him. And then, afterward, they devour him all but the head, and then they sit and weep over the head" (ibid., p. 106–107).

[68]Richard Barber, *Bestiary: Being an English Version of the Bodleian Library, Oxford M.S. Bodley 764* (Rochester: Boydell Press, 1993).

[69]"They have feet and legs which are twelve feet long, sides with chest seven feet long [tr. bodies seven feet wide across the chest]" (Gibb, *Wonders*, p. 104).

[70]John Block Friedman, *The Monstrous Races in Medieval Art and Thought.* (Cambridge, MA: Harvard University Press, 1981), p. 23.

[71]Although the earliest use in English of "host" in the sense of hospitaller is late thirteenth-century, it appears as Old French "*hoste*" as early as the mid-twelfth cen-tury, meaning "host, guest, stranger, foreigner." Interestingly, the earliest use in English of "host" to mean guest occurs in Gower's story of "Lichaon," in the *Confessio Amantis*, who "his hostes slough and into mete / He made the bodies to ben ete." See *OED* for this reference.

[72]This particular illustration is especially reminiscent of illustrations of the medieval wild man. See Richard Bernheimer, *Wild Men in the Middle Ages: A Study in Art, Sentiment, and Demonology* (Cambridge, Harvard University Press, 1952).

[73]"Damnation is eternal swallowing and digestion, eternal partition; the mouth of hell is a real mouth; second, final, definitive death is mastication" (Caroline Walker Bynum, *The Resurrection of the Body in Western Christianity 200–1336* [New York: Columbia University Press, 1995], p. 186).

[74]"*non beatum amplius reputasset quem deus comedisset.*" Tertullian, *Scorpiace*, in *Quinti Septimi Florentis Tertulliani Opera*, eds. Augusti Reifferscheid and Georgü Wissowa (Vindobonae; Pragae: F. Tempsky, 1890–1957), p. 7, 1082, ll. 10–11.

[75]Irenaeus of Lyons, *Adversus Haereses.* Quoted in Bynum, *Resurrection*, pp. 38–39.

[76]"*Cresce et mandacabis me, nec to me in to mutabis sicut carnis tuae sed to muta-beris in me*" (Augustine, *Confessions*, tr. R. S. Pine-Coffin [Harmondsworth: Penguin. 1961], 7:10; p. 147).

[77]Herrad of Hohenbourg, *Hortus Deliciarum*, ed. Rosalie Green et al. (London and Leiden: Warburg Institute/University of London and Brill, 1979), plate 93, drawing 211, p. 173.

[78]*Peter of Celle: Selected Works*, tr. Hugh Feiss (Kalamazoo, MI: Cistercian Publications, 1989), pp. 112–13.

[79]Martha Himmelfarb, *Tours of Hell: An Apocalyptic Form in Jewish and Christian Literature* (Philadelphia: Fortess, 1983), p. 62. See Jonah 1:17 and 2:10, and especially Job 41: 14–21: "Who can open the doors of his face? His teeth [are] terrible round about. . . . Out of his mouth go burning lamps, [and] sparks of fire leap out. Out of his nostrils goeth smoke, as [out] of a seething pot or caldron. His breath kindleth coals, and a flame goeth out of his mouth."

[80]Jacques Le Goff, *The Birth of Purgatory*, tr. Arthur Goldhammer (Chicago: University of Chicago Press, 1984), p. 28.

[81]Himmelfarb, *Tours of Hell*, p. 141. Alan E. Bernstein, *The Formation of Hell: Death and Resurrection in the Ancient and Christian Worlds* (Ithaca: Cornell University Press, 1993), p. 284ff.

[82]Bernstein, *The Formation of Hell*, p. 286.

[83]Himmelfarb, *Tours of Hell*, p. 101.

[84]Ibid., p. 99.

[85]Ibid., p. 101.

[86]Le Goff, *The Birth of Purgatory*, p. 195.

[87]Ibid., p. 187.

[88]Rodney Mearns, ed. *The Vision of Tundale*, Middle English Texts Series (Heidelberg: Carl Winter, Universitätsverlag, 1985), p. 7.

[89]Ibid., cap. 3.

[90]Ibid., ll. 427–328.

[91]Ibid., l. 534.

[92]Ibid., ll. 561–64.

[93]Ibid., cap. 4.

[94]Ibid., ll. 599–604.

[95]Ibid., l. 800.

[96]Ibid., ll. 815–16.

[97]Ibid., cap 6.

[98]Ibid., l. 958.

[99]Ibid., ll. 1313–1418.

[100]One could argue, too, for a form of digestion in Canto XXV, where souls in reptilian form temporarily reassume human shape by biting into and fusing with other sinners.

[101]"*Da ogni bocca dirompea co' denti / un peccatore, a guisa di maciulla, / sì che tre ne facea così dolente*" (*The Divine Comedy of Dante Alighieri*, tr. John D. Sinclair [New York: Oxford University Press, 1961], canto XXXIV, ll. 55–57, pp. 422–23).

[102]Bynum, *Resurrection*, passim.

[103]"*Non altrimenti i cuoci a' lor vassalli / fanno attuffare in mezzo la caldaia / la carne con li uncin, perchè non galli*" (Dante, *Divine Comedy*, ll. 55–57, pp. 262–63).

[104]"*ch'eran già cotin dentro dalla crosta*" (ibid., Canto XXII, l. 150, p. 277;).

[105]Maggie Kilgour, *From Communion to Cannibalism: An Anatomy of Metaphors of Consumption* (Princeton: Princeton University Press, 1990), p. 69.

[106]"*ambo le man per lo dolor mi morsi*" (Dante, *Divine Comedy*, Canto XXXIII, l. 58, pp. 406–7).

[107]"*poscia, più che 'l dolor, potè 'l digiuno,*" (ibid., Canto XXXIII. l. 75, pp. 408–409).

[108]"*e come 'l pan per fame si manduca, / così 'l sovran li denti all'altro pose / là 've 'l cervel s'aggiugne con la nuca*" (Canto XXXII ll. 127–129, pp. 400– 401). On Ugolino and cannibalism, see John Freccero, "Bestial Sign and Bread of Angels

(*Inferno* 32–33)." *Yale Italian Studies*. 1: Winter 1977: pp. 53–66, and Robert Durling, "Deceit and Digestion in the Belly of Hell," *Allegory and Representation*, ed. Stephen Greenblatt (Baltimore: Johns Hopkins Press, 1981), pp. 61–93.

[109]Carol Zaleski, *Otherworld Journeys: Accounts of Near-Death Experience in Medieval and Modern Times* (New York & Oxford: Oxford University Press, 1987), p. 37.

[110]Piero Camporesi, *The Fear of Hell: Images of Damnation and Salvation in Early Modern Europe* (University Park, PA: Pennsylvania State University Press, 1991), p. 18.

[111]Ibid., p. 166.

[112]N. Tanner, ed. *Heresy Trials in the Diocese of Norwich, 1428–31* (London: Offices of the Royal Historical Society, 1977), p. 45. On this concern, see also Anne Hudson, "The Mouse in the Pyx: Popular Heresy and the Eucharist," *Trivium*, vol. 26 (1991), pp. 40–53.

[113]A. M. Gietl, *Die Sentenzen Rolands Nachmals Papstes Alexander III* (Freiburg, 1891), pp. 232–33.

[114]Note, however, that the holy could, and did, live exclusively on the eucharist. Bynum discusses a number of holy women who achieved this feat in *Holy Feast and Holy Fast: The Religious Significance of Food to Medieval Women* (Berkeley: University of California Press, 1987).

[115]"Cannibalism . . . is primarily a medium for non-gustatory messages—messages having to do with the maintenance, regeneration, and, in some cases, the foundation of the cultural order" (Peggy Reeves Sanday, *Divine Hunger: Cannibalism as a Cultural System* [Cambridge: Cambridge University Press, 1986], p. 3).

[116]Mikhail Bakhtin, *Rabelais and His World*, tr. Helene Iswolsky (Bloomington: Indiana University Press, 1984), p. 221.

[117]Cannibalism is almost always a threat, rarely an opportunity. The exceptions, of course, are the Richard I material, where identification is clearly assumed with the English Christian king rather than the bestial Saracen victims, and the "Lay of Ignaure," discussed in chapter two, where cannibalism is both symbolic and literal, and as such, ultimately ambivalent.

[118]Peggy Phelan, *Unmarked: The Politics of Performance* (London: Routledge, 1993). In the same vein, see also Mary Daly's definition of "fetal identification syndrome": "masculine identification with fetal tissue resulting from male apprehension that men 'live' by connecting themselves to women and to 'Mother Earth' as forever fetal inhabitors, possessors, and parasites" (Mary Daly, *Websters' First New Intergalactic Wickedary of the English Language* [Boston: Beacon Press, 1987], pp. 198–99).

[119]For further discussion of links between cannibalism and accusations of sodomy, see chapter five.

[120]Claude Levi-Strauss, *The Naked Man*, tr. John and Doreen Weightman (New York: Harper and Row, 1981), p. 141. William Arens, *The Man-Eating Myth:*

Anthropology and Anthropophagy (New York : Oxford University Press, 1979), p. 146.

[121]John Gower, *The Complete Works of John Gower*, ed. George Campbell Macauley, 4 vols. (Oxford: Clarendon, 1899–1901); *Confessio Amantis*, Book III, ll.309–310.

[122]Ibid., ll. 406–7.

[123]Ibid., ll. 2586–89.

NOTES TO CHAPTER TWO

[1]J. Forshall, and F. Madden, eds. *The Holy Bible: Translated from the Latin Vulgate by John Wycliffe and His Followers* (Oxford: At the University Press, 1850). John 6:52–56.

[2]Miri Rubin, *Corpus Christi: The Eucharist in Late Medieval Culture* (Cambridge: Cambridge University Press, 1991), p. 15.

[3]Kilgour, *From Communion*, p. 81.

[4]Peter of Vaux, "The Life of Colette of Corbie," *Acta Sanctorum* (Paris: Apud Victorem Palme, 1863), p. 558.

[5]The lower case form here is apparently an error, since "he" obviously refers to Jesus, not to Goddeschalk.

[6]Caesarius of Heisterbach, *Dialogus Miraculorum* Vol II (London: Routledge, 1929), pp. 108–09. The collection emphasizes overcoming the repulsiveness of the body, such as in the stories of the bishop who uses his tongue to wipe away the rotting flesh of a leper (pp. 31–33), or the bishop of Salzburg who consumes the sacrament after a leper vomits it forth (pp. 33–34). In both cases, the leper is Jesus, testing His elect. Benedicta Ward refers to the appearances of Christ in the bread as "counter-miracles," since they allow the recipient to see beneath the miraculous but illusory appearance of the bread to the reality of the god beneath. (*Miracles and the Medieval Mind: Theory, Record, and Event, 1000–1215* [Philadelphia: University of Pennsylvania Press, 1982], p. 15.)

[7]Caesarius, *Dialogus*, pp. 210–211.

[8]Ibid., p. 110.

[9]Caroline Walker Bynum, *Holy Feast*, p. 177.

[10]Caesarius, *Dialogus*, p. 110. It is significant that the sin of the offending priest is a sexual one, since unsanctioned sexuality, like cannibalism itself, represents a trespassing over the borders of the body. Thus one violation of the body's wholeness and individualism is punished by the threat of a second. See Mary Douglas, *Purity and Danger: An Analysis of the Concepts of Pollution and Taboo* (London: Routledge and Kegan Paul, 1966), pp. 120–121.

[11]For more on the theological threat of Donatism, see chapter three.

[12]Caesarius, *Dialogus*, p. 121.

[13]Caroline Walker Bynum, *Fragmentation and Redemption: Essays on Gender and the Human Body in Medieval Religion* (New York: Zone, 1991), p. 130.

[14]Bynum, *Holy Feast*, p. 93.

[15]Rubin, *Corpus Christi,* pp. 175–76. See also Ernest W. McDonnell, *The Beguines and Beghards in Medieval Culture with Special Emphasis on the Belgian Scene* (New Brunswick: Rutgers University Press, 1954), pp. 300–317.

[16]Ibid., p. 316.

[17]Rubin, *Corpus Christi,* pp. 118–19; Leah Sinanoglou, "The Christ Child as Sacrifice: A Medieval Tradition and the Corpus Christi Plays," *Speculum* 48:3 (1973): p. 493.

[18]Miri Rubin, "Desecration of the Host: the Birth of an Accusation," Diana Wood, ed. *Christianity and Judaism: Papers Read at the 1991 Summer and the 1992 Winter Meeting of the Ecclesiastical History Society* (Oxford; Blackwell, 1972), p. 173. For the significance of the industrial "*fornax*" of this tale, as opposed to the domestic "*clibanum,*" see Carra Ferguson O' Meara, "In the Hearth of the Virgin Womb," *Art Bulletin* 63: 1 (1981): p. 82.

[19]It is therefore doubly significant that Jewish children receive eucharistic visions—not only are the children untutored in matters of faith, but also in the supposedly deliberate Jewish rejection of Christ. This leads to some interesting conclusions about nature and nurture, including the idea that both the Jewish faith and the supposed Jewish hardheartedness may have been considered to have been social rather than genetic developments.

[20]For a similar point, see Bynum, *Holy Feast,* p. 62: ". . . If women, who were more vulnerable to sin than men, less rational and strong, could receive Christ in the eucharist . . . how heinous by comparison were the crimes of male self-indulgence and clerical corruption."

[21]Rubin, *Corpus Christi,* p. 121.

[22]J. Migne, ed. *Patrologia Latina,* LXXIII, col, 979, in Sinanoglou, "Christ Child as Sacrifice," pp. 492–493.

[23]Hermann J. Strack, *The Jew and Human Sacrifice: Human Blood and Jewish Ritual, an Historical and Sociological Inquiry,* tr. Henry Beauchamp (New York: Blom, 1971), p. 34.

[24]Rubin, *Corpus Christi,* p. 15.

[25]*L'Elucidarium et les Lucidaires,* ed. Yves Le Fevre (Paris: E. de Boccard, 1954) Book 1, pp. 394–95.

[26]*De eukaristia,* BL Add, 24660. In Rubin, *Corpus Christi,* p. 91.

[27]R. Po-Chia Hsia, *The Myth of Ritual Murder: Jews and Magic in Reformation Germany* (New Haven: Yale University Press, 1988), p. 55.

[28]For a similar narrative, see also the *Croxton Play of the Sacrament.*

[29]*The Minor Poems of the Vernon Ms.,* ed. C. Horstmann and F. J. Furnivall (London: EETS, 1892–1901) ll. 197–98, p. 177. A variant appears as the classic Mass of St. Basil. Note that the vision can in fact be seen as both a blessing and a punishment—it is because of his heritage that the Jew sees the bloody Christ, but the vision is also the instrument of his salvation.

[30]Decima L. Douie and Dom Hugh Farmer, eds. *The Life of St. Hugh of Lincoln,* Vol. II. (London: Nelson, 1962), p. 94.

[31]Rubin, *Corpus Christi*, p. 121. See also Robert Mannyng of Brunne, *Handlyng Synne*, ed. I. Sullens (Binghamton: *Medieval and Renaissance Texts and Studies* 14, 1983), ll. 10.006–82, pp. 249–50 for another doubting monk.

[32]Bynum, *Fragmentation*, p. 123.

[33]See Bynum, *Holy Feast*, p. 67—but cp. p. 116, where she is said to taste honeycomb in this situation. A modern account of a similar eucharistic miracle is that of Julia Kim in Naju, Korea, who tasted blood and felt the host moving during a mass in September 1995. Witnesses saw a piece of bloody "dark red living flesh" in her mouth. A photograph of this is available at http://web.frontier.net/ Apparitions/jkim.gif.

[34]As Caroline Bynum has pointed out, the contemporary academic equation of the medieval body with sexuality is limiting and anachronistic, failing to take into account the physical certainties of both fertility and decay. See *Fragmentation and Redemption*, p. 182ff, and pp. 79–118. During the following argument, I draw heavily on Bynum's work on the significance of ritual eating for medieval women in *Holy Feast and Holy Fast*.

[35]Bynum, *Holy Feast*, p. 103 and pp. 131–133.

[36]Ibid., p. 118. Lutgard is ingesting at His wounds neither morbidity nor physical nourishment, but spiritual sustenance. It should be recalled that medieval biology identified breast milk as transmuted menstrual blood, purified and whitened so that nursing, like communion, should not be repellent.

[37]Ibid., p. 145; p. 172.

[38]Ibid., p. 126; pp. 122–23.

[39]Ibid., p. 114.

[40]Macy, *Theologies of the Eucharist*, p. 40.

[41]Ibid.

[42]Stephen Benko, *Pagan Rome and the Early Christians* (Bloomington: Indiana University Press, 1984), p. 54.

[43]Ibid., p. 1.

[44]One wonders, for instance, exactly how much dough would be required to completely hide a child, even a newborn, how its movements would have been stifled, and how the most innocent novice would have been fooled by the weight of the "dough," or by the force required to pierce it.

[45]Ibid., p. 3.

[46]Gavin I. Langmuir, *Toward a Definition of Antisemitism* (Berkeley: University of California Press, 1990), p. 212.

[47]Strack, *The Jew and Human Sacrifice*, p. 136.

[48]Norman Cohn, *Europe's Inner Demons: An Enquiry Inspired by the Great Witch-Hunt* (New York: Basic, 1975), p. 6.

[49]Although note that Langmuir has convincingly argued that medieval interest in the text of *Against Apion* was probably too late to influence the development of either the twelfth-century ritual murder accusation or the thirteenth-century blood libel (*Toward a Definition*, p. 214).

[50]Hyam Maccoby, *The Sacred Executioner: Human Sacrifice and the Legacy of Guilt* (New York: Thames and Hudson, 1982), p. 150. Maccoby identifies this charge as a phantasy stemming from a misinterpretation of the book of Psalms (ibid.).

[51]The following is a noninclusive list of ritual murders/blood libels and host desecrations. Locations indicate ritual murder/blood libel only unless otherwise marked: 1144 Norwich, 1168 Gloucester, 1171 Blois, 1181 Bury St. Edmonds, 1182 Pontoise, 1182 Braisne, 1182 Saragossa, 1190 Winchester, 1234 Lauda, 1235 Fulda, 1235 Norwich, 1243 Belitz HD, 1247 Valréas, 1255 Lincoln, 1261/7 Pforzheim, 1270 Weissenberg, 1271 Berne, 1279 London, 1283 Mainz, 1285 Munich, 1286 Oberwesel RM and HD, 1287 Berne, 1290 Paris HD, 1293 Krems, 1321 Spain and France HD (poison), 1329 Savoy, 1337 Deckendorf HD, 1338 Bohemia HD, 1347 Lake Geneva HD (poison), 1389 Prague HD, 1410 Segovia HD, 1420 Vienna RM/HD, 1453 Breslau HD, 1470 Endingen, 1470 Regensburg HD, 1475 Trent, 1476 Baden, 1477 Passau HD, 1482 Rinn, 1490 La Guardia, 1492 Sternbach, 1494 Tyrnau, 1504 Waldkirch, 1507 Cracow HD, 1510 Brandenberg RM/HD, 1510 Berlin HD, 1514 Halle HD, 1529 Poesing. "More than 150 charges of ritual murder are listed in the standard works of reference; yet these do not constitute, in all probability, more than a fraction of the whole" (Joshua Trachtenberg, *The Devil and the Jews: The Medieval Conception of the Jew and its Relation to Modern AntiSemitism* [New Haven; Yale University Press, 1943]).

[52]Ibid., p. 135.

[53]Langmuir, *Toward a Definition*, p. 281. By "cannibalism" here, Langmuir appears to mean that the case alleged medicinal consumption of blood rather than its external application, the latter representing the most typical medieval use of blood-healing. See Trachtenberg, *The Devil and the Jews*, p. 140ff.

[54]Strack, *The Jew and Human Sacrifice*, p. 278; Langmuir, *Toward a Definition*, p. 265.

[55]Strack, *The Jew and Human Sacrifice*, p. 190.

[56]Ibid.

[57]Trachtenberg, *The Devil and the Jews*, p. 134.

[58]Ibid., p. 135.

[59]Ibid., p. 140ff.

[60]Ibid., p. 113.

[61]Ibid., p. 114.

[62]Hsia, *The Myth of Ritual Murder*, p. 58.

[63]Strack, *The Jew and Human Sacrifice*, p. 185.

[64]Bernard Glassman, *Anti-Semitic Stereotypes without Jews: Images of the Jews in England, 1290–1700* (Detroit : Wayne State University Press, 1975), pp. 30–31.

[65]Hsia, *The Myth of Ritual Murder*, p. 56.

[66]Trachtenberg, *The Devil and the Jews*, p. 113; it is not clear whether this is a reference to the Deckendorf case, or a different occurrence in the same area at roughly the same time.

[67]Ibid. p. 115.

[68]Ward, *Miracles*, p. 166; Trachtenberg, *The Devil and the Jews*, p. 101 and p. 104; Hsia, *The Myth of Ritual Murder*, p. 10.

[69]Rubin, *Corpus Christi*, p. 24. Indeed, Lateran IV never defined "*transubstantiatio*," including the terminology, according to Gary Macy, only as a common term for an assertion of Christ's real presence (Macy, *Theologies*, p. 140).

[70]Trachtenberg, *The Devil and the Jews*, p. 116.

[71]An example of the motif that does not fit into this format is the enigmatic vision of Dante in chapter three of *Vita Nuova*.

[72]Rita Lejeune, ed. *Le Lai d'Ignaure ou Lai du Prisonnier* (Liege: Vaillant-Carmanne, 1938), ll. 45–51:

A toutes douse s'acointa;
Et tant chascune l'en creanta
S'amour trestout a son voloir,
Et, s[el] de li voloit avoir,
K'il seroit servis comme quens,
Chascune cuide k'il soit siens
Si s'en fait molt jolie et cointe.

Tr. R. Howard Bloch. "The Lay and the Law: Sexual/Textual Transgression in *La Chastelaine de Vergi*, The *Lai d'Ignaure*, and the *Lais* of Marie de France," *Stanford French Review*, XIV, 1–2 Spring-Fall (1990): pp. 181–210.

[73]"[s]oris ki n'a c'un trau poi dure." Ibid., l. 373.

[74]   *Mangié avés le grant desir*
Ki si vous estoit em plaisir
Car d'autre n'aviés vous envie.
En la fin en estes servie!
Vostre drut ai mort et destruit:
Toutes, partirés au deduit
De chou que femme plus goulouse
(ibid., ll. 567–73).

For a parallel historical report in which a woman is "fed" her lover's genitals, see Aelred of Rievaulx's commentary on the nun of Watton, translated and discussed by Giles Constable in "Aelred of Rievaulx and the Nuns of Watton: An Episode in the Early History of the Gilbertine Order," *Medieval Women*, ed. Derek Baker (Oxford: Blackwell, 1978), pp. 205–26.

[75]"*Et l'autre plaignoit son douch cuer: / Ja mais nul n'en ert de tel fuer.*" Ibid., ll. 597–8.

[76]Milad Doueihi, "The Lure of the Heart," *Stanford French Review* 14, 1–2 (1990): p. 65.

[77]Ibid., p. 56.

[78]Mark Burde, "Cannibals at Communion: Parody in the 'Lai d'Ignaure.'" Paper delivered at the 32nd International Conference on Medieval Studies, May, 1997.

[79]Rubin, *Corpus Christi*, p. 360.

NOTES TO CHAPTER THREE

[1]Note that the especial focus on the eucharist of the eleventh and twelfth centuries coincided with both the rise of regionalism and protonationalism and the attempts to establish universal papal primacy. On this, see Sarah Beckwith, *Christ's Body: Identity, Culture, and Society in Late Medieval Writings* (London: Routledge, 1993).

[2]Rubin, *Corpus Christi*, p. 36.

[3]James, *Sacrifice and Sacrament*, p. 59.

[4]Joseph A. Jungmann, *Missarum Sollemnia: Eine Genetische Ekklärung der Römischen Mosse* (Vienna: Herder, 1962), Vol. 1, p. 166. On this, see also Joel T. Rosenthal, *The Purchase of Paradise: Gift Giving and the Aristocracy, 1307–1485* (London: Routledge & Kegan Paul, 1972).

[5]Rubin, *Corpus Christi*, p. 353.

[6]*Self and Society in Medieval France: The Memoirs of Abbot Guibert of Nogent*, ed. John F. Benton (New York, Harper & Row, 1970), Book 1: 25–26; p. 115.

[7]*"Id solum quod de frumento est transubstantiatur"* ("De Sacramentis," in *The "Historia Occidentalis" of Jacques de Vitry*, ed. J. F. Hinnebusch [Fribourg: The University Press, 1972], p. 219).

[8]*The Panarion of Epiphanius of Salamis*, tr. Frank Williams (New York: Brill, 1987), Nag Hammadi Studies Vol. XXXV. Vol. 1, p. 60.

[9]Ibid., p. 186.

[10]Martin Del Rio, *Disquisitionum Magicarum Libri Sex* (Venice: apud Ioan. Antonium et Iacobum de Franciscis, 1606), Lib. II, quaest. XVI. Quoted in Julio Caro Baroja, *The World of the Witches*, tr. Nigel Glendinning (London: Weidenfeld, 1964), p. 120.

[11]John W. Baldwin, *The Language of Sex: Five Voices from Northern France around 1200* (Chicago: University of Chicago Press, 1994), p. 213.

[12]John Noonan, *Contraception: A History of Its Treatment by the Catholic Theologians and Canonists* (Cambridge, MA; Harvard University Press, 1986), p. 236.

[13]Ibid.

[14]Geoffrey Chaucer, *The Complete Poetry and Prose of Geoffrey Chaucer*, ed. John H. Fisher (New York: Holt, Rinehart and Winston, 1977). "The Parson's Tale," ll. 575–76 and 581, p. 371.

[15]Noonan, *Contraception*, p. 95.

[16]Ibid., p. 98.

[17]Aristotle, *The Generation of Animals* (Cambridge, MA: Harvard University Press, 1963).

[18]Noonan, *Contraception*, p. 73.

[19]Soranus of Ephesus, *Soranus's Gynecology* (Baltimore: Johns Hopkins Press, 1956), 1.12.43. Quoted in Noonan, *Contraception*, p. 89.

[20]Baldwin, *The Language of Sex*, p. 95. John Noonan agrees, citing Augustine's *On Genesis according to the Letter*, 10.18.32. See also Noonan, *Contraception*, p. 89

for the similar views of Jerome and of Clement of Alexandria.

[21]Baldwin, *The Language of Sex*, p. 95.

[22]"If a Christian writer adopted Soranos's view, as Tertullian does in *The Soul*, he would have reason to invest the male seed with special significance. Under the other theories he would have had a general notion that male seed was important" (Noonan, *Contraception*, p. 89).

[23]Ibid., p. 91.

[24]Ibid., p. 89.

[25]Ibid., p. 237.

[26]Ibid., p. 298.

[27]Ibid., p. 297.

[28]For a more accurate view of the body in Gnostic thought, see Michael A. Williams, "Divine Image—Prison of Flesh: Perceptions of the Body in Ancient Gnosticism," *Zone* 5: pp. 128–47.

[29]Williams, *Panarion*, pp. 86–87.

[30]Noonan, *Contraception*, p. 96.

[31]*Right Ginza*, 229, 20–22 and 228, pp. 14–27, quoted by Williams in *Panarion*, p. 86.

[32]Benton, *Self and Society*, p. 218 ff. See also Seth Lerer, "*Transgressio Studii*: Writing and Sexuality in Guibert of Nogent," *Stanford French Review*, XIV, 1–2 Spring-Fall, 1990: pp. 243–66.

[33]Bynum, *Resurrection*, n. 110, p.149.

[34]Ibid.

[35]Benton, *Self and Society*, p. 93.

[36]Ibid., pp. 212–13.

[37]Ibid., n. 2, p. 213..

[38]Norman Cohn, *Europe's Inner Demons*, p. 1.

[39]Ibid., p. 16.

[40]Ibid., p. 18.

[41]Ibid., p. 19.

[42]Ibid., p. 56.

[43]Noonan, *Contraception*, p. 116.

[44]Leonard George, *Crimes of Perception: An Encyclopedia of Heresies and Heretics* (New York: Paragon, 1995), p. 250.

[45]Noonan, *Contraception*, p. 116.

[46]R. I. Moore, *The Origins of European Dissent* (London: Penguin, 1977), p. 153.

[47]Benton, *Self and Society*, pp. 212–13.

[48]*Corpus Christi*, p. 9.

[49]Benton, *Self and Society*, p. 214.

[50]Ibid.

[51]Edward Peters, *Heresy and Authority in Medieval Europe: Documents in Translation* (Philadelphia: University of Pennsylvania Press, 1980), p. 24.

[52]Walter L. Wakefield and Austin P. Evans, *Heresies of the High Middle Ages: Selected Sources, Translated and Annotated* (New York: Columbia University Press, 1969), pp. 116–17.

[53]Samuel R. Maitland, *Facts and Documents Illustrative of the History, Doctrine and Rites of the Ancient Albigenses and Waldenses* (London: C. J. G. and F. Rivington, 1832), p. 344ff.

[54]"The Passau Anonymous: On the Origins of Heresy and the Sect of the Waldensians." c. 1260. Peters, *Heresy and Authority*, p. 159.

[55]It is not clear here whether "knowing the words" refers to the ability to recite the Latin or to consecrate in the vernacular. Edward Peters has suggested that the appearance of women priests may owe something to Cathar practices (*Heresy and Authority*, p. 106).

[56]Malcolm Lambert, *Medieval Heresy: Popular Movements from the Gregorian Reform to the Reformation* (Oxford University: Cambridge, MA: B. Blackwell, 1992), p. 103.

[57]"Burchard of Worms in his canon law collection at the beginning of the eleventh century had felt it needful to include a penance for those who held the Donatist view that sacraments administered by unworthy priests were not valid" (ibid., p. 29).

[58]Ibid., p. 197.

[59]Lambert, on the philosophy of Bohemian reformer Matthias of Janov, p. 292. Yet their insistence on Utraquism, touching on the very heart of church ritual, was at the root of their formal rift with the orthodox church (ibid., p. 316).

[60]Ibid., p. 339.

[61]Maitland, *Facts and Documents*, p. 392ff.

[62]Peters, *Heresy and Authority*, p. 278. Later Lollard teaching on the eucharist came to be vastly different from the consubstantiation which Wyclif himself came to endorse. See Lambert, *Medieval Heresy*, p. 260ff.

[63]Lambert, *Medieval Heresy*, p. 252.

[64]For eucharistic variations within a particular sect, see Lambert, *Medieval Heresy*, p. 171 on the Waldensians, and p. 260 on the development of Lollard eucharistic views.

[65]Ibid., p. 122.

[66]Williams, *Panarion*, p. 65.

[67]Ibid., p. 131; p. 99.

[68]Ibid., p. 298; p. 229.

[69]Lambert, *Medieval Heresy*, p. 122. For a definitive medieval association of a religious group with the animal it refused to eat, see Isaiah Shachar, *The Judensau: A Medieval Anti-Jewish Motif and its History* (London: The Warburg Institute, 1974).

[70]Lambert, *Medieval Heresy*, p. 165.

[71]Bynum, *Resurrection*, p. 219.

[72]Lambert, *Medieval Heresy*, p. 391.

[73]Ibid., p. 316.

[74]Ibid., p. 94.

[75]Ibid., p. 392.

[76]J. Crompton, "Leicester Lollards," *Transactions of the Leicestershire Archeological and Historical Society* 44 (1968–69), p. 17. See also Miri Rubin on the role of the eucharist in Wyclif's loss of ecclesiastical support: "It is only when Wyclif significantly commented upon the eucharist that he became really dangerous, and only then that he lost his position in Oxford and his patron. In his *Chronicon* Henry Knighton (d. 1396) reported that the Blackfriars council of 1382 placed the acceptance of eucharistic orthodoxy at the centre of the requirements made of suspected Wycliffites. . . . Views on the eucharist were thus the very centre of criticism, and the one which the church could least allow to pass uncorrected . . . Anti-Lollard tracts such as the Dominican John's *Ferretra Sacramenti* of c.1380 were often devoted solely to combating Lollard eucharistic error" (*Corpus Christi*, p. 327). Rubin continues: "Within the language of religion, with the eucharist as its heart many objections, criticism and attacks could be tolerated as long as they were not aimed at that heart. Thus Wyclif's trenchant criticism of papal authority, the wealth of the church, the religious orders, images and pilgrimages were all tolerated early in his career, until he began to pronounce on the eucharist" (ibid., p. 350).

[77]Ibid., p. 353.

[78]Ibid., p. 347.

[79]Keith Thomas, *Religion and the Decline of Magic: Studies in Popular Beliefs in Sixteenth- and Seventeenth-Century England* (New York: Oxford University Press, 1971), passim, especially pp. 53–54, and pp. 273–274.

[80]Rubin, *Corpus Christi*, p. 341.

[81]Caesarius of Heisterbach, *Dialogus*, Chapter IX. "Of a woman who was stricken with paralysis because she had spread the Lord's body over her cabbages." p. 115.

[82]Trachtenberg, *The Devil and the Jews*, pp. 115–16.

[83]Rossell Hope Robbins, *The Encyclopedia of Witchcraft and Demonology* 2nd ed. (New York: Bonanza Books, 1981), p. 518.

[84]Trachtenberg, *The Devil and the Jews*, p. 116; Venetia Newall, ed. *The Witch Figure: Folklore essays by a group of scholars in England honoring the 75th birthday of Katharine M. Briggs* (London: Routledge and Kegan Paul, 1973), p. 115.

[85]Aldous Huxley, *The Devils of Loudun* (New York: Carroll and Graf, 1952). "The etymologists agree, at all events, that sabbat has nothing whatsoever to do with the number seven, or the Jewish Sabbath" (Pennethorne Hughes, *Witchcraft* [London: Longmans, 1952], p. 123).

[86]Trachtenberg, *The Devil and the Jews*, p. 101; Robbins, *Encyclopedia*, p. 415.

[87]Henry Charles Lea, *Materials Toward a History of Witchcraft* Vol. 1. (Philadelphia: University of Pennsylvania Press, 1939).

[88]Anne Llewellyn Barstow, *Witchcraze: A New History of the European Witch Hunts* (San Francisco: Pandora, 1994), p. 61.

[89]Trachtenberg, *The Devil and the Jews*, p. 212.

[90]Caesarius, *Dialogue*, pp. 112–13.

[91]Trachtenberg, *The Devil and the Jews*, p. 212. The suggestion here is of a concentration of evil facilated by a chain of consumption.

[92]Robbins, *Encyclopedia*, p. 415.

[93]Trachtenberg, *The Devil and the Jews*, p. 212.

[94]Robbins, *Encyclopedia*, p. 459. The fact that both infant cannibalism and eucharistic parody are sometimes both said to occur at a single sabbat, as at Avignon in 1582, is not evidence against the function being played by eucharistic parody, but rather a proliferation indicative of the complexity and psychological importance of the simultaneous flesh/not-flesh of the eucharist.

[95]Cf. here *The Malleus Maleficarum of Heinrich Kramer and James Sprenger*, ed. Montague Summers (New York: Dover, 1971), pp. 141–42, and *The Record of the Trial and Condemnation of a Witch, Matteuccia di Francesco, at Todi, 20 March 1428*, ed. Dominico Mammoli (Rome: np, 1972), passim, especially p. 36ff.

[96]Kramer and Sprenger, *Malleus* 2:1, p. 102.

[97]Ibid., 3:15, p. 229.

[98]Robbins, *Encyclopedia*, p. 421.

[99]Hughes, *Witchcraft*, p. 142.

[100]Joseph Klaits, *Servants of Satan: The Age of the Witch Hunts* (Bloomington: Indiana University Press, 1985), p. 53.

[101]Arthur Evans, *Witchcraft and the Gay Counterculture: A Radical View of Western Civilization and Some of the People It Has Tried to Destroy* (Boston: Fag Rag Books, 1978). He asserts, even more credulously, "the heretics at Orleans probably performed some abortion rite, especially since Cathars considered giving birth as a grave sin" (p. 55).

[102]Kramer and Sprenger, *Malleus* 2:1, p. 141. The analogy between this rhetoric and that associated with dilation and extraction abortions seems striking.

[103]For the birthchamber as a form of women-only carnival, see Adrian Wilson, "The Ceremony of Childbirth and its Interpretation," in Valerie Fildes, ed., *Women as Mothers in Preindustrial England: Essays in Memory of Dorothy McLaren* (London: Routledge, 1990), pp. 68–107.

[104]Lyndal Roper, *Oedipus and the Devil: Witchcraft, Sexuality, and Religion in Early Modern Europe* (London: Routledge, 1994), p. 202.

[105]Deborah Willis, *Malevolent Nurture: Witch-Hunting and Maternal Power in Early Modern England* (Ithaca: Cornell University Press, 1995), p. 6.

[106]Willis, *Malevolent Nurture*, pp. 50–51.

[107]Ibid., p. 8; p. 10.

[108]Ibid., p. 34.

[109]Roper, *Oedipus and the Devil*, p. 202.

[110]Ibid., p. 203.

[111]Merrall Llewelyn Price, "Bitter Milk: The *Vasa Menstrualis* and the Cannibal(ized) Virgin." *College Literature* 28.1, (Winter 2001): pp. 144–154. See also Charles T. Wood, "The Doctor's Dilemma: Sin, Salvation, and the Menstrual

Cycle in Medieval Thought" *Speculum* 56 no. 4 (1981): pp. 710–22.

[112]Erich Neumann, *The Great Mother: An Analysis of the Archetype* (New York: Pantheon, 1955), p. 32.

[113]Bynum, *Holy Feast*, p. 269ff.

[114]Felix Graefe, *Jan Sanders van Hemesson and Seine Identification mit dem Braunschweiger Monogrammisten* (Leipzig: K. W. Hiersemann, 1909). Like indigenous peoples believed by western culture to practice cannibalism in order to absorb the admired bravery of their enemies, a breastfed infant, in continuing to suck blood as it did in the womb, was believed to be taking into itself its nurse's physical, mental, moral, and emotional characteristics in the form of her blood—hence the care one should take to find a wetnurse of healthy appearance and good moral character. See Margaret R. Miles, "The Virgin's One Bare Breast: Female Nudity and Religious Meaning in Tuscan Early Renaissance Culture," pp. 193–208. In Susan Rubin Suleiman, *The Female Body in Western Culture: Contemporary Perspectives* (Cambridge: Harvard University Press, 1985).

[115]At the same time as the bloodfeeding of the familiars transgressed cannibalism taboos, the shedding of the witch's blood to nourish her helpmeets was "an unholy parody of the sacrifice of Christ" (Willis, *Malevolent Nurture*, pp. 52–55). Moreover, the repeated accusations against witches that they caused cows to give blood instead of milk is further evidence of an imagined reversal of the normal generative process.

[116]Ibid., p. 52.

[117]Valerie Fildes, *Breasts, Bottles, and Babies: A History of Infant Feeding* (Edinburgh: Edinburgh University Press, 1986), p. 262ff.

[118]Roper, *Oedipus and the Devil*, p. 25.

[119]Roper describes Augsburg cases in which the lying-in maid allegedly diabolically corrupts or poisons food intended for the mother in order to pass the ill-effects on to the nursing child (*Oedipus and the Devil*, p. 207).

[120]For bloodsucking, sometimes "*in musipulam conversa*," in the form of a fly, see the account of the 1428 trial of Matteuccia di Francesco, at Todi: "Furthermore, not content with these things, adding evil to evil and aided by an infernal spirit, she often went to Stregato to ruin the health of children by sucking their blood. She also sucked the blood of babies on various occasions and in various places" (Mammoli, *Trial and Condemnation*, p. 36).

[121]Roper, *Oedipus and the Devil*, p. 207.

[122]Ibid., p. 208. For ages of accused witches, see John Demos, *Entertaining Satan: Witchcraft and the Culture of Early New England* (New York: Oxford University Press, 1982); for elderly women being particularly guilty of cannibalism, see Bernadette Bucher, *Icon and Conquest: A Structural Analysis of the Illustrations of de Bry's Great Voyages* (Chicago University of Chicago Press, 1981), passim.

[123]J. Döpler, *Theatrum Poenarum* Vol. 1 (Sondershausen: Döpler, 1693), p. 959. In Michael Kunze, *Highroad to the Stake* (Chicago: University of Chicago Press, 1987), p. 407.

[124]Barstow, *Witchcraze*, p. 150. This "dewomanning" of Anna was followed by the "unmanning" of her elderly husband, who was impaled on a stick driven through his anus. "By this brutish parody of anal intercourse, he received not only intense physical torture but also was branded a sodomite . . ." Barstow, *Witchcraze*, p. 145. For links, including the highly speculative, between homosexuality and witchcraft allegations, see Evans, *Witchcraft and the Gay Counterculture*, passim.

[125]Miles, *Carnal Knowing*, p. 156.

[126]Marilyn Yalom, *A History of the Breast* (London: HarperCollins, 1997), p. 4.

[127]Christiane Olivier, *Jocasta's Children: The Imprint of the Mother*, tr. George Craig (London: Routledge, 1989), p. 15.

[128]Yalom, *A History of the Breast*, p. 63.

[129]Douglas, *Purity and Danger*, p. 115.

[130]Beckwith, *Christ's Body*, p. 41.

[131]Rubin, *Corpus Christi*, p. 29.

NOTES TO CHAPTER FOUR

[1]Gary Larson, *The Far Side Gallery 4* (Kansas City: Andrews and McMeel, 1993), p. 97.

[2]Even less gruesome contemporary manifestations of maternal murder provoke tremendous public outcry in the United States—witness the hysterical (with all the implications of the word) national response to Susan Smith drowning her sons in late 1993. Moreover, reports that Iraqi troops had taken premature babies from incubators during the invasion of Kuwait in 1990 were seized upon as justification for US involvement in the Gulf War. Later reports suggested that the story was unreliable. See, among others, *The Houston Chronicle*, 7 March 1992, A 21.

[3]In his six-volume *Motif Index of Folk Literature* (Bloomington: Indiana University Press, 1932–36), Stith Thompson lists variants that include Celtic, Spanish, Greek, Talmudic, Indian, Hawaiian, New Zealand, Greenland, Senecan, Angolan, and Zulu under the rubric G72 "Unnatural parents eat children."

[4]Another redaction of the story appears in the hagiography of St. Vincent Ferrer: "According to one version, he restored to life an infant whose mother had dismembered it, cooked it, and was about to offer it as food to the father and to the saint, who had returned from preaching a sermon. The author attributes her deed to an attack of insanity, such as afflicted her from time to time" (*Acta Sanctorum* cited in Shulamith Shahar, *Childhood in the Middle Ages* [London: Routledge, 1990], p. 300 n. 73). A second miracle attributed to St. Vincent Ferrer involves a pregnant woman who dismembers her existing child because she craves meat. The distraught father brings the dismembered body to the saint's shrine, and the child is reconstituted.

[5]Gaalya Cornfeld, ed. and tr., *Josephus: The Jewish War* (Grand Rapids, MI: Zondervan, 1982), p. 6.

[6]Ibid., pp. 416–17 (bk. 6, sec.201–13).

[7]Ibid., pp. 418 (bk. 6, sec.218).

[8]For an alleged right to paternal cannibalism during a siege in the High Middle Ages, see John Boswell, *The Kindness of Strangers: The Abandonment of Children in Western Europe from Late Antiquity to the Renaissance* (New York: Pantheon, 1988). Boswell quotes a thirteenth-century Castilian law that permitted certain besieged citizens to consume their children with legal impunity: "according to the true law of Spain a father who is besieged in a castle he holds from his lord may, if so beset with hunger that he has nothing to eat, eat his child with impunity rather than surrender his castle without permission of the lord. If he can do this for his lord, it is appropriate that he be able to do this for himself as well" (p. 329). Boswell adds that the mother did not enjoy the authority either to sell or eat her child.

[9]Josephus has earlier taken care to establish that the rebels were similarly brutal to the helpless, with less cause: "They beat old men who were clutching their victuals; they dragged women by their hair as they concealed what was in their hands; they had no pity for gray hairs or infants, but picked them up as they clung to their scraps and dashed them to the ground. . . . It was not that the tormentors were hungry—their actions would have been less barbarous had they sprung from necessity, but they were keeping their reckless passions exercised and providing supplies for themselves to use in the coming days" (Cornfeld, *Josephus,* pp. 386–88).

[10]Stephen K. Wright, *The Vengeance of our Lord: Medieval Dramatizations of the Destruction of Jerusalem* (Toronto: Pontifical Institute of Mediaeval Studies, 1989), p. 21 n. 48. The confusion is exacerbated by the fact that St. Hegesippus is known to have composed a no longer extant work dealing with the second-century Jewish Bar-Kochba uprising. See Michael E. Hardwick, *Josephus as an Historical Source in Patristic Literature through Eusebius* (Atlanta: Scholars Press, 1989), p. 46, and Eusebius Pamphilus, *The Ecclesiastical History of Eusebius Pamphilus, Bishop of Cesarea in Palestine* (Grand Rapids, Mich.: Guardian Press, 1976), p. 135 (sec. 4:8). Eusebius refers in section 2.23 (pp. 76–78) to Hegesippus's discussion in his *Commentaries* of the taking of Judea by Vespasian as a punishment for the death of James the Just.

[11]Wright, *Vengeance,* p. 23.

[12]In a number of versions, both Titus and Vespasian convert and are baptized after a miraculous healing. The war against the Jews is therefore a Christian endeavor, undertaken primarily to avenge Jesus's death.

[13]Note, in contrast, Josephus's attempt to deflect accusations of sensationalism in sections 199–200: "But why should I go on to describe the inanimate things that hunger made them unashamed enough to eat, as I now describe an act of which there is no parallel in the annals of Greece or any other country, a horrible and unspeakable deed and one incredible to hear. I hope that I shall not be suspected by posterity of grotesque inventions and would have gladly passed over this calamity in silence, had there not been countless contemporary witnesses to bear me out. Moreover, my country would have little reason to thank me if I suppressed the narrative of the horrible miseries that it had to endure" (Cornfeld, *Josephus,* p. 416). There is a suggestion here, I think, not only that Josephus sees the Maria episode as

testament to the dreadful suffering of the Jews, but that he felt that news of the extent of their suffering could be mitigating, or even redemptive.

[14]Or "breath," or "life."

[15]Carolyn Dinshaw, *Chaucer's Sexual Poetics* (Madison: University of Wisconsin Press, 1989), p. 21.

[16]I have in mind here Barbara Creed's distinction between the dyadic/devouring mother and the phallic/castrating mother. See *The Monstrous Feminine: Film, Feminism, Psychoanalysis* (London: Routledge, 1993). It is surprising that the symbolic conflation of stomach and womb has been overlooked in recent work on the gendered iconography of cannibalism.

[17]The translation of Eusebius's *Ecclesiastical Histories* is entire, with the exception of Book 10. See here Eva Matthews Sanford, "Propaganda and Censorship in the Transmission of *Josephus*," *Transactions and Proceedings of the American Philological Association* 6 (1935), p. 136: "It is not always possible to determine whether mediaeval references depend on the Rufinus translation or on 'Hegesippus'; the latter is sometimes cited by his own name and sometimes simply as Josephus, while Otto of Freising played safe with 'Iosephus seu Egesippus.'"

[18]Lotario Dei Segni, *De Miseria Condicionis Humane*, ed. Robert E. Lewis (Athens: University of Georgia Press, 1978), pp. 138–39. 1 am using Lewis's translation except where otherwise noted, but see also *On the Misery of the Human Condition*, ed. Donald R. Howard, tr. Margaret Mary Dietz (Indianapolis: Bobbs-Merrill, 1969), pp. 30–31.

[19]Note also that Innocent himself encountered a case of Christian cannibalism during his papacy: see *Die Register Innocenz' III*, ed. Othmar Hageneder (Rome; Verlag der Österreichischen Akademie der Wissenschaften, 1979), pp. 155–56. 1 would like to thank John C. Moore for bringing this to my attention.

[20]Michele Maccarrone believes that the future pope's source was John of Salisbury's *Policraticus* 2:6, which was published in Latin in 1159; see Michele Maccarrone, ed., *De Miseria Humane Conditionis* (Lucani: In Aedibus Thesauri Mundi, 1955), p. xli. However, John of Salisbury's material comes directly from Rufinus's Latin translation of Eusebius, and thus provides little of interest in terms of the development of the motif. The importance of the *Polycraticus* here resides primarily in its popularity, since it remains extant in some hundred manuscripts, and to the subsequent enormous popularity of the papal version it influenced, but also in the fact that it also contains a sustained allegory of the body politic, against which, I argue with Mary Douglas, the individual, and particularly the monstrous maternal body, is polarized. See John of Salisbury, *Polycraticus*, ed. Clemens C. I. Webb (Oxford: Clarendon Press, 1909); Mary Douglas, *Natural Symbols: Explorations in Cosmology* (New York: Pantheon, 1970), p. 101.

[21]Price, "Bitter Milk," p. 146.

[22]Guy N. Deutsch, *Iconographie de l'illustration de Flavius Joséphe au temps de Jean Fouquet* (Leiden: E. J. Brill, 1986), p. 181.

[23]Dante, *Divine Comedy; Purgatorio* 23, ll. 29–30.

[24]Laurent De Premierfait, *Des Cas des Nobles Hommes et Femmes*, ed. Patricia May Gathercole (Chapel Hill: University of North Carolina Press, 1968).

[25]Chaucer, *Complete Poetry; The Legend of Good Women*, G-prologue, ll. 414–15, p. 30.

[26]Segni, *De Miseria Condicionis Humane*, p. 29.

[27]A more influential and widely known English version, however, may have been the brief and condemnatory reference in John Lydgate's *The Fall of Princes* (c. 1430), a free translation of Boccaccio by way of Premierfait:

> A certeyn woman, thus seith the cronicleer,
> Rosted hir child whan vitaile dide faille,—
> She hadde of stoor non othir apparaille,—
> Theron be leiseer hirself she dide feede.
> Which in a woman was to horrible a deede!
> (VII: ll. 1484–88).

See *Lydgate's Fall of Princes*, ed. Henry Bergen, 4 vols. (Washington: Carnegie Institute of Washington, 1923–27), p. 816.

[28]   On Marie, a myld wyf, for mischef of foode
> Hir owen barn that go bar go brad on the gledis,
> Rostyth rigge & rib with rewful wordes
> Sayth: "Sone upon eache side our sorow is a-lofte.
> Batail a-boute the borwe, our bodies to quelle.
> Withyn hunger so hote that nez our herte brestyth;
> Therfor yeld that I the yaf & agen tourne,
> & entr ther thou cam out!" & etyth a schoulder.
> (ll. 1077–1108, pp. 62–63).

See *The Siege of Jerusalem* (London: Oxford University Press, 1932), pp. 62–63.

[29]Barbara Creed (*Monstrous Feminine*, p. 109) writes that "the image of the toothed vagina, symbolic of the all-devouring woman, is related to the subject's infantile memories of its early relation with the mother, and the subsequent fear of its identity being swallowed up by the mother."

[30]Stephen Wright suggests (*Vengeance*, p. 29) that the *Vindicta Salvatoris* narrative dates from "perhaps as early as 700," thus predating Walafrid.

[31]A comprehensive analysis of the origin and transmission of the *Vengeance* texts may be found in Ernst von Dobschütz, *Christusbilder: Untersuchungen zur Christlichen Legende* (Leipzig: J. C. Hinrichs, 1899).

[32]Alvin E. Ford, ed., *La Vengeance de Nostre-Seigneur: The Old and Middle French Prose Versions: The Version of Japheth* (Toronto: Pontifical Institute of Mediaeval Studies, 1984).

[33]Granger Ryan and Helmut Ripperger, tr., *The Golden Legend of Jacobus de Voragine* (London: Longman, Green, 1941), pp. 267–68.

[34]Ibid., p. 264. However, Sherry L. Reames in *The Legenda Aurea: A Reexamination of its Paradoxical History* (Madison: University of Wisconsin Press, 1985), argues for the text as less anti-Semitic than its predecessors and successors:

"Even the chapter on James the Lesser, which recounts the siege and destruction of Jerusalem in grisly detail, shows noticeable restraint for a medieval narrative of its kind. . . . Jacobus's account goes on to emphasize the proofs of God's desire to save the Jews, rather than see them punished for rejecting Christ (pp. 298–99). The message that Jews are human beings capable of redemption is reinforced elsewhere in the *Legenda* by Jacobus's tendency to retell stories in which they are converted, rather than condemned, by miracles" (p. 262 n. 9).

[35] "*Dame, Dieux vous mende par moy que vous mengés de l'enfant afin que ce que Dieux dist soit fet. Car il dist le jour de pasques flouries, le jour qu 'il entra en ceste ville sur une asnesse, que en ceste generacion seroit en Jherusalem sy grant pestilense et famine, si grant que la mere mengeroit son enfant*" (Ford, *Vengeance de Nostre-Seigneur*, pp. 149–50). The initial reference-point here is the entry of Jesus into Jerusalem in Luke 19:41–44, discussed above, but the cannibalism reference seems to have been imported here, perhaps from Leviticus 27:29. See note 54.

[36] ll. 974–75. There is the strong suggestion here that, unlike in the negative Maria versions, the emperor and his advisors have not heard of the death and consumption of the children. Divinely commanded, this act does not cause the uproar that it does in the other versions.

[37] Wright, *Vengeance*, p. 7. For the Corpus Christi plays as a means of reinscribing social and civic boundaries "at the expense of those constructed as the enemies of Christ," see Sarah Beckwith, "Ritual, Church and Theatre: Medieval Dramas of the Sacred Body," in *Culture and History, 1350–1600: Essays on English Communities, Identities, and Writing*, ed. David Aers (Detroit: Wayne State University Press, 1992), pp. 72–73.

[38] Wright, *Vengeance*, p. 195.

[39] However, the material within the *Siege of Jerusalem* corpus seemed also to have the potential for controversy. Stephen Wright, in *Vengeance*, pp. 111–12, mentions a historical lampoon performed in Lignerolles in 1549, *La Prophetie de Jeremie et la destruction de Jerusalem*, based possibly and loosely on the *Vengeance* tradition, and quotes Pierre de Pierrefleur, *Mémoires de Pierrefleur*, ed. A. Vermeil (Lausanne: D. Mattignier, 1856): "*La ditte histoire tendant la pluspart en derision des prestres et de toutes gens ecclesiastiques*" [The said history was for the most part aimed at deriding priests and other ecclesiastical people].

[40] Wright, *Vengeance*, p. 113.

[41] Wright argues that "it can be shown that every surviving example of the *Vengeance of Our Lord* in France is based directly on Marcadé's text" (ibid., p. 112).

[42] Eustache Marcadé, *La Vengance Jesucrist d'Eustache Marcadé*, ed. Andrée Marcelle Fourcade Kail (Ph.D. diss., Tulane University, 1955), ll. 12,713–14.

[43] Wright, *Vengeance*, p. 138.

[44] This is the suggestion of Wright, who dates the panels at around 1530 (*Vengeance*, p.142). However, A. M. Nagler, in *The Medieval Religious Stage: Shapes and Phantoms*, tr. George M. Schoolfield (New Haven and London: Yale University Press, 1976), suggests that they may have been imaginative post-performance "the-

atrical impressions" (p. 81).

⁴⁵For developments in the manuscript illustrations of the Maria episode, see Deutsch, *Iconographie*, passim. Deutsch also sees Maria as a deliberate perversion of the Virgin Mary, as I argue below.

⁴⁶Marcadé's character of Josephus in fact, not only is shaken by the mother's act, but indicts all the inhabitants of the city as more cruel and terrible than carnivorous beasts young ("[*q*]*ue chiens, luppars, lyons ou leupx*"), that after all feed rather than feed on their own young (Marcadé, *La Vengance*, l. 12,731).

⁴⁷The Middle English poetic *Siege of Jerusalem* is the text that echoes this development most clearly: Mary "[r]ostyth rigge & rib with rewful wordes," and then "etyth a schoulder" (pp. 62–63, ll. 1079, 1084).

⁴⁸These figures, which appear in Deutsch, *Iconographie*, as plates 145 and 146, also appear in Millard Meiss, *French Painting in the Time of Jean De Berry: the Boucicaut Master* (London: Phaedon, 1968). The scene does not capture her offer of food to the rebels (or, as in fig. 2, to the soldiers) but rather she is caught in the act by male figures who exhibit varying manifestations of authority and of disapproval. Perhaps one is, as in figure 4, Josephus himself.

⁴⁹Wright, *Vengeance*, p. 131, and Jehan Pussot, cited in Louis Paris, *Le Théâtre à Reims depuis les Romains jusqu'à nos jours* (Reims: F. Michaud, 1885), p. 52. Perhaps, however, the commercial enterprise proved more trouble than it was worth, since the theatrical project was never repeated.

⁵⁰This is Wright's description (*Vengeance*, p. 188). By my count, there are 679 lines in the *Aucto de la Destruicion de Jerusalen*, ed. Léo Rouanet, *Colección de Autos, Farsas, y Coloquios del Siglo XVI* (Barcelona: L'Avenc, 1901).

⁵¹Ibid., between ll. 455–56.

⁵²Wright, *Vengeance*, p. 195.

⁵³In addition to those of 2 Kings and Lamentations 4 already discussed, several other Old Testament verses address the devastation of a godless Israel with the metaphor of familial cannibalism. Leviticus 27:29 forecasts, "You shall eat the flesh of your sons, and you shall eat the flesh of your daughters." Deuteronomy 28:53 threatens, "And you shall eat the offspring of your own body, the flesh of your sons and daughters, whom the Lord your God has given you, in the siege and in the distress with which your enemies shall distress you." Jeremiah 19:9: "And I will make them eat the flesh of their sons and their daughters and everyone shall eat the flesh of his neighbor in the siege and in the distress with which their enemies and those who seek their life afflict them." Lamentations 2:20: "Look, O Lord, and see! / With whom has thou dealt thus? / Should women eat their offspring, the children of their tender care?" Ezekiel 5:10: "Therefore fathers shall eat their sons in the midst of you, and sons shall eat their fathers."

⁵⁴Boswell, *Kindness*, pp. 329–30.

⁵⁵Shahar, *Childhood*, p. 135.

⁵⁶Frank Lestringant, *Mapping the Renaissance World: The Geographical Imagination in the Age of Discovery*, tr. David Fausett (Berkeley: University of

California Press, 1994).

[57]George Tyler Northup, ed. and tr., *Letter to Piero Soderini, Gonfaloniere: The Year 1504* (Princeton: Princeton University Press, 1916), p. 5; Matthew Letts, ed. and tr., *Hans Staden: The True History of his Captivity 1557* (New York: R. M. McBride, 1929), p. 128; Jean de Léry, *History of a Voyage to the Land of Brazil, Otherwise Called America,* ed. and tr. Janet Whatley (Berkeley: University of California Press, 1990), p. 128. See the following chapter for a discussion of the uses of cannibalism accusations in the New World.

[58]Mary B. Campbell, *The Witness and the Other World: Exotic European Travel Writing, 400–1600* (Ithaca: Cornell University Press, 1988), p. 82; emphasis in the original. See also Rosi Braidotti, "Signs of Wonders and Traces of Doubt: On Teratology and Embodied Differences," in *Between Monsters, Goddesses, and Cyborgs: Feminist Confrontations with Science, Medicine, and Cyberspace,* eds. Nina Lykke and Rosi Braidotti (London: Zed, 1996), p. 142ff.

[59]Debbie Nathan and Michael Snedeker, *Satan's Silence: Ritual Abuse and the Making of a Modern American Witch Hunt* (New York: Basic Books, 1995), p. 31. Each of these taboo behaviors is ascribed to medieval and early modem dissenters, from Jews to heretics to witches. William Arens points out in *The Man-Eating Myth: Anthropology and Anthropophagy* (New York: Oxford University Press, 1979) that, as in the Maria trope, the fantasy of cannibalism is often framed in terms of incest, one member of the family devouring another as the ultimate horror (p. 146). For twentieth-century connections between filicide and incest, see Phillip J. Resnick, "Child Murder by Parents: A Psychiatric Review of Filicide," *American Journal of Psychiatry 126* (1969). Resnick writes that filicidal women "eroticized relationships with their murdered children; destructive wishes aimed at the initial incest object were reactivated and vented on the current incest object—the child" (p. 79).

[60]The role of protective, although inadequate father, is sometimes filled by the character of Joseph(us) in later dramatic variants, such as the *Aucto de la Destruicion de Jerusalen.* Note that Edward Stern's somewhat dated article, "The Medea Complex: the Mother's Homicidal Wishes to her Child," *Journal of Mental Science* 94 (1948), argues that, in the case of maternal infanticide, "a search should always be made for a conscious or unconscious hatred of the husband" (p. 330). While the androcentrism of this statement is clear, it opens the possibility of infanticide as a political act. Also apparent here is what Mary Daly calls "fetal identification syndrome"—patriarchal identification of self with offspring (*Websters',* pp. 198–99).

[61]Shahar, *History of Childhood,* p. 138.

[62]MS. Engl. Poet. e. I. Lyric 3344 in Carleton Brown and Rossell Hope Robbins, *The Index of Middle English Verse* (New York: Columbia, 1943). The poem continues: "The Jewes dide crien her parlement, / On the day of juggement; / They weren aferd they sholde ben shent: / I thonke a mayden everydel. / To the piler he was bounde, / To his herte a spere was stongen; / For us he suffred a deedly wounde; / I thonke a mayden everydel." Lyrics with a similar theme include "O lytel whyle lesteneth to me," MS. BL Royal 18. A. 10, *Index* 2481, in which Mary becomes rec-

onciled to the cross to the extent that she kisses it, and "As I walked me this endre day," B. M. Addit. MS. 5465, *Index 364*, in which standard roles are reversed, and a laughing Mary comforts a crying Jesus about his future sacrifice.

[63]See Michael P. Carroll, *Madonnas That Maim: Popular Catholicism in Italy since the Fifteenth Century* (Baltimore: Johns Hopkins, 1992), especially p. 67ff.

[64]Marina Warner, *Alone of All Her Sex: The Myth and the Cult of the Virgin Mary* (London: Weidenfeld and Nicolson, 1976), p. 220. She adds, "like Ishtar, who sent Tammuz down into the dustbowl of shadows and ghosts as her substitute, Mary participated in the immolation of her son, the conqueror of death" (p. 323).

[65]The contemporary rises in popularity of the cults of the Virgin and of the Passion are generally linked in terms of heterodox responses to dualistic heresies like Catharism, but Michael P. Carroll suggests that the link is more fundamental: "Since it is this same desire that gives rise to intense Marian devotion, a masochistic emphasis upon Christ's Passion will be most evident in those regions where support for the Mary cult is strongest" (*The Cult of the Virgin Mary: Psychological Origins* [Princeton: Princeton University Press], p. 67).

[66]Alan Dundes, ed., *The Blood Libel Legend: A Casebook in Anti-Semitic Folklore* (Madison: University of Wisconsin Press, 1991), p. 352.

[67]Carroll, *Cult of the Virgin*, p. 34.

[68]Gunilla Theander Kester, "The Forbidden Fruit and Female Disorderly Eating: Three Versions of Eve," in *Disorderly Eaters: Texts in Self-Empowerment*, ed. Lilian R. Furst and Peter W. Graham (University Park: Pennsylvania State University Press, 1992), p. 232.

[69]On this, see Lilian R. Furst: "Disorderly eating can thus represent that last protest left to the socially disempowered and at the same time, paradoxically, a means for them to achieve a kind of domination" (ibid., p. 6). For a use of an infanticide narrative to unlock the horrors of patriarchy in fiction, see Toni Morrison, *Beloved: A Novel* (New York: Knopf, 1987). Compare also Betty S. Travitsky on the infanticidal mother in "Child Murder in English Renaissance Life and Drama," *Medieval and Renaissance Life and Drama in England: An Annual Gathering of Research, Criticism, and Reviews*, vol. 6, ed. Leeds Barroll (New York: AMS Press, 1993): "Do we see her machinations as acts for which we should have some sympathy, or as acts which are unnatural and hideous, even 'female'? Is there any intimation, for example, that these female characters are dissatisfied—legitimately or not—with their frustrations in their patriarchal worlds, that they cannot achieve their ends in law-abiding ways, that some aspect of patriarchy (such as militarism, for example) has provided a rationale for their behavior?" (p. 64).

NOTES TO CHAPTER FIVE

[1]Bartolomé de Las Casas, *Historia de las Indias* (México: Fondo de Cultura Económica, 1951), p. 517.

[2]José de Acosta, *De Procuranda Indorum Salute* (Madrid: Ediciones Atlas, 1954), p. 373.

[3]Tzvetan Todorov, *The Conquest of America: The Question of the Other*, tr. Richard Howard (New York: Harper and Rowe, 1982), p. 31, and David Beers Quinn, "New Geographical Horizons: Literature," *First Images of America: The Impact of the New World on the Old*, ed. Fredi Chiapelli et al. (Berkeley: University of California Press, 1976), p. 637.

[4]These comments included the reminder: "wild men who eat human flesh; their faces are ugly and loathsome . . ." The issue of the grim appearance of man-eaters was to reappear in his own writings. John Cummins, ed. and tr., *The Voyage of Christopher Columbus: Columbus's Own Journal of Discovery Newly Restored and Translated* (New York: St. Martin's Press, 1992), p. 33.

[5]Ibid., p. 125.

[6]Ibid., p. 13.

[7]J. M. Cohen, ed. and tr., *The Four Voyages of Christopher Columbus; being his own log-book, letters and dispatches with connecting narrative drawn from the Life of the Admiral by his son Hernando Colon and other contemporary historians* (Harmondsworth: Penguin, 1969), p.12.

[8]Cummins, *Voyage*, p. 127.

[9]Ibid., pp. 130–31.

[10]Quinn, *New Geographical Horizons*, p. 637.

[11]Greenblatt, *Marvelous Possessions*, p. 75.

[12]Cummins, *Voyage*, pp. 122–23.

[13]Ibid., p. 137.

[14]Ibid., p. 129. See also Las Casas on this point: "It is unlikely that they were remnants of people they had eaten for, if they ate human flesh as much as it said, a house would not accommodate all the bones and heads—which there would be no reason to keep anyway, unless as relics of their most famous enemies, and all of this is pure guesswork" (Bartolomé de Las Casas, *History of the Indies* tr. and ed. Andrée Collard [New York: Harper and Rowe, 1971], p. 45).

[15]Cohen, *Four Voyages*, p. 137.

[16]Ibid., p. 193; see also Kirkpatrick Sale, *The Conquest of Paradise: Christopher Columbus and the Columbian Legacy* (New York: Knopf, 1990), p. 132.

[17]Francisco Guerra, *The Pre-Columbian Mind: A Study in the Aberrant Nature of Sexual Drives, Drugs Affecting Behaviour, and the Attitude Towards Life and Death, with a Survey of Psychotherapy, in Pre-Columbian America* (London: Seminar, 1971), p. 220.

[18]Cummins, *Voyage*, p. 170.

[19]Ibid., p. 33.

[20]Anthony Pagden, *The Fall of Natural Man: The American Indian and the Origins of Comparative Ethnology* (Cambridge: Cambridge University Press, 1986), p. 86.

[21]David E. Stannard, *American Holocaust: Columbus and the Conquest of the New World* (Oxford: Oxford University Press, 1992), p. 205.

[22]Cohen, *Four Voyages*, p. 298.

[23]Peter Hulme calls this point in the voyage "the defeat of the Oriental discourse as the articulating principle of the *Journal*" (*Colonial Encounters*, p. 31).

[24]Cummins, *Voyage*, p. 165.

[25]Ibid., p. 168.

[26]Ibid., p. 142.

[27]Todorov, *Conquest*, p. 40.

[28]Valentin Y. Mudimbe, "*Romanus Pontifex* (1454) and the Expansion of Europe," *Race, Discourse, and the Origin of the Americas: A New World View*, eds. Vera Lawrence Hyatt and Rex Nettleford (Washington: Smithsonian Institution Press, 1995), p. 61.

[29]Neil L. Whitehead, "Carib Cannibalism," *Journal de la Societe des Americanistes* LXX (1984), p. 72.

[30]Ibid.

[31]Helen Carr, "Woman/Indian: 'The American' and His Others," *Europe and Its Others*, eds. Francis Barker et al. (Colchester: University of Essex, 1985), p. 50.

[32]Clare Le Corbeiller, "Miss America and Her Sisters," *Metropolitan Museum of Art Bulletin* xix: (1961), passim.

[33]Anne McClintock, *Imperial Leather: Race, Gender, and Sexuality in the Colonial Contest* (New York: Routledge, 1995), p. 26.

[34]Louis Montrose, "The Work of Gender in the Discourse of Discovery," in *New World Encounters*, ed. Stephen Greenblatt (Berkeley: University of California Press, 1993), p. 180.

[35]Northup, *Letter to Piero*, pp. 5–12.

[36]Ibid., pp. 5–6.

[37]Ibid., p. 36.

[38]Montrose, "The Work of Gender," p. 180.

[39]Patricia de Fuentes, ed. and tr., *The Conquistadors: First-Person Accounts of the Conquest of Mexico* (New York: Orion, 1963), p. 181.

[40]Ibid., p. 123 n. 32. See also Natalie Zemon Davis, "Women on Top," *Society and Culture in Early Modern France: Eight Essays* (Stanford: Stanford University Press, 1975), pp. 124–51, and Barbara A. Babcock, ed., *The Reversible World: Symbolic Inversion in Art and Society* (Ithaca: Cornell University Press, 1978), passim.

[41]Cummins, *Voyage*, p. 130.

[42]Margaret Zamora, "Christopher Columbus's 'Letter to the Sovereigns': Announcing the Discovery," *New World Encounters*, ed. Stephen Greenblatt (Berkeley: University of California Press, 1993), p. 8.

[43]Fuentes, *The Conquistadors*, pp. 7–8.

[44]Lesley Byrd Simpson, ed. and tr., *Cortés: The Life of the Conqueror by His Secretary, Francisco López de Gómara* (Berkeley, University of California Press, 1964), p. 303.

[45]Lestringant, *Mapping the Renaissance World*, p. 79.

[46]Ibid., p. 81.

[47]Northup, *Letter*, p. 5.

[48]Simpson, *Cortés* , p. 149.

[49]Letts, *Hans Staden*, p. 155. As William Arens points out, however, Staden was among the Tupi for less than a year, and therefore could not have witnessed the process he describes (*The Man-Eating Myth*, p. 23).

[50]de Léry, *History of a Voyage*, p. 128.

[51]Guerra, *Pre-Columbian Mind*, p. 94.

[52]Frank Lestringant, *Cannibals: The Discovery and Representation of the Cannibal from Columbus to Jules Verne*, tr. Rosemary Morris (Cambridge: Polity Press, 1997), p. 24.

[53]Samuel Eliot Morison, ed. and tr., *Journals and Other Documents on the Life and Voyages of Christopher Columbus* (New York: Heritage Press, 1963), p. 134.

[54]Guerra, *Pre-Columbian Mind*, p. 45.

[55]Morison, *Journals*, p. 219.

[56]Jonathan Goldberg, *Sodometries: Renaissance Texts, Modern Sexualities* (Stanford: Stanford University Press, 1992), p. 198.

[57]Letts, *Hans Staden*, pp. 160–61

[58]de Léry, *History of a Voyage*, p. 127.

[59]Janet Whatley, "Food and the Limits of Civility: The Testimony of Jean de Léry," *Sixteenth-Century Journal* 15 (1984): p. 397. The punishments inflicted here suggest connections with either witchcraft or heresy, or both: the father is burned alive, the mother strangled, the remains of the old woman disinterred and burned.

[60]Bucher, *Icon and Conquest*, p. 82.

[61]Robert F. Berkhofer, *The White Man's Indian: Images of the American Indian from Columbus to the Present* (New York: Knopf, 1978), p. 9.

[62]Clément Marot, *Oeuvres Poetiques*, ed. Gérard Defaux (Paris: Bordas, 1990).

[63]Greenblatt, *Marvelous Possessions*, pp. 15–16.

[64]Sara Castro-Klaren, "What Does Cannibalism Speak? Jean de Léry and the Tupinamba Lesson," *Carnal Knowledge: Essays on the Flesh, Sex, and Sexuality in Hispanic Letters and Film*, ed. Pamela Bacarisse (Pittsburgh: Ediciones Tres Rios, 1991), p. 40.

[65]Claude J. Rawson, "'Indians' and Irish: Montaigne, Swift, and the Cannibal Question," *Modern Language Quarterly* 53: 3 (September, 1992): p. 304.

[66]Morison, *Journals*, p. 286.

[67]Lestringant, *Cannibals*, p. 61.

[68]Carl Gustav Jung, *Four Archetypes: Mother, Rebirth, Spirit, Trickster* (London: Ark, 1986), p. 16.

[69]Michael Palencia-Roth, "Cannibalism and the New Man of Latin America in the Fifteenth- and Sixteenth-Century European Imagination," *Comparative Civilizations Review* 12 (Spring 1985), p. 20.

[70]Morison, *Journals*, p. 236.

[71]Palencia-Roth, "Cannibalism and the New Man," p. 5.

[72]Morison, *Journals*, p. 211. A less explicit example occurs in Cuneo: "On the

28th we went ashore where we found all our above-mentioned men dead and still lying on the ground without eyes, which we thought to have been eaten; because as soon as they have beheaded anyone, immediately they scoop out their eyes and eat them" (ibid., p. 213).

[73]Cohen, *Four Voyages*, p. 137.

[74]Guerra, *Pre-Columbian Mind*, pp. 45–46.

[75]Goldberg, *Sodometries*, p. 193.

[76]Guerra, *Pre-Columbian Mind*, p. 56.

[77]Ibid., pp. 23–24; pp. 31–36.

[78]Clark L. Taylor, "Homosexuality in Pre-Columbian and Colonial Mexico," *Male Homosexuality in Central and South America*, ed. Stephen O. Murray (San Francisco: Instituto Obregon, 1987), p. 12.

[79]Byrne Fone, *Homophobia: A History* (New York: Metropolitan, 2000), p. 193ff.

[80]Las Casas, *Historia*, p. 276.

[81]Pietro Martire d'Anghiera, *The Decades of the Newe Worlde or West India. Englysshe by Richarde Eden* (London: William Powell, 1555), p. 90.

[82]John Grier Varner and Jeannette Johnson Varner, *Dogs of the Conquest* (Norman: University of Oklahoma Press, 1983), p. 45.

[83]Michel Foucault, *History of Sexuality*, tr. Robert Hurley (New York: Pantheon, 1978–86), vol. 1, p. 101.

[84]Goldberg, *Sodometries*, p. 196. See also "Mundus Novus": "they are comely, too, of countenance which they nevertheless themselves destroy; for they bore their cheeks, lips, noses and ears . . . a thing so unwonted and monstrous" (Northup, *Letter to Piero*, V, p. 5).

[85]Letts, *Hans Staden*, p. 160.

[86]Fuentes, *The Conquistadors*, p. 176.

[87]Ibid., p. 242 n. 26.

[88]Peter A. G. M. de. Smet, *Ritual Enemas and Snuffs in the Americas* (Amsterdam: Centre for Latin American Research and Documentation, 1985), passim.

[89]Morison, p. 220.

[90]Richard C. Trexler, *Sex and Conquest: Gendered Violence, Political Order, and the European Conquest of the Americas* (Ithaca: Cornell University Press, 1995), p. 145.

[91]Ibid., p. 84.

[92]Ibid.

[93]Diego Durán, *The History of the Indies of New Spain*, tr. Doris Heyden (Norman, OK: University of Oklahoma Press, 1994), p. 5.

[94]Goldberg, *Sodometries*, p. 181.

[95]Peter Mason, *Deconstructing America: Representations of the Other* (London: Routledge, 1990), p. 173.

[96]After surrendering their sodomites, the Indians explain that sodomitical

actions have been the cause of "many thunderinges, lyghtninge, and tempests," but are also recorded as associating thunder and lightning with the sound of Spanish military technology: "they beleved that owre menne caryed thunder and lyghtenynge about with them" (Goldberg, *Sodometries*, pp. 186–87).

[97]Taylor reports that ". . . the Aztecs, who were so blatant in public but puritanical in private, shouted 'Cuilone, Cuilone' ('queer, queer') from their canoes at the Spaniards during the 'Noche Triste' when Cortés was forced to retreat from Mexico City losing many soldiers." He goes on to add that "[t]he warriors' epithets, of course, may only have been another example of labeling one's enemies homosexual" ("Homosexuality in Pre-Columbian," p. 11). It is at least inconsistent that Taylor doesn't read accusations of Toltec sodomy in the same way.

[98]Guerra, *The Pre-Columbian Mind*, p. 219.

[99]Ibid.

[100]Ibid.

[101]Bucher, *A Structural Analysis*, p. 10.

[102]de Léry, *History of a Voyage*, pp. 212–213.

[103]Morison, *Journals*, p. 251.

[104]Bernal del Castillo Díaz, *The Discovery and Conquest of Mexico, 1517–1521*, ed. Genaro Garcia, tr. A. P. Maudsley (New York: Farrar, Straus, and Cudahy, 1956), p. 125.

[105]de Léry, *History*, p. 94.

[106]In Fuentes, *The Conquistadors*, p. 221 n. 16.

[107]Todorov, *Conquest*, p. 175.

[108]Díaz, *Discovery and Conquest*, p. 238.

[109]Fuentes, *The Conquistadors*, pp. 111–112.

[110]Simpson, *Córtes*, p. 287.

[111]Ibid., pp. 284–85.

[112]Gómara reports at one point that the Mexicans "said to themselves . . ." Ibid., p. 127.

[113]de Léry, *History*, p. 147.

[114]Ibid., p. 245, n. 8.

[115]Ibid., p. xxix.

[116]Letts, *Hans Staden*, p. 160. This suggests that ritual cannibalism must be mutual and self-perpetuating—a closed system. However, see Arens, *The Man-Eating Myth*, p. 25ff. for the unlikelihood of Staden being able to understand such an exchange.

[117]Letts, *Hans Staden*, p. 103, 81.

[118]Díaz, *Discovery and Conquest*, p. 140. "Teules" are daemons, either benign or malign.

[119]Simpson, *Córtes*, p. 105.

[120]Fuentes, *The Conquistadors*, p. 31.

[121]Guerra, *The Pre-Columbian Mind*, p. 85.

[122]Arens, *The Man-Eating Myth*, p. 69.

[123]Todorov, *Conquest,* p. 64.

[124]Arens. *The Man-Eating Myth,* p. 69.

[125]Simpson, *Córtes,* p. 253. Trexler, however, suggests that such a tradition is a shared cultural characteristic: "common to both cultures was a deeply engrained tradition that, beginning with verbal sexual insults, ranged up to castration, perhaps to circumcision, even to a fear of cannibalism" (Trexler, *Sex and Conquest,* p. 174).

[126]Ibid., pp. 209–210.

[127]Fuentes, *The Conquistadors,* p. 112.

[128]Ibid., p. 115.

[129]Sale, *Conquest,* p. 133.

[130]Robert A. Myers, "Island Carib Cannibalism," *Nieuwe West-Indische* Gids 58 (1988), p. 172.

[131]Ibid.

[132]Ibid.

[133]William C. Sturtevant, "First Visual Images of Native America," in Chiapelli, pp. 432–39.

[134]Letts, *Hans Staden,* pp. 15–16.

[135]Myers, "Island Carib Cannibalism," p. 172.

[136]Guerra, *The Pre-Columbian Mind,* p. 99.

[137]Fuentes, *The Conquistadors,* p. 16; p. 210, n. 4.

[138]See *Jews and the Encounter with the New World, 1492/1992* (Ann Arbor, Michigan: University of Michigan Press, 1992), passim.

[139]Durán, *The History of the Indies,* pp. 3–10.

[140]Greenblatt, *Marvelous Possessions,* pp. 131–32.

[141]Todorov, *Conquest,* p. 210.

[142]Greenblatt, *Marvelous Possessions,* p. 25.

[143]de Léry, *History,* p. 41.

[144]Ibid., p. 141. See also Greenblatt, *Marvelous Possessions,* p. 15.

[145]Fernando Cervantes, *The Devil in the New World: The Impact of Diabolism in New Spain* (New Haven: Yale University Press, 1994), p. 25.

[146]Castro-Klaren, "What Does Cannibalism Speak?" p. 39.

[147]Guerra, *The Pre-Columbian Mind,* p. 277.

[148]Greenblatt, *Marvelous Possessions,* p. 136.

Bibliography

Anderson, Andrew Runni. *Alexander's Gate, Gog, and Magog, and the Inclosed Nations.* Cambridge, MA: The Mediaeval Academy of America, 1932.

Arens, William. *The Man-Eating: Myth: Anthropology and Anthropophagy.* New York: Oxford University Press, 1979.

Aristotle. *The Generation of Animals.* Cambridge, MA: Harvard University Press, 1963.

Augustine, *Confessions,* tr. R. S. Pine-Coffin. Harmondsworth: Penguin, 1961.

Babcock, Barbara A., ed. *The Reversible World: Symbolic Inversion in Art and Society.* Ithaca: Cornell University Press, 1978.

Bakhtin, Mikhail. *Rabelais and His World.* Tr. Helene Iswolsky. Bloomington: Indiana University Press, 1984.

Baldwin, John W. *The Language of Sex: Five Voices from Northern France around 1200.* Chicago: University of Chicago Press, 1994.

Barber, Richard. *Bestiary: Being an English Version of the Bodleian Library, Oxford MS. Bodley 764.* Rochester: Boydell Press, 1993.

Baroja, Julio Caro. *The World of the Witches.* Tr. Nigel Glendinning. London: Weidenfeld, 1964.

Barstow, Anne Llewellyn. *Witchcraze: A New History of the European Witch Hunts.* San Francisco: Pandora, 1994.

Beckwith, Sarah. "Ritual, Church and Theatre: Medieval Dramas of the Sacred Body." *Culture and History, 1350–1600: Essays on English Communities Identities and Writing,* ed. David Aers. Detroit: Wayne State University Press, 1992.

———. *Christ's Body: Identity, Culture, and Society in Late Medieval Writings.* London: Routledge, 1993.

Benko, Stephen. *Pagan Rome and the Early Christians.* Bloomington: Indiana University Press, 1984.

ography

Bennett, Josephine Waters. *The Rediscovery of Sir John Mandeville.* New York: MLA, 1954.

Benton, John F., ed. *Self and Society in Medieval France: The Memoirs of Abbot Guibert of Nogent.* Toronto: University of Toronto Press, 1984.

Bernheimer, Richard. *Wild Men in the Middle Ages: A Study in Art, Sentiment, and Demonology.* Cambridge: Harvard University Press, 1952.

Berkhofer, Robert F. *The White Man's Indian: Images of the American Indian from Columbus to the Present.* New York: Knopf, 1978.

Bernstein, Alan E. *The Formation of Hell: Death and Resurrection in the Ancient and Christian Worlds.* Ithaca: Cornell University Press, 1993.

Bloch, R. Howard. "The Lay and the Law: Sexual/Textual Transgression in *La Chastelaine de Vergi*, The *Lai d'Ignaure*, and the *Lais* of Marie de France." *Stanford French Review* XIV, 1–2 Spring-Fall (1990): 181–210.

Boenig, Robert. *The Acts of Andrew in the Country of the Cannibals: Translations from the Greek, Latin, and Old English.* New York: Garland, 1991.

Boswell, John. *The Kindness of Strangers: The Abandonment of Children in Western Europe From Late Antiquity to the Renaissance.* New York: Pantheon, 1988.

Braidotti, Rosi. "Signs of Wonders and Traces of Doubt: On Teratology and Embodied Differences." In *Between Monsters, Goddesses, and Cyborgs: Feminist Confrontations with Science, Medicine, and Cyberspace*, eds. Nina Lykke and Rosi Braidotti. London: Zed, 1996.

Brooks, Kenneth R., ed. *Andreas and the Fates of the Apostles.* Oxford: Clarendon, 1961.

Browe, Peter. *Die Eucharistischen Wunder des Mittelalters.* Breslau: Verlag Muller & Seiffert, 1938.

Brown, Carleton and Rossell Hope Robbins. *The Index of Middle English Verse.* New York: Columbia, 1943.

Brunner, Karl. *Der Mittelenglische Versroman über Richard Löwenherz.* Wiener Beitrage zur Englischen Philologie 42. Vienna: Braunmüller, 1913.

Bucher, Bernadette. *Icon and Conquest: A Structural Analysis of the Illustrations of de Bry's Great Voyages.* Tr. Basia Miller Gulati. Chicago: University of Chicago Press, 1981.

Budge, E. A. T. Wallis. *The Contendings of the Apostles.* London: Oxford University Press, 1935.

Burde, Mark. "Cannibals at Communion: Parody in the 'Lai d'Ignaure.'" Paper delivered at the 32nd International Congress on Medieval Studies, May, 1997.

Bynum, Caroline Walker. *Holy Feast and Holy Fast: The Religious Significance of Food to Medieval Women.* Berkeley: University of California Press, 1987.

———. *Fragmentation and Redemption: Essays on Gender and the Human Body in Medieval Religion.* New York: Zone, 1991.

————. *The Resurrection of the Body in Western Christianity.* New York: Columbia University Press, 1995.

Caesarius of Heisterbach. *Dialogus Miraculorum.* Vol II. Tr. H. von E. Scott and C. C. Swinton-Bland. London: Routledge, 1929.

Campbell, Mary B. *The Witness and the Other World: Exotic European Travel Writing, 400–1600.* Ithaca: Cornell University Press, 1988.

Camporesi, Piero, *The Fear of Hell: Images of Damnation and Salvation in Early Modern Europe.* University Park, PA: Pennsylvania State University Press, 1991.

Carr, Helen. "Woman/Indian: 'The American' and His Others." In *Europe and Its Others*, eds. Francis Barker, Peter Hulme, Margaret Iversen, and Diana Loxley. Colchester: University of Essex, 1985: 46–60.

Carroll, Michael P. *The Cult of the Virgin Mary: Psychological Origins.* Princeton: Princeton University Press, 1986.

————. *Madonnas That Maim: Popular Catholicism in Italy since the Fifteenth Century.* Baltimore: Johns Hopkins University Press, 1992.

Castro-Klaren, Sarah. "What Does Cannibalism Speak? Jean de Léry and the Tupinamba Lesson." In *Carnal Knowledge: Essays on the Flesh Sex and Sexuality in Hispanic Letters and Film*, ed. Pamela Bacarisse. Pittsburgh: Ediciones Tres Rios, 1999: 23–44.

Cervantes, Fernando. *The Devil in the New World: The Impact of Diabolism in New Spain.* New Haven: Yale University Press, 1994.

Chaucer, Geoffrey. *The Complete Poetry and Prose of Geoffrey Chaucer.* Ed. John H. Fisher. New York: Holt, Rinehart, and Winston, 1977.

Cohen, J. M. *The Four Voyages of Christopher Columbus: Being His Own Logbook, Letters and Dispatches with Connecting Narrative Drawn from the Life of the Admiral by His Son Hernando Colon and Other Contemporary Historians.* Harmondsworth: Penguin, 1969.

Cohn, Norman. *The Pursuit of the Millennium: Revolutionary Millenarians and Mystical Anarchists of the Middle Ages.* New York: Oxford University Press, 1970.

————. *Europe's Inner Demons: An Enquiry Inspired by the Great Witch-Hunt.* New York: Basic, 1975.

Constable, Giles. "Aelred of Rievaulx and the Nuns of Watton: An Episode in the Early History of the Gilbertine Order." In *Medieval Women*, ed. Derek Baker. Oxford: Blackwell, 1978: 205–26.

Cornfeld, Gallya, ed and tr. *Josephus: The Jewish War.* Grand Rapids, MI: Zondervan, 1982.

Creed, Barbara. *The Monstrous Feminine: Film, Feminism, Psychoanalysis.* London: Routledge, 1993.

Crompton, J. "Leicester Lollards." *Transactions of the Leicestershire Archaeological* and Historical Society 44 (1968–69).

Cummins, John. *The Voyage of Christopher Columbus: Columbus's Own Journal of Discovery Newly Restored and Translated.* New York: St. Martin's Press, 1992.

Daly, Mary. *Websters' First New Intergalactic Wickedary of the English Language.* Boston: Beacon, 1987.

d'Anghiera, Pietro Martire. *The Decades of the Newe Worlde or West India. Englysshe by Richarde Eden.* London: William Powell, 1555.

Dante. *The Divine Comedy of Dante Alighieri.* Tr. John D. Sinclair. New York: Oxford University Press, 1961.

Davis, Natalie Zemon. "Women on Top." In *Society and Culture in Early Modern France: Eight Essays by Natalie Zemon Davis.* Stanford: Stanford University Press, 1975.

de Acosta, José. *De Procuranda Indonum Salute.* Madrid: Ediciones Atlas, 1954.

de Fuentes, Patricia, ed. and tr. *The Conquistadors: First Person Accounts of the Conquest of Mexico.* New York: Orion, 1963.

dei Segni, Lotario. *De Miseria Condicionis Humane.* Ed. Robert E. Lewis. Athens: University of Georgia Press, 1978.

de las Casas, Bartolomé. *History of the Indies.* Tr. and ed. Andrée Collard. New York: Harper and Rowe, 1971.

de Léry, Jean. *History of a Voyage to the Land of Brazil Otherwise Called America.* Ed. and tr. Janet Whatley. Berkeley: University of California Press, 1990.

Del Rio, Martin. *Disquisitionum Magicarum Libri Sex.* Venice: Apud Ioan. Antonium et Iocabum de Franciscis, 1606.

Demos, John Putnam. *Entertaining Satan: Witchcraft and the Culture of Early New England.* New York: Oxford University Press, 1982.

de Pierrefleur, Pierre. *Memoires de Pierrefleur.* Ed. A. Vermeil. Lausanne: D. Mattignier, 1856.

de Premierfait, Laurent. *Des Cas des Nobles Hommes et Femmes.* Ed. Patricia M. Gathercole. Chapel Hill: University of North Carolina Press, 1968.

Deutsch, Guy N. *Iconographie de l'Illustration de Flavius Josephe au Temps de Jean Fouquet.* Leiden: Brill, 1986.

Díaz, Bernal del Castillo. *The Discovery and Conquest of Mexico, 1517–1521.* Ed. Genaro Garcia. Tr. A. P. Maudsley. New York: Farrar, Straus and Cudahy, 1956.

Dinshaw, Carolyn. *Chaucer's Sexual Poetics.* Madison: University of Wisconsin Press, 1989.

Dobschütz, Ernst von, *Christusbilder: Untersuchungen zue Christlichen Legende.* Leipzig: J. C. Hinrichs, 1899.

Döpler, J. *Theatrum Poenarum.* Vol. 1. Sondershausen: Döpler, 1693.

Doueihi, Milad. "The Lure of the Heart." *Stanford French Review* 14. 1–2 (1990): 51–68.

Douglas, Mary. *Purity and Danger: An Analysis of the Conceits of Pollution and Taboo.* London: Routledge and Kegan Paul, 1966.

———. *Natural Symbols: Explorations in Cosmology.* New York: Pantheon, 1970.

Douie, Decima L., and Dom Hugh Farmer, eds. *The Life of St. Hugh of Lincoln.* Vol. 2. London: Nelson, 1962.

Dundes, Alan. *The Blood Libel Legend: A Casebook in Anti-Semitic Folklore.* Madison: University of Wisconsin Press, 1991.

Durân, Fray Diego. *The History of the Indies of New Spain.* Tr. Doris Heyden. Norman: University of Oklahoma Press, 1994.

Durling, Robert. "Deceit and Digestion in the Belly of Hell." *Allegory and Representation,* ed. Stephen Greenblatt. Baltimore: Johns Hopkins Press, 1981.

Epiphanius. *The Panarion of Epiphanius of Salamis.* Tr. Frank Williams. New York: Brill, 1987. Nag Hammadi Studies Vol. XXXV.

Evans, Arthur. *Witchcraft and the Gay Counterculture: A Radical View of Western Civilization and Some of the People It Has Tried to Destroy.* Boston: Fag Rag Books, 1978.

Fildes, Valerie. *Breasts, Bottles, and Babies: A History of Infant Feeding.* Edinburgh: Edinburgh University Press, 1986.

Floovant. *Chanson de Geste du XIIe Siecle.* Ed. Sven A. Andolf. Uppsala: Almqvist and Wiksells, 1941.

Fone, Byrne. *Homophobia: A History.* New York: Metropolitan, 2000.

Ford, Alvin E., ed. *La Vengeance de Nostre-Seigneur: The Old and Middle French Prose Versions: The Version of Japheth.* Toronto: The Pontifical Institute of Mediaeval Studies, 1984.

Forshall, J. and F. Madden, eds. *The Holy Bible: Translated from the Latin Vulgate by John Wycliffe and His Followers.* Oxford: Oxford University Press, 1850.

Foucault, Michel. *History of Sexuality.* Tr. Robert Hurley. New York: Pantheon, 1978–86. Vol. 1.

Freccero, John. "Bestial Sign and Bread of Angels (*Inferno* 32–33)." *Yale Italian Studies* 1 (Winter 1977).

Friedman, John Block. *The Monstrous Races in Medieval Art and Thought.* Cambridge, MA: Harvard University Press, 1981.

———. "The Marvels-of-the-East Tradition in Anglo-Saxon Art." In *Sources of Anglo-Saxon Culture,* ed. Paul E. Szarmach. Kalamazoo, MI: Medieval Institute, 1986: 319–341.

Fulcher of Chartres. *A History of the Expedition to Jerusalem, 1095–1127.* Tr. Frances R. Ryan. Ed. Harold Fink. Knoxville: University of Tennessee Press, 1969.

George, Leonard. *Crimes of Perception: An Encyclopedia of Heresies and Heretics.* New York: Paragon, 1995.

Gibb, Paul Allen. *Wonders of the East: A Critical Edition and Commentary.* Ph.D. thesis: Duke, 1977.

Gietl, A. M. *Die Sentenzen Rolands Nachmals Papstes Alexander III.* Freiburg, 1891.

Glassman, Bernard. *Anti-Semitic Stereotypes without Jews: Images of the Jews in England, 1290–1700.* Detroit: Wayne State University Press, 1975.

Goldberg, Jonathan. *Sodometries: Renaissance Texts, Modern Sexualities.* Stanford: Stanford University Press, 1992.

Gower, John. *The Complete Works of John Gower.* Ed. George Campbell Macaulay. 4 vols. Oxford: Clarendon, 1899–1901.

Graefe, Felix. *Jan Sanders van Hemesson and Seine Identification mit dem Braunschweiger Monogrammisten.* Leipzig, K. W. Hiersemann, 1909.

Greenblatt, Stephen J. *Marvelous Possessions: The Wonder of the New World.* Chicago: University of Chicago Press, 1991.

Guerra, Francisco. *The Pre-Columbian Mind: A Study in the Aberrant Nature of Sexual Drives, Drugs Affecting Behaviour, and the Attitude towards Life and Death, with a Survey of Psychotherapy, in Pre-Columbian America.* London: Seminar, 1971.

Guibert of Nogent. *The Deeds of God through the Franks: A Translation of Guibert de Nogent's Gesta Dei Per Francos.* Tr. and ed. Robert Levine. Rochester: Boydell Press, 1997.

Guzman, Gregory G. "Reports of Mongol Cannibalism in the Thirteenth-Century Latin Sources: Oriental Fact or Western Fiction?" In *Discovering New Worlds: Essays on Medieval Exploration and Imagination*, ed. Scott D. Westrem. New York: Garland, 1991: 31–68.

Hageneder, Othmar, ed. *Die Register Innocenz' III.* Rome: Verlag der Ostereichischen Akademie der Wissenschaften, 1979.

Hamelius, Paul, ed. *Mandeville's Travels, Translated from the French of Jean d'Outremeuse, Edited from MS. Cotton Titus CXVI in the British Library.* London: Oxford University Press, 1919.

Hardwick, Michael E. *Josephus as an Historical Source in Patristic Literature through Eusebius.* Atlanta: Scholars Press, 1989.

Hauer, Stanley R. "Richard Coeur de Lion: Cavalier or Cannibal?" *Mississippi Folklore Register* (14) 1980: 88–95.

Heng, Geraldine. "Cannibalism, the First Crusade, and the Genesis of Medieval Romance." *Differences: A Journal of Feminist Cultural Studies* 10:1 (Spring, 1998): 98–174.

Herrad of Hohenbourg. *Hortus deliciarum.* Ed. Rosalie Green et al. London and Leiden: Warburg Institute/University of London and Brill, 1979.

Higden, Ranulf. *Polychronicon.* Rolls Series no. 41, pt. 4. London: Longman, 1972.

Himmelfarb, Martha. *Tours of Hell: An Apocalyptic Form in Jewish and Christian Literature.* Philadelphia: Fortess, 1983.

Hogg, Gary. *Cannibalism and Human Sacrifice.* London: Hale, 1958.

Horstmann, C. and F. J. Furnivall, eds. *The Minor Poems of the Vernon Ms.* London: EETS, 1892–1901.

Hsia, R. Po-Chia. *The Myth of Ritual Murder: Jews and Magic in Reformation Germany.* New Haven: Yale University Press, 1988.

Hudson, Anne. "The Mouse in the Pyx: Popular Heresy and the Eucharist." *Trivium*, vol. 26, (1991): 40–53.

Hughes, Pennethorne. *Witchcraft.* London: Longman, 1952.

Hulme, Peter. *Colonial Encounters: Europe and the Native Caribbean, 1492–1797.* London: Methuen, 1986.

Huxley, Aldous. *The Devils of Loudun.* New York: Carroll and Graf, 1952.

James of Vitry. *The "Historia Occidentalis" of Jacques de Vitry.* Ed. J. F. Hinnebusch. Fribourg: The University Press, 1972.

James, E. O. *Sacrifice and Sacrament.* London: Thames and Hudson, 1962.

Jews and the Encounter with the New World, 1492/1992. Christopher Columbus Quincentenary Jubilee Commission Ann Arbor: University of Michigan Press, 1992.

John of Salisbury. *Polycraticus.* Ed. Clemens C. I. Webb. Oxford: Clarendon Press, 1909.

Jung, Carl Gustav. *Four Archetypes: Mother, Rebirth, Spirit, Trickster.* London: Ark, 1986.

Jungmann, Joseph A. *Missarum Sollemnia: Eine Genetische Ekklärung der Römischen Mosse.* Vienna: Herder, 1962.

Kester, Gunilla Theander. "The Forbidden Fruit and Female Disorderly Eating: Three Versions of Eve." In *Disorderly Eaters: Texts in Self-Empowerment,* eds. Lilian R. Furst and Peter W. Graham. University Park: Pennsylvania State University Press, 1992.

Kilgour, Maggie. *From Communion to Cannibalism: An Anatomy of Metaphors of Consumption.* Princeton: Princeton University Press, 1990.

Klaits, Joseph. *Servants of Satan: The Age of the Witch Hunts.* Bloomington: Indiana University Press, 1985.

Kolbing, E. and Mabel Day. *The Siege of Jerusalem, edited from ms. Laud. Misc. 656 with variants from all other extant mss.* London: EETS, 1932.

Kunze, Michael. *Highroad to the Stake.* Chicago: University of Chicago Press, 1987.

La Conquete de Jérusalem. Ed. Celestin Hippeau. Paris: A. Aubry, 1868.

Lambert, Malcolm. *Medieval Heresy: Popular Movements from the Gregorian Reform to the Reformation.* 2nd ed. Oxford University: Cambridge, MA: B. Blackwell, 1992.

Langmuir, Gavin I. *Toward a Definition of Antisemitism.* Berkeley and Los Angeles: University of California Press, 1990.

Larson, Gary. *The Far Side Gallery 4.* Kansas City: Andrews and McMeel, 1993.

Lea, Henry Charles. *Materials Toward a History of Witchcraft.* Vol. 1. Philadelphia:

University of Pennsylvania Press, 1939.

Le Corbeiller, Clare. "Miss America and Her Sisters." *Metropolitan Museum of Art Bulletin* xix (1961).

Le Goff, Jacques. *The Birth of Purgatory.* Tr. Arthur Goldhammer. Chicago: University of Chicago Press, 1984.

Lejeune, Rita, ed. *Le Lai d'Ignauré ou Lai du Prisonnier.* Liège: Vaillant-Carmanne, 1938.

Le "Liber" de Raymond d'Aguilers. Ed. John Hugh and Laurita Lyttleton Hill. Paris: P. Geuthner, 1969.

L' Elucidarium et les Lucidaires. Ed. Yves Le Fevre. Paris: E. de Boccard, 1954.

Lerer, Seth. "Transgressio Studii: Writing and Sexuality in Guibert of Nogent." *Stanford French Review* XIV, 1–2 (Spring-Fall 1990): 243–66.

Lestringant, Frank. *Mapping the Renaissance World: The Geographical Imagination in the Age of Discovery.* Tr. David Fausett. Berkeley and Los Angeles: University of California Press, 1994.

———. *Cannibals: The Discovery and Representation of the Cannibal from Columbus to Jules Verne.* Tr. Rosemary Morris. Cambridge: Polity Press, 1997.

Letts, Matthew, ed. and tr. *Hans Staden: The True History of His Captivity, 1557.* New York: R. M. McBride, 1929.

Levi-Strauss, Claude. *The Naked Man.* Tr. John and Doreen Weightman. New York: Harper & Row, 1981.

Lydgate, John. *Lydgate's Fall of Princes.* Ed. Henry Bergen, 4 vols. Washington: Carnegie Institute of Washington, 1923–27.

Maccarrone, Michele, ed. *De Miseria Humane Conditionis.* Lucani: In Aedibus Thesauri Mundi, 1955.

Maccoby, Hyam. *The Sacred Executioner: Human Sacrifice and the Legacy of Guilt.* New York: Thames and Hudson, 1982.

Macy, Gary. *The Theologies of the Eucharist in the Early Scholastic Period: A Study of the Salvific Function of the Sacrament According to the Theologians, c. 1080–c. 1220.* Oxford: Clarendon, 1984.

Maitland, Samuel R. *Facts and Documents Illustrative of the History, Doctrine, and Rites of the Ancient Albigenses and Waldenses.* London: C. J. G. and F. Rivington, 1832.

The Malleus Maleficarum of Heinrich Kramer and James Sprenger. Ed. Montague Summers. New York: Dover, 1971.

Mannyng, Robert of Brunne, *Handlyng Synne.* Ed. I. Sullens. Binghamton: Medieval and Renaissance Texts and Studies 14, 1983.

Marcadé, Eustache. *La Vengance Jesucrist d'Eustache Marcadé.* Ed. Andrée Marcelle Fourcade Kail. PhD. diss., Tulane University, 1955.

Marot, Clément. *Oeuvres Poetiques.* Ed. Gérard Defaux. Paris: Bordas, 1990.

Marvin, Julia. "Cannibalism as an Aspect of Famine in Two English Chronicles." In

Food and Eating in Medieval Europe, eds. Martha Carlin and Joel T. Rosenthal. London: Hambledon, 1998: 73–86.

Mason, Peter. *Deconstructing America: Representations of the Other*. London: Routledge, 1990.

McClintock, Anne. *Imperial Leather: Race, Gender, and Sexuality in the Colonial Contest*. New York: Routledge, 1995.

McDonnell, Ernest W. *The Beguine and Beghards in Medieval Culture with Special Emphasis on the Belgian Scene*. New Brunswick: Rutgers University Press, 1954.

McGinn, Bernard. *Visions of the End: Apocalyptic Traditions in the Middle Ages*. New York: Columbia University Press, 1979.

Mearns, Rodney, ed. *The Vision of Tundale*. Heidelberg: Carl Winter, Universitätsverlag, 1985. Middle English Texts Series.

Meiss, Millard. *French Painting in the Time of Jean De Berry: The Boucicaut Master*. London: Phaidon, 1968.

Miles, Margaret R. "The Virgin's One Bare Breast: Female Nudity and Religious Meaning in Tuscan Early Renaissance Culture." In *The Female Body in Western Culture: Contemporary Perspectives*, ed. Susan Rubin Suleiman. Cambridge: Harvard University Press, 1985: 193–208.

———. *Carnal Knowing: Female Nakedness and Religious Meaning in the Christian West*. Boston: Beacon, 1989.

Montrose, Louis. "The Work of Gender in the Discourse of Discovery." In *New World Encounters*, ed. Stephen Greenblatt. Berkeley and Los Angeles: University of California Press, 1993: 177–217.

Moore, R. I. *The Origins of European Dissent*. London: Penguin, 1977.

Morison, Samuel Eliot, ed. and tr. *Journals and Other Documents on the Life and Voyages of Christopher Columbus*. New York: The Heritage Press, 1963.

Morrison, Toni. *Beloved: A Novel*. New York: Knopf, 1987.

Mudimbe, Valentin Y. "*Romanus Pontifex* (1454) and the Expansion of Europe," In *Race, Discourse, and the Origin of the Americas: A New World View*, eds. Vera Lawrence Hyatt and Rex Nettleford. Washington: Smithsonian Institution Press, 1995.

Murray, Stephen O., ed. *Male Homosexuality in Central and South America*. New York: Gai Saber Monograph, 1987.

Myers, Robert A. "Island Carib Cannibalism." *Nieuwe WestIndische Gids* 58 (1988): 147–84.

Nagler, A. M. *The Medieval Religious Stage: Shapes and Phantoms*. New Haven and London: Yale University Press, 1976.

Nathan, Debbie and Michael Snedeker. *Satan's Silence: Ritual Abuse and the Making of a Modern American Witch Hunt*. New York: Basic, 1995.

Neumann, Erich. *The Great Mother: An Analysis of the Archetype*. New York:

Pantheon, 1955.

Newall, Venetia, ed. *The Witch Figure: Folklore essays by a group of scholars in England honouring the 75th birthday of Katharine M. Briggs*. London: Routledge and Kegan Paul, 1973.

Noonan, John. *Contraception: A History of Its Treatment by the Catholic Theologians and Canonists*. Cambridge, MA: Harvard University Press, 1986.

Northup, George Tyler, ed. and tr. *Letter to Piero Soderini, Gonfaloniere. The Year 1504*. Princeton: Princeton University Press, 1916.

Olivier, Christiane. *Jocasta's Children: The Imprint of the Mother*. Tr. George Craig. London: Routledge, 1989.

O'Meara, Carra Ferguson. "In the Hearth of the Virgin Womb." *Art Bulletin* 63: 1 (1981).

On the Misery of the Human Condition. Ed. Donald R. Howard. Tr. Margaret Mary Dietz. Indianapolis: Bobbs-Merrill, 1969.

Ovid. *Metamorphoses*. Tr. Rolfe Humphries. Bloomington: Indiana University Press. 1955.

Pagden, Anthony. *The Fall of Natural Man: The American Indian and the Origins of Comparative Ethnology*. Cambridge: Cambridge University Press, 1986.

Palencia-Roth, Michael. "Cannibalism and the New Man of Latin America in the Fifteenth- and Sixteenth-Century European Imagination." *Comparative Civilizations Review* 12 (Spring 1985): 1–27.

Pamphilus, Eusebius. *The Ecclesiastical History of Eusebius Pamphilus, Bishop of Cesarea in Palestine*. Grand Rapids, MI: Guardian Press, 1976.

Paris, Louis. *Toiles Peintes et Tapisseries de la Ville de Reims, ou, la Mise en Scène de Théâtre des Confrères de la Passion*. Paris: Bruslart, 1843.

———. *Le Théâtre à Reims Despuis les Romains Jusqu'à Nos Jours*. Reims: F. Michaud, 1885.

Paris, Matthew. *Matthéi Parisiensis, Monachi Sancti Albani, Chronica Majiora*. London: Longman & Co., 1872–83.

Peter of Celle. *Selected Works*. Tr. Hugh Feiss. Kalamazoo, MI: Cistercian Publications, 1989.

Peter of Vaux. "The Life of Colette of Corbie." *Acta Sanctorum*. Paris: Apud Victorem Palme, 1863.

Peters, Edward. *Heresy and Authority in Medieval Europe: Documents in Translation*. Philadelphia: University of Pennsylvania Press, 1980.

Phelan, Peggy. *Unmarked: The Politics of Performance*. London: Routledge, 1993.

Polo, Marco. *The Travels of Marco Polo*. New York: Orion, 1958.

Price, Merrall Llewelyn. "Bitter Milk: The *Vasa Menstrualis* and the Cannibal(ized) Virgin." *College Literature* 28.1, (Winter 2001): 144–154.

Quinn, David Beers. "New Geographical Horizons: Literature." In *First Images of America: The Impact of the New World on the Old*, eds. Fredi Chiapelli,

Michael J. B. Allen and Robert L. Benson. Berkeley and Los Angeles: University of California Press, 1976: 635–58.

Rawson, C. J. "'Indians' and Irish: Montaigne, Swift, and the Cannibal Question." *Modern Language Quarterly* 53: 3. (September 1992): 299–363.

Reames, Sherry L. *The Legenda Aurea: A Reexamination of Its Paradoxical History.* Madison: University of Wisconsin Press, 1985.

The Record of the Trial and Condemnation of a Witch. Matteuccia di Francesco, at Todi. 20 March 1428. Ed. and tr. Dominico Mammoli. Rome: np, 1972.

Resnick, Phillip J. "Child Murder by Parents: A Psychiatric Review of Filicide." *American Journal of Psychiatry* 126 (1969).

Riley-Smith, Jonathan. *The First Crusade and the Idea of Crusading.* London: Athlone, 1986.

Robbins, Rossell Hope. *The Encyclopedia of Witchcraft and Demonology.* New York: Bonanza, 1959.

Romm, James S. *The Edges of the Earth in Ancient Thought: Geography, Exploration, and Fiction.* Princeton, NJ: Princeton University Press, 1992.

Roper, Lyndal. *Oedipus and the Devil: Witchcraft, Sexuality, and Religion in Early Modern Europe.* London: Routledge, 1994.

Rosenthal, Joel T. *The Purchase of Paradise: Gift Giving and the Aristocracy, 1307–1485.* London: Routledge and Kegan Paul, 1972.

Rouanet, Leo. *Coleccion de Autos, Farsas, y Coloquios del Siglo XVI.* Barcelona: L'Avenc, 1901.

Rubin, Miri. *Corpus Christi: The Eucharist in Late Medieval Culture.* Cambridge: Cambridge University Press, 1991.

———. "Desecration of the Host; the Birth of an Accusation." In *Christianity and Judaism: Papers Read at the 1991 Summer Meeting and the 1992 Winter Meeting of the Ecclesiastical History Society,* ed. Diana Wood. Oxford: Blackwell, 1992.

Ryan, Granger and Helmut Ripperger, trs. *The Golden Legend of Jacobus de Voragine.* London: Longmans, 1941.

Sale, Kirkpatrick. *The Conquest of Paradise: Christopher Columbus and the Columbian Legacy.* New York: Knopf, 1990.

Sanday, Peggy Reeves. *Divine Hunger: Cannibalism as a Cultural System.* Cambridge: Cambridge University Press, 1986.

Sanford, Eva Matthews. "Propaganda and Censorship in the Transmission of Josephus." *Transactions and Proceedings of the American Philological Association* 6 (1935).

Schlesinger, Roger, and Arthur P. Stabler, eds. and trs. *André Thevet's North America: A Sixteenth-Century View.* Kingston and Montreal: McGill Queen's University Press, 1986.

Shachar, Isaac. *The Judensau: A Medieval Anti-Jewish Motif and its History.* London:

Warburg Institute, 1974.

Shahar, Shulamith. *Childhood in the Middle Ages.* London: Routledge, 1990.

Simpson, Lesley Byrd. *Cortés: The Life of the Conqueror by His Secretary, Francisco Lôpez de Gômara.* Berkeley, University of California Press, 1964.

Sinanoglou. Leah. "The Christ Child as Sacrifice: A Medieval Tradition and the Corpus Christi Plays." *Speculum* 48:3 (1973): 491–509.

Slessarev, Vsevolod. *Prester John: The Letter and the Legend.* Minneapolis: University of Minnesota Press, 1959.

Smet, Peter A. G. M. de. *Ritual Enemas and Snuffs in the Americas.* Amsterdam: Centre for Latin American Research and Documentation, 1985.

Soranus of Ephesus. *Soranus's Gynecology.* Baltimore: Johns Hopkins Press, 1956.

Stannard, David E. *American Holocaust: Columbus and the Conquest of the New World.* Oxford: Oxford University Press, 1992.

Stern, Edward. "The Medea Complex: the Mother's Homicidal Wishes to Her Child." *Journal of Mental Science* 94 (1948).

Stock, Brian. *The Implications of Literacy: Written Language and the Models of Interpretation in the Eleventh and Twelfth Centuries.* Princeton: Princeton University Press, 1983.

Strack, Hermann L. *The Jew and Human Sacrifice. Human Blood and Jewish Ritual, an Historical and Sociological Inquiry.* New York: Blom, 1971.

Sturtevant, William C. "First Visual Images of Native America." In *First Images of America: The Impact of the New World on the Old,* eds. Fredi Chiapelli, Michael J. B. Allen and Robert L. Benson. Berkeley and Los Angeles: University of California Press, 1976: 417–454.

Sumberg, Lewis A. "The 'Tafurs' and the First Crusade." *Mediaeval Studies,* XXI (1959): 224–46.

Tannahill, Reay. *Flesh and Blood: A History of the Cannibal Complex.* New York: Stein and Day, 1975.

Tanner, N., ed. *Heresy Trials in the Diocese of Norwich, 1428–31.* London: Offices of the Royal Historical Society, 1977.

Tattersall, Jill. "Anthropophagi and Eaters of Raw Flesh in French Literature of the Crusade Period: Myth, Tradition and Reality." *Medium Aevum* v. 57 no. 2 (88): 240–53.

Taylor, Clark L. "Homosexuality in Pre-Columbian and Colonial Mexico." In *Male Homosexuality in Central and South America,* ed. Stephen O. Murray. San Francisco: Instituto Obregon, 1987.

Tertullian. *Scorpiace.* In *Quinti Septimi Florentis Tertulliani Opera,* eds. Augusti Reifferscheid and Georgü Wissowa. Vindobonae; Pragae: F. Tempsky, 1890–1957.

Thomas of Kent. *The Anglo-Norman Alexander (Roman de Toute Chevalerie).* Ed. Brian Foster. London: Anglo-Norman Text Society, 1976–1977.

Thomas, Keith. *Religion and the Decline of Magic: Studies in Popular Beliefs in Sixteenth- and Seventeenth-Century England.* New York: Oxford University Press, 1971.

Thompson, Stith. *Motif Index of Folk Literature.* Bloomington: Indiana University Press, 1932–36.

Todorov, Tzvetan. *The Conquest of America: The Question of the Other.* Tr. Richard Howard. New York: Harper and Row, 1982.

Trachtenberg, Joshua. *The Devil and the Jews: The Medieval Conception of the Jew and Its Relation to Modern AntiSemitism.* New Haven: Yale University Press, 1943.

Travitsky, Betty S. "Child Murder in English Renaissance Life and Drama." *Medieval and Renaissance Life and Drama in England: An Annual Gathering of Research, Criticism, and Reviews* Vol. VI. Ed. Leeds Barroll. New York: AMS Press, 1993: 63–84.

Trexler, Richard C. *Sex and Conquest: Gendered Violence, Political Order, and the European Conquest of the Americas.* Ithaca: Cornell University Press, 1995.

Varner, John Grier and Jeannette Johnson Varner. *Dogs of the Conquest.* Norman: University of Oklahoma Press, 1983.

Wakefield, Walter L. and Austin P. Evans. *Heresies of the High Middle Ages: Selected Sources Translated and Annotated.* New York: Columbia University, 1969.

Ward, Benedicta. *Miracles and the Medieval Mind: Theory, Record, and Event, 1000–1215.* Philadelphia: University of Pennsylvania Press, 1982.

Warner, Marina. *Alone of All Her Sex: the Myth and the Cult of the Virgin Mary.* London: Weidenfeld and Nicolson, 1976.

Whatley, Janet. "Food and the Limits of Civility: The Testimony of Jean de Léry." *Sixteenth Century Journal* 15 (1984).

White, David Gordon. *The Myths of the Dog-Man.* Chicago: University of Chicago Press, 1991.

Whitehead, Neil L. "Carib Cannibalism." *Journal de la Societe des Americanistes* LXX (1984): 69–88.

Williams, Michael A. "Divine Image—Prison of Flesh: Perceptions of the Body in Ancient Gnosticism." *Zone* 5:128–47.

Willis, Deborah. *Malevolent Nurture: Witch-Hunting and Maternal Power in Early Modern England.* Ithaca: Cornell University Press, 1995.

Wilson, Adrian. "The Ceremony of Childbirth and its Interpretation." In *Women as Mothers in Pre-Industrial England: Essays in Memory of Dorothy McLaren,* ed. Valerie Fildes. London: Routledge, 1990: 68–107.

Wolohojian, Albert Mugrdich. *The Romance of Alexander the Great by Pseudo-Callisthenes.* New York: Columbia University Press, 1969.

Wood, Charles T. "The Doctor's Dilemma: Sin, Salvation and the Menstrual Cycle in Medieval Thought." *Speculum* 56 no. 4 (1981): 710–22.

Wright, Stephen K. *The Vengeance of Our Lord: Medieval Dramatizations of the Destruction of Jerusalem.* Toronto: Pontifical Institute of Mediaeval Studies, 1989.

Yalom, Marilyn. *A History of the Breast.* London: HarperCollins, 1997.

Yule, Henry, tr. and ed. *Cathay and the Way Thither: Being a Collection of Medieval Notices of China.* Series II; Volume II. London: The Hakluyt Society, 1913.

Zaleski, Carol. *Otherworld Journeys: Accounts of Near-Death Experience in Medieval and Modern Times.* New York: Oxford University Press, 1987.

Zamora, Margarita. "Christopher Columbus's 'Letter to the Sovereigns': Announcing the Discovery." In *New World Encounters,* ed. Stephen Greenblatt. Berkeley and Los Angeles: University of California Press, 1993: 1–11.

Index